Advance Praise for *The Network Is Your Customer*

Rogers's work is thought-provoking and practical. It's important reading for any marketer trying to engage the ever-evolving consumer in the digitally networked space. His synthesis of vast amounts of information and application of deep analytical rigor deliver a strategically grounded, highly relevant, and, most important, applicable operating model.
—**Antonio J. Lucio,** Global CMO, Visa Inc.

The Network Is Your Customer shows in real terms how networks have changed our lives as customers as well as citizens. The book explains how marketing and customer service demand constant engagement and commitment to customers, and it shows you how any business can meet that challenge for better returns.
—**Craig Newmark,** founder of craigslist

This book will shake up your business and change the way you think about the Internet. With more than a hundred real-world cases, Rogers shows how customer networks impact the bottom line of every business and how you can make them work for you.
—**Bernd Schmitt,** CEO of the EX Group, author of *Big Think Strategy*

In this groundbreaking new book, Rogers reveals the science and the psychology behind our ever more connected lives. More important, he shows how to build the products, services, and organizations of the future that your customers will flock to join.
—**John Gerzema,** Chief Insights Officer, Young & Rubicam, and best-selling author of *The Brand Bubble* and *Spend Shift*

Every marketer who wants to stay relevant should read this book. Rogers shows five strategies for how customer networks can drive bottom-line results at companies of every size and industry. Tap into the digital world and make the network work for you!
—**Sandy Carter,** Vice President, Software Business Partners, IBM Corporation

Your customers are changing your business model. Looking for answers? This book holds key insights to understanding customers in a digital world. With its five strategies and straightforward advice for responding to change in your own business, it's a must read for any manager.
—**Jeff Fleischman,** Chief Digital Officer, TIAA-CREF

Rogers weaves great storytelling, compelling examples, and real business insight into an important book that transforms our understanding of twenty-first-century business and what it will take to win in this new customer-powered reality.
—**Dwayne Spradlin,** CEO of InnoCentive

Don't miss this book. *The Network Is Your Customer* is a great choice for anyone, from entry-level worker to CEO, who wants to cut through the clutter and discover brilliant ways every marketer can create value in the age of the Web. With dozens of inspired case studies, Rogers clearly illustrates how smart brands are using digital channels to satisfy the need for individuality in consumer choice.
—**John Mayo-Smith,** Chief Technology Officer, R/GA

For anyone looking to understand the future of customers in the digital age, Rogers has written a fascinating business guide. He focuses not only on the technological speed warp we're living in but on the behaviors and motivations that give it meaning and what organizations should be doing about it now!
—**Lisa Hsia,** Senior Vice President, Bravo Digital Media

I call it Listenomics. Others call it The Relationship Era. You can think of it as salvation. What Rogers details in this compelling book is that the very forces that are destroying mass marketing—that is, the digital revolution—also power the bright and bold future of commerce.
—**Bob Garfield,** host of NPR's *On the Media,* editor for *Ad Age,* and author of *The Chaos Scenario*

Rogers uses great real-life case studies to show you how to stop thinking about your customers as a mass audience and start leveraging the knowl-edge and conversations in their networks.
—**Francois Gossieaux,** founder and partner, Human 1.0, and author, *The Hyper-Social Organization*

In a hyperconnected world, a great switch has been flicked: the power formerly vested in boardrooms is surging to the people formerly known as consumers. Asking your customers, then, to connect with you only in yes-terday's terms—through the practice formerly known as mass marketing—is a surefire recipe for irrelevance. So if you want to understand why your customers might be tuning you out—and how to start tuning into the thicker, stronger, more meaningful signals they're already listening to—then this thoroughly practical book should be your guide.
—**Umair Haque,** Director, Havas Media Lab

THE NETWORK IS YOUR CUSTOMER

The Network Is Your Customer

Five Strategies to Thrive in a Digital Age

DAVID L. ROGERS

Yale

UNIVERSITY PRESS

New Haven & London

Yale University Press books may be purchased in quantity for educational,
business, or promotional use. For information,
please e-mail sales.press@yale.edu (U.S. office)
or sales@yaleup.co.uk (U.K. office).

Designed by James J. Johnson and set in Electra type by
Integrated Publishing Solutions.
Printed in the United States of America.

Library of Congress Cataloging-in-Publication Data

Rogers, David L., 1970–
The network is your customer : five strategies to thrive in a
digital age / David L. Rogers.
p. cm.
Includes bibliographical references and index.
ISBN 978-0-300-16587-6 (clothbound : alk. paper) 1. Business
networks. 2. Social networks. 3. Digital media—Social aspects. 4. Digital
media—Economic aspects. 5. Strategic planning. I. Title.
HD69.S8R646 2010
658.8′12—dc22   2010029162

A catalogue record for this book is available from the British Library.

This paper meets the requirements of ANSI/NISO Z39.48-1992
(Permanence of Paper).
10 9 8 7 6 5 4 3 2 1

For my family, my most cherished network

Contents

Contents

Preface

The spark for this book began at the BRITE conference. I started the BRITE conference series in 2008 at Columbia Business School, where I am executive director of our Center on Global Brand Leadership. The focus of BRITE is on "brands, innovation, and technology." Over three years, I have led half a dozen large BRITE conferences and smaller senior leadership summits at Columbia and with the Center's partner business schools in Asia and Europe. These conferences have brought together innovative companies and nonprofits, cutting-edge entrepreneurs, and big thinkers of all kinds to share ideas about the ways emerging technologies are changing business. Topics we have explored include: open innovation, viral media, customer influence on brands, and the disruption of long-standing business models by the Internet.

One of the things I was amazed to see at BRITE was that our most exciting new digital business ideas were not just coming from Web companies like Google. The intense disruption wrought by the Web and its digitally empowered customers was transforming businesses far beyond the usual suspects of record labels and newspapers. I saw innovative new practices emerging in industries like consumer packaged goods, automobiles, fashion, finance, education, philanthropy, and politics, as well as in technology and new media.

At the same time, a lot of hype and overheated speculation were being generated about what the digital future might hold (revolution! capitalism reborn! power to the people!). I saw a need for a practical and evidence-based approach to digital business strategy. Through our research center and independently, I had advised and consulted on strategy for numerous companies in a wide range of industries. What I found they needed most were some basic frameworks for how businesses that are not aiming to be the next Facebook or Google might still harness the power of the Web. I wanted to distill some fundamental strategies and approaches that could work for businesses in the digital age, whether they were selling shoes or news, software or health care.

So I decided to write my next book.

The research was fun and always surprising. It took me (virtually) from Iowa to Afghanistan and Tel Aviv to Tokyo. I got to investigate not just consumer behaviors and innovative companies but insurgent political campaigns and creative musicians (of whom I am also one, although I got better business ideas from looking at my musical peers). In keeping with my subject, I read voraciously on my smartphone, in my RSS reader, on Web sites, and, yes, in printed books. My network was always with me. In the Mumbai airport, at a bar in Barcelona, or riding a rickshaw in Singapore, I shared articles with my research team via Evernote, reached out to business leaders on LinkedIn, followed the discoveries of other writers on Twitter (@david_rogers), and sketched my emerging themes on my blog (www.davidrogers.biz).

The key insight I found as my research progressed is that customers have changed. To thrive in our digital age, businesses need to reimagine our customers: not as a mass of isolated individual actors but as networks—with each customer as a node linking and dynamically interacting with each other and with us. The network is your customer.

This was not where I started. Like most observers, I started out thinking a lot about new media—"social media"—and all its latest shiny new forms. But I quickly realized this was a distraction. If we instead take a careful look at the changes in our *customers*—their behaviors, their motivations, and what they value—we can develop a broad strategic view of how to create value and reinvent our businesses for a digital future.

By focusing on customers, I identified five core strategies that any organization can use. Equally important, I realized that customer network strategy is not just something that impacts communications, social networking, or public relations. It has the potential to drive sales, to enhance innovation, to generate customer insights, to reduce operational costs, and much more.

As I wrote, I was lucky to have the chance to speak about my ideas to business leaders, small entrepreneurs, students, advertising agencies, nonprofits, and the press, in interviews, classrooms, and conferences in the United States, Europe, and Asia.

Their responses convinced me of the importance of my topic, as many explained how networks have transformed their relationship to customers and offer great opportunities for their business.

I also heard a lot of great questions: What is the business impact of customer networks? Is it better for some companies to *not* engage with networks? How does a network strategy work in different business categories? Can you measure the return on investment? How do different customer network behaviors relate? How does a network strategy work if I'm selling something that isn't a sexy consumer product? This book distills two years of hard thinking to answer these questions.

Some friends asked me, why write a book about the Web? (Isn't that like painting a picture of a television?) But I'm not sure books are as antiquated as we imagine. Unlike my previous two books (on marketing, brands, and customer experience), this one will not be read only on paper. Many of you will read these words on an e-reader like the Kindle or Nook, on a tablet like the iPad, or even on your phones (squint, squint). Some have proclaimed that our ever more cluttered media environment demands that writing become ever shorter if it is to find an audience. I disagree. I think the unique value of long-form writing is not diminished; indeed, it may have grown (even as we find it harder to make the time for it).

A book offers a unique opportunity to explore an idea in depth and vet a hypothesis in meticulous detail to see how it holds up after the initial thrill of a bold discovery has worn off. It offers the challenge of tying many ideas together and teasing out the complexities of their relationships to one another.

The biggest challenge in writing a book like this is that you are writing for the future. The first words you commit to the page will likely be read by your average reader two or more years later. This forces you to step back from the news of the moment, the trends of the day, and take a much broader view of your subject. Technology is changing too fast for me to write about it here in an up-to-the-minute fashion. (As I write this, my latest speeches already contain new cases that are too recent to make it in the book.) This forced me to focus not on technology but on the underlying behaviors that shape our adoption of technology and give it impact and meaning.

By understanding our behaviors, as individuals linked and living together in the seamless web of our digital networks, I hope to shed some light on the opportunities that lie ahead for us all.

Acknowledgments

This book would not have been possible without my own network of supporters, contributors, teachers, advisers, and readers.

Numerous companies, nonprofits, and entrepreneurs contributed cases to this book by dint of their exceptional work with customer networks. I am especially grateful to those whom I met through their appearances at the BRITE conferences that I lead at Columbia Business School. These include: Dave Carroll ("United Breaks Guitars"), Robin Chase (Zipcar), Carol Koh Evans (Microsoft), Bob Greenberg (R/GA), Marty Homlish (SAP), Lisa Hsia (Bravo Media), David Hsieh (Cisco), Tony Jebara (Sense Networks), Pamela Kaufman (Nickelodeon), Mark Kershisnik (Eli Lilly), Sylvia Marino (Edmunds), John Mayo-Smith (R/GA), Alyson Meranze (American Express), Freddy Mini (Netvibes), Ed Moran (Deloitte), Adam Nash (LinkedIn), Craig Newmark (craigslist), Bre Pettis (Makerbot), Penry Price (Google), Avner Ronen (Boxee), Vivian Schiller (NPR), Adam Selig (Visible Technologies), Dwayne Spradlin (InnoCentive), Paal Smith-Meyer (LEGO), Stephen Voltz (Eepy Bird), Luke Williams (Frog Design), and the many other companies and speakers at BRITE that did not make it into the book but inspired and informed it. I'd like to give a special thanks for additional in-depth interviews with Richard Binham-

Acknowledgments

mer (Dell), Sandy Carter (IBM), Thomas Gensemer (Blue State Digital), and Mark Yolton (SAP).

Thanks are also due to the writers who have joined me at BRITE and helped shape my thinking on networks, customers, and business, including: Seth Godin, Francois Gossieaux, Umair Haque, Jeff Howe, Jeff Jarvis, and Steve Rubel. A handful of others contributed critical ideas, though we never met offline: Albert-László Barabási, Kevin Kelly, Clay Shirky, and Fred Wilson, thank you, as well.

But ideas are one thing; a finished book is quite another.

This book would not have happened without my agent, Jim Levine, and my editor, Michael O'Malley. Each gave his enthusiastic support and commitment to the project from the earliest stages and provided valuable feedback as I developed the ideas into the full work you see today. Kerry Evans at Levine Greenberg and Niamh Cunningham and the editorial team at Yale University Press were constant supporters at each stage of the process.

Bernd Schmitt was an invaluable advocate for this project, prodding me to write the book and supporting its development at every stage, beginning with the BRITE conference where so many of my ideas began to take shape.

Jim, Michael, and Schmitt each gave detailed and invaluable feedback to the manuscript at various stages, asking the right questions, pushing for clarity, and letting me know when I was on the right track. Matthew Quint, Francois Gossieaux, and Richard Cacciato were generous with their time in reading the manuscript and offering excellent suggestions. Karen Vrotsos was a matchless editor, bringing a fresh eye, an inquiring sensibility, and a keen sense of cadence to the final prose. Laura Jones Dooley gave an expert and invaluable final edit.

The research for the book was critically assisted by several staff at our Center on Global Brand Leadership at Columbia Business School. Danielle Bailey was my lead research assistant, tracking

Acknowledgments

down countless sources, pitching cases and examples for my consideration, and serving as a sounding board. David Platt and Eileen Alhasic were of great help as I gathered my citations at the end of writing. Anna Fokina did a wonderful job bringing my scribbled illustrations to life, as did Stephanie Shieh for the "A-E-triple-C" icons that helped me remember the chapters of my own book.

I'd like to give a special thank you to Matthew Quint, Nancy Oti, Dina Shapiro, Nick Peterson, John Davis, Jin Han, Cara Toh, Joshua Safier, Jennifer Tromba, Yaron Samid, Lloyd Trufleman, Bill Sobel, and all our tireless staff and volunteers who have made the BRITE conference possible each year—and to the more than one thousand insightful attendees and speakers who make up the vibrant BRITE community.

My greatest and most enduring thanks go to Karen and George, who supported, encouraged, fed, nudged, and loved me through months of work while I wrote this book.

And thank you for reading it!

How to Read This Book

This is meant to be a practical book.

It has a lot of stories—about a networked improv comedy act, a Japanese newlywed writing a novel on her phone, Barack Obama's highly encrypted BlackBerry, American soldiers blogging in the war zone, and a young Israeli entrepreneur's quest to make his television work better, among others.

The book also offers more than a hundred case studies and examples of businesses applying strategic and innovative thinking to customer networks. And it is organized to provide a few key frameworks that should help you do the same in your own organization, whatever it may be.

Depending on where you are in developing your strategy for customers in the digital age, you may want to choose certain parts of this book to focus on or read the parts in a different order.

So let me offer a quick user's guide to this book.

Chapter 1

In this chapter you will find an overview of the book's key concepts: what customer networks are, why they matter, and the range of impact they can have on organizations. The chapter introduces the five core behaviors of customer networks and the five strategies that any organization can use to leverage them.

Use this chapter to orient yourself for the whole book.

Chapter 2

This chapter provides a more detailed and formal definition of what a "customer network" is. It also steps back to provide some background—from the science of networks and the history of technology—in order to shed light on the bewildering changes being wrought by today's digital tools. It concludes with a rethinking of the purchase funnel and some of our other basic models of business.

Depending on questions you may have after chapter 1, you may want to dig into this chapter next or come back later for additional background.

Chapters 3 to 7

This is the case study–filled "how to" heart of the book.

Each of these five chapters explains one of the five core customer network strategies. Each chapter also presents several different approaches to that strategy—for example, six approaches you might use for an ENGAGE strategy. My aim is to make each strategy extremely concrete for readers, and to show how each strategy might work in your organization.

Each chapter presents over two dozen case examples, highlighting the best practices of different businesses. Cases were carefully chosen to reflect a variety of organizations: large and small, business and nonprofit, as well as consumer goods and services, B2B, media, and technology companies. Most important, cases were chosen for having proven benefits and clearly achieved business objectives.

As you begin developing your own customer network strategy, you may refer back to chapters 3 to 7 for specific approaches and case examples.

These chapters also explore key customer behaviors shaping each strategy (for example, the rise of an on-demand culture, the splintering of our attention among media, or the desire to collaborate with others around shared values).

Each chapter ends with a peek at emerging trends ("The Future of . . ."). These trends are already starting to impact customer network behavior, but they are too nascent to offer case studies of how companies will use them for business goals. I hope they may spur your own thinking, so that your organization might provide one of the first case studies that we can learn from.

Chapter 8

Many business leaders see a promising new digital strategy and simply jump in, trying to emulate another company's success without thinking through their own objectives or how the strategy might best fit their own business, customers, and competitive landscape.

Chapter 8 provides a five-step planning and implementation process to guide this thinking, so that customer network strategy is not just driven by enthusiasm but is as carefully developed as any other business strategy.

For larger and long-standing organizations, this management process will help you apply a new conceptual framework (customer network strategy) to your existing departments and business processes.

For any reader, whether a division manager or a CEO, it should give you a road map to begin developing a customer network strategy for your own organization.

Chapter 9

As a leader, you need to consider more than just having the right strategy. Dwayne Spradlin, CEO of InnoCentive, told me once, "Culture eats strategy for lunch."

Leadership for customer networks requires more than just

planning and implementing a single project or initiative. It requires a fundamental shift in the orientation of an organization.

In chapter 9, I address the questions of "What will the organization of the future look like?" and "How do we create an organization that is not just customer-focused, but customer network–focused?" Drawing on interviews from inside some of the most forward-looking organizations in business, technology, and politics, I offer a few key principles that will define the customer network–focused organization.

Leaders of established businesses that grew up before the rise of customer networks need to ask themselves: What assumptions about our business do we need to reconsider? How does our culture need to change? What new skills and capacities do we need to foster? This chapter will help you answer these questions.

Self-Assessment Quiz

One of my readers got to the end of my manuscript and said, "I love this and want to get my team working on our customer network strategy now. Can you give me a simple assessment tool that I can give them, before they've read the whole book?"

That's what this is. The list of questions here should help you start thinking through where your business is right now, where your customers are, and what your objectives might be.

How to Continue the Conversation Online

Because the subject of customer networks is so dynamic, there will surely be much more to say, and many cases to explore, as this book comes to print.

I hope you will join me at my Web site, www.davidrogers.biz, where I will continue to write about cases and trends in customer networks, and where I will ask for your input and contributions as readers and experts in your own fields.

PART I

A New Model for Customers in the Digital Age

CHAPTER 1

The Customer Network Revolution

Look closely at a bee.

You may see it flying from tree to bush, seeking the best nectar to drink. You may watch it gather pollen on the bristles of its hind legs. Or you may marvel as it secretes wax to build hexagonal cells in its hive. Observing the bee up close, you might mistake this industrious insect for a solitary hunter-gatherer, seeking food, building a shelter, acting alone.

But look at the bigger picture, and you see a different story. This single bee is part of a vast, thriving colony of more than ten thousand bees: highly social insects that cooperate closely in seeking food, building a hive, and reproducing. The colony is capable of coordinated action, but it has almost no formal hierarchy or leadership, no more than a school of fish or a flock of gulls. The "queen" bee is really more of an indentured servant, tasked with producing thousands of eggs. She is in charge of very little else. Yet despite the simple roles played by each of its members, a powerful group intelligence emerges from the colony as a whole. This is networked intelligence.

The organization of a bee colony depends on a web of constant communication. The bees communicate as they build the brood comb together, place the pupae of offspring into cells, and seek out new and better sources of food. The precise means of bee communication remain a mystery. But they appear to include a combination of pheromones, low-frequency sounds, and a miniature dance of figure eights and body shakes (the bee's "waggle"). The lone bee that you see hovering in a field of clover has most likely found its chosen flower by following the directions communicated by others in the hive. And when the time comes to resettle en masse, a signal among them will trigger thousands of bees to swarm out of the hive and establish a new colony for the future.

Like the swarming bees in a hive, we humans are linked together today by an invisible web of communications. But instead of waggles, hums, and pheromones, we communicate by the digital technologies that permeate every aspect of our lives.

These technologies include the Web browsers that connect us to the trillion-plus pages of the World Wide Web via our computers and our smartphones. They include such messaging technologies as email, instant messaging, Skype, texting, and Twitter. They include technologies to download or stream radio podcasts, videos, photos, and songs to our pocket-sized media players, to our laptops, or to Net-enabled boxes attached to our TVs. These Internet technologies run on devices that are increasingly embedded not just in our computers and phones but in our game consoles, our cars, and even our shoes.

Our constantly multiplying digital tools connect us to more than just products, companies, and media channels. Far more important, they connect us all to one another. The digital flow of our data, our ideas, our commerce, and our identity turns each of us into a node in an enormously powerful network of human interaction. It is a network capable of spreading ideas, running businesses, organizing political action, and subverting institutions. We are the network, and the network is us.

A New Paradigm: Customer Networks

The impact of this new network on businesses and organizations of all kinds is profound. As the Internet links us in networks, it is transforming customers' relationships to each other and to organizations. Every organization today must realize that its customers—whether shoppers, business clients, charitable donors, or election voters—are behaving radically differently than in the predigital era. Our approach to business must change to match.

Business in the twentieth century was based on a model that viewed customers as isolated and passive individuals. With the rise of mass media, such as radio and television, businesses could reach extremely large audiences of customers, but businesses could not market to each of them as individuals. Business practice was therefore designed to suit the paradigm of a mass audience. Under this paradigm, product development, manufacturing, and communications were all designed to suit the aggregate behaviors of masses of individuals.

Today, business needs a new paradigm: the customer network. In customer networks, customers are no longer viewed as isolated individuals but are seen as dynamic and interactive participants in a network. These customers are constantly responding, connecting, and sharing among themselves and with businesses they care about. To succeed, businesses, nonprofits, and organizations of all kinds need new strategies that match the behavior of customer networks. But first we need to rethink our image of our customers, from individuals to networks. We need to stop thinking about the bee and focus on the hive.

Four Stories of Customer Networks

Businesses need to change the way they think about customers because the rise of customer networks has given much more power, independence, and influence to individuals.

To illustrate, let me start with four short stories that show the influence of customer networks.

Challenging Authority

Until recently, if a government controlled its country's mass media, individual citizens had no way to spread their own point of view, to get their voices heard outside their borders, or to organize themselves easily on a large scale. With the rise of customer networks, however, even the most authoritarian government has much less control over the flow of information.

In the summer of 2009, the supreme leader of Iran announced that incumbent president Mahmoud Ahmadinejad had won reelection in a landslide during the first round of voting. The announcement was widely disbelieved by supporters of the opposition candidate, who had expected that a close vote would force Ahmadinejad into a second-round run-off election.

Iranians took to the streets in the hundreds of thousands, but they didn't just march. They used every variety of digital technology available to communicate with each other and the outside world, including the Twitter microblogging service. Although the Iranian government ruled the airwaves and promptly ejected every foreign reporter from the country, still the protesting citizens were able to report their own view of events on the ground. The U.S. State Department even requested that the owners of Twitter delay a scheduled maintenance that would have taken down the service in order to leave it accessible to citizens of Iran during the protests.

As days of turmoil led to a brutal crackdown in the streets of Iranian cities, local citizens spread images of the violence online to viewers around the world as evidence against the regime. The murder by security forces of one young Iranian woman, Neda Agha-Soltan, was filmed on a cell phone, and the video clips spread rapidly online, making her a martyr and symbol of the struggle for Iranians. The protesters' call for a rerun of the election was not successful. But in this new globally networked world, the government could not easily squelch the voices of their protest.

Bashing a Brand

It used to be that if a customer had a terrible experience with your business, you might lose a customer for life. Perhaps, if that customer told family members or friends, your company might lose a handful of customers. That would have been the worst that could happen. Now, because of the power of customer networks, one bad customer experience can potentially have a huge impact on the image of a business or brand.

Take the experience of singer-songwriter Dave Carroll, who was traveling from Halifax to Nebraska with his band, Sons of Maxwell, when United Airlines badly damaged his guitar. The airline admitted the damage, but for nine months it passed the buck, refusing to compensate Carroll for the $3,500 in repairs to his instrument. After speaking to the last customer service agent who refused to help, Carroll promised United that he would write three songs about his experience. The first song, "United Breaks Guitars," turned into a comical YouTube video that hit a nerve with customers everywhere. The video featured country-style lyrics and comical images: luggage handlers ineptly tossing guitar cases through the air, a crime-scene outline of the "victim," sour and indifferent airline officials, and Carroll's band singing woeful harmony while gazing over his broken instrument in a burial casket.

Within two days, the video had been watched more than a million times and United was contacting Carroll to apologize and offer him compensation (he declined but suggested they donate the money to charity). United promised to mend its customer service ways, but it was too late to prevent the hit to the company's reputation. Within a few months, the video had been viewed more than five million times and attracted thirty-five thousand comments from customers. Those millions of viewers did not find United's actions a laughing matter: an independent analysis found "the vast majority of comments citing bad experiences, boycotts, and even other broken guitars."[1]

When United Airlines finally met with Carroll and announced new luggage policies, the company told him that they had never made the policies before because his problem was "statistically insignificant." In the world of customer networks, every customer experience can be significant.

Loving a Brand

Customer networks don't only hurt brands; they spread positive word of mouth as well. In 2008, a Facebook page for one of the world's most popular brands, Coca-Cola, rocketed to the number two spot on the social networking site, with more than three million fans "friending" and visiting the page to express their affection and affinity for Coke.

What was surprising, though, was that the page was not created by anyone in Coca-Cola's marketing department or any of its advertising agencies. It was created by two customers: Dusty Sorg, an aspiring actor in Los Angeles, and his friend Michael Jedrzejewski. Facebook users around the world soon began to come to the site and post their own photos of Coke advertising and packaging, Coke delivery trucks, Coke vending machines around the world, Coke tattoos, Coke memorabilia, and themselves drinking Coke. They also posted comments in many languages:

> "I was at Disneyland yesterday . . . drinking a Classic Coca-Cola :-)"
>
> "i lv coke......................................."
>
> "hımm:)seni her türlü içerim"
>
> "COKE ZERO MY FAVE THOUGH"
>
> "Para mi es más necesaria la Coca Cola que el aire que respiro!!!"
>
> "I just cannot live without you hahah. Coca Cola 4 life! (drinkin cola every sec of the day :p)"[2]

Within a few weeks, the page had 750,000 fans; within four months, the number was well over a million. The exact reason was a mystery to Dusty and Michael. They hadn't launched an advertising campaign, gone on the radio to tell the world, or otherwise publicized it. In fact, there were more than two hundred other Coca-Cola pages on Facebook, but none had come close to their growth. Something about their page or, more likely, the network of Facebook friends that they were linked to, and that their friends and friends' friends were linked to, had tapped into a powerful connection to the Coke brand and spread their page through the network of Facebook users.

Then, three months after the page had been posted, Facebook announced a new rule forbidding fan pages for brands that were not owned by the company they represented. Dusty and Michael's page would either have to be shut down or given to Coca-Cola to manage. Coke's management was not pleased. They had no interest in squelching the enthusiasm of their customers or putting them under the corporate thumb. So instead, when Facebook handed the page's ownership over to the company, Coca-Cola handed management of the page right back to Dusty and Michael. The page, and its network on Facebook, continued to grow and thrive.

Driving Your Business

Customer networks are not just influencing brand image and corporate reputations, however. They are also creating whole new business models for companies.

It used to be that if you wanted to start a clothing company, you needed to invest a lot of capital in product design, in marketing and promoting your brand, and in manufacturing and launching a variety of styles for each season—knowing that many styles would inevitably fail.

Jake Nickell and Jacob DeHart couldn't afford the traditional model for a clothing business when they started their company as nineteen-year-olds. They had only a thousand dollars to launch the hip, urban T-shirt business they called Threadless. The two Jakes couldn't rely on the old business model, so they built a new one driven by the power of their customer network.

Instead of hiring designers, the Jakes invite their customers to create designs for T-shirts and upload them at the Threadless Web site to compete in design contests. Winners receive a cash prize (which has grown from $100 to $2,500), but submissions are motivated just as much by the customers' desire to see their T-shirt designs come to life and be worn by others. Once their designs have been submitted, customers have a strong incentive to send everyone they know to the Threadless site to check out the contest and to vote for their design. Instead of advertising, the company lets its own customers spread the word. The winning contest designs get printed by Threadless and are then sold back to the same customers who voted for them.

Jake and Jacob now have a thirty-million-dollar clothing business with a 30 percent profit margin, thanks to some unusual features: zero advertising cost, virtually no product development costs, and a 100 percent success rate for their product launches, because every one of them has already been preselected and voted on by the customers who will buy it.[3]

The Challenge of Customer Networks

Faced with the growing power of networked customers, every business today faces a stark choice: Will your customers be your biggest competitor? Or will they be your biggest business driver?

Right now, two college kids with a Wi-Fi connection could be starting up the next craigslist, Napster, or YouTube. Your customers can easily become your biggest competitive threat. They can also become your best focus group, product developers, and volunteer marketing force. To choose the right course, however, a business must develop a strategy to engage with customer networks at every stage of the enterprise.

Let me be clear: Pursuing the same mass-market business strategies of the past and slapping up a Facebook page or launching a Twitter account is *not* a customer network strategy.

As companies seek to respond to the growing power of customer networks, they too often fall prey to the same basic mistakes:

- *Infatuation with Technology:* Executives read the business press, see a list of the latest hot social media, and tell their managers: Let's get some of that!

- *Lack of Customer Insight:* Companies launch plans without taking the time to understand the networked behavior of their customers and what is driving that behavior.

- *Lack of Clear Objectives:* Without a clear vision for how the strategy will affect the business's bottom line, efforts become unfocused, lack impact, and are impossible to measure.

- *Limited Scope and Vision:* A few people in public relations or communications are tasked with managing customer networks, with no vision of how networks could transform other divisions such as market research, innovation, sales, or marketing.

The results of these mistakes are all too clear. Large, successful brands launch Twitter accounts without considering who will follow them and why, only to see them languish with few followers and even fewer customers actually interacting with the brand. Other companies vainly hire ad agencies to film funny videos that they hope will go "viral" online. According to the 2009 Tribalization of Business Study, one third of all online communities launched by businesses fail to attract even a hundred participants.[4] Without clear strategic planning, such investments lead to efforts that neither inspire nor engage customers and have zero impact on business.

An effective customer network strategy can be a powerful driver of product innovation, brand engagement, and cost savings for business. But to effectively inspire sales, loyalty, innovation, or word of mouth among customer networks, businesses need to do more than post a funny video or jump on the latest social networking site. They need to do more than harness tomorrow's technology to sell last year's products.

To survive and thrive today, companies need to understand the core underlying behaviors of customer networks. And then they need to innovate products, services, and experiences that help customer networks get *what they want*.

So . . . what do customer networks want?

To learn the answer, companies need to stop focusing just on new *technologies* and start paying attention to new and emerging customer *behaviors*. They need to understand the network dynamics that persist even as technologies rapidly change and evolve. How do customers behave in networks? What do they value? What will they pay for?

Five Customer Network Behaviors

We now have four decades of experience living with the Internet, a network of networks; fifteen years of broad public use of the World Wide Web; and nearly a decade since the adoption of widespread social media tools in the Web 2.0 era. By observing which media have been embraced and how customers have used them, which new businesses have flourished, and which old brands have successfully adapted to customer networks, we can begin to identify a few broad, underlying usage patterns. I call these core customer network behaviors.

First, customers in networks seek to freely *access* digital data, content, and interactions as quickly, easily, and flexibly as possible. Whether it is instant communication on our smartphones, on-demand television from our digital cable boxes, or having a world of information at our fingertips with search engines, we want it all and we want it now. Increasingly, wherever we go, our choice of where to work or play is influenced by the availability of Internet access without logins, firewalls, or fees. The next generation of real-time data, location-aware mobile services, and cloud-computing technology will put each of us in even closer and more constant contact with our networks.

Second, customers seek to *engage* with digital content that is sensory, interactive, and relevant to their needs. We may be reading fewer newspapers and magazines than five years ago, but major news publishers have more readers than ever. In Japan, a new literary genre has emerged, the cell-phone novel, written for the smallest screen. Internet video has become an established medium for everything from amateur musicians to corporate communications. Gaming has moved from a niche activity of hardcore fanboys to a medium for all ages that is used for pleasure, learning, and even work. New mobile operating systems are turning portable devices like phones, tablets, and e-readers into our newest tools for engaging text, audio, and video.

Third, customers seek to *customize* their experiences in networks by choosing and modifying a wide assortment of information, products, and services. Online retailers have accustomed us to a vast range of choices that could never be matched by a physical book, music, or video store. The Web itself is the ultimate customizable medium, with a trillion pages to choose from as you browse for content, news, or commerce. Hypertext, RSS feeds, and widgets have made digital content highly customizable and point to the future of an increasingly personalized Web. But an overload of choices will make recommendation engines and filtering tools increasingly important.

Fourth, customers seek to *connect* with one another by sharing their ideas and opinions in text, images, videos, and social links. Every day, tens of thousands of hours of video are uploaded to the Web for sharing, along with countless photos, customer product reviews, status updates, blog posts, and comments in discussion forums. Across the world, people, brands, book clubs, and rock bands connect with their "friends" on various social networking sites. They spend time there for diverse goals, from friendship and dating to business networking and self-expression. Chronically ill patients are even using social networks to compare results on different therapies. Increasingly, our relationships in social networks are portable to other Web sites, allowing us to personalize and enrich all of our digital experiences.

Fifth, customers seek to *collaborate* on collective projects and goals through open platforms. Beyond just sharing ideas and conversations, networked customers are mobilizing together to measure traffic flows, write computer software, and elect political candidates. Millions of voters have joined online networks to raise money and organize in the offline world of phone calls, door-to-door canvassing, and hosting house parties. With varying skills, others are collaborating online to write encyclopedias, sustain journalism under totalitarian regimes, or design clothes for their friends. Today's digital tools allow groups to form and collaborate easily across great distances, whether motivated by curiosity, personal interests, or deeply held social values.

The order of these five behaviors reflects a progression from fundamental value (to the customer) to complex value (to the customer). This can be thought of as a parallel to psychologist Abraham Maslow's Hierarchy of Needs, which ranks human needs from the most basic (physiological needs such as air, food, and water) to those that are related to identity and purpose (the need for esteem, respect, and morality).[5] Although they do not match Maslow's categories, the five customer network behaviors are similarly ordered from the most basic to the most complex value to the customer:

- *Access:* The ability to actually connect to networks easily, flexibly, and effectively
- *Engage:* The ability to find relevant and valuable content and experiences in networks
- *Customize:* The ability to match or adapt those network experiences to unique customer needs
- *Connect:* The ability to express oneself and communicate with other customers in networks

- *Collaborate:* The ability to engage in purposeful action, with shared goals, in networks

The relative priority of these values is not fixed. We cannot generalize and say that "it is always more important to a customer to *collaborate* than it is to *connect*," or even that "if a customer has achieved some ability to *engage*, then he or she will focus on trying to *customize*."

Nor do these five behaviors exist in isolation. In many digital experiences, a customer may be simultaneously fulfilling multiple core behaviors (for example, seeking easy access to customized content). But understanding the unique value and importance of each of these behaviors by itself can shed light on their cumulative effect. Understanding them together offers a unique view into the motivations that continue to shape customer choice and actions as the technology of our digital networks rapidly evolves.

Last, the impact of these behaviors does not remain solely in the world of digital bits and online experiences. Each of these five behaviors in online networks shapes our choices and actions in the offline world as well, whether it is the places we travel, the votes we cast, or the products and services we purchase. Ideas and conversations that start in digital networks quickly spread over into offline relationships and interactions, and back again.

Five Customer Network Strategies

For organizations and businesses, the five customer network behaviors—*accessing, engaging, customizing, connecting,* and *collaborating*—can provide the key to creating value, building strong relationships, and designing products and services for customers in our digital age.

These five core behaviors provide the basis for five powerful strategies for customer networks: the ACCESS, ENGAGE, CUSTOMIZE, CONNECT, and COLLABORATE strategies (fig. 1.1). You may remember these as A-E-C-C-C, or "A-E-triple-C."

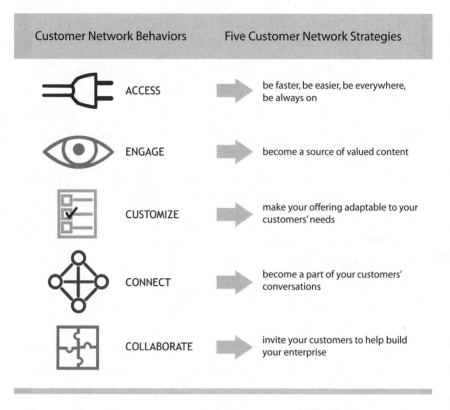

Customer Network Behaviors	Five Customer Network Strategies
ACCESS	be faster, be easier, be everywhere, be always on
ENGAGE	become a source of valued content
CUSTOMIZE	make your offering adaptable to your customers' needs
CONNECT	become a part of your customers' conversations
COLLABORATE	invite your customers to help build your enterprise

Figure 1.1 Five customer network behaviors and five core customer network strategies. *Illustration by Anna Fokina.*

This book explores each of these five strategies in detail and examines how they have been successfully applied by a variety of businesses and organizations. Here is a brief overview.

The ACCESS Strategy: Be Faster, Be Easier, Be Everywhere, Be Always On

Every organization today faces the expectations of an always-on world. To compete, businesses must find ways to provide customers an easier, faster, more pervasive connection to digital networks. Providing always-on Web connections to customers allows a service business like Virgin America airline to differentiate itself from competitors. On-demand business models—such as USAA's digital banking and Zipcar's auto rentals—meet customers' desire for more flexible service. As smartphones make our networks increasingly mobile and location aware, companies from Urbanspoon to Sears are finding new ways to let customers browse, discover, and purchase on the go. Meanwhile, cloud computing makes data accessible from anywhere, and real-time feeds make it accessible at anytime, allowing companies from Coca-Cola to Serena Software to communicate faster and better with employees. Businesses like Nike and Lifescan are connecting customers to their data by embedding digital access in more and more products, from cars to medical sensors to running shoes. And e-tailers such as Amazon.com and products like the Flip Video camcorder demonstrate how offering simpler and easier digital access can increase sales and market share. By providing new and better kinds of network access, businesses can make themselves indispensable to customers' lives.

The ENGAGE Strategy: Become a Source of Valued Content

In the predigital age, companies could piggyback on mass media such as television and radio to buy customers' captive attention and blast them with advertising messages. But in an environment of abundant media and rampant ad-skipping, businesses that want to engage customer networks need to create content that customers will actually want to consume. Today, every business needs to think like a media business. On sites like the American Express OPEN Forum and Dell's digitalnomads.com, companies are engaging audiences by creating content that is extremely useful for their core customers. Others, from Methodist University Hospital to the Broadway musical *Spring Awakening* to New Jersey retailer Wine Library, are engaging customers by showing an authentic and personal face in their media. By focusing on niche audiences and their particular interests, companies from General Electric to Mercedes-Benz are creating content that engages influential segments.

And businesses from IBM's consultants to the makers of Webkinz stuffed animals are engaging audiences and driving profits via interactive online gaming. By becoming a source of valued content, media, and information, companies can deepen relationships with customer networks that are increasingly difficult to sway with conventional advertising.

The CUSTOMIZE Strategy: Make Your Offering
Adaptable to Your Customers' Needs

Networked customers are not looking for cookie-cutter experiences, identical content, and mass-produced products, especially in the digital realm. By giving them tools to customize products, services, and content to suit their needs and interests, businesses can add real value that will differentiate them from competitors and engage their customers more deeply. Personalized playlists allow brands like Nissan and media companies like Pandora and NPR to provide customers with exactly the content they are looking for. Thanks to Web interfaces and digital prototyping, customers can also "mash up" and customize physical products and services, such as the Nike ID shoe line or the services at Affinia Hotels. Choice can give your business a human face, as the charity Kiva found when it let donors choose the project they wished to fund online, whether it was a mother in Guatemala who needed four hundred dollars for equipment to start a tailoring business or a farmer in Angola who needed three hundred dollars for new goats to milk. Other businesses have created platforms for choice, among them HP's Magcloud for custom magazine design and Ponoko's Web-based service for the custom manufacturing of furniture, toys, or jewelry. But companies need to beware of what psychologists have called the paradox of choice and not overwhelm customers with disorganized options. This is why Netflix offered a million-dollar prize to help improve its Cinematch movie recommendations. Choice schemas, recommendation engines, and new social filtering tools are essential to the future of digitally customized experiences.

The CONNECT Strategy: Become a Part of Your Customers' Conversations

Customers are constantly sharing ideas and opinions on the Web today in social media conversations that shape brand perception. Companies can benefit by joining these conversations—either in popular forums like Facebook and Twitter or by creating their own forums where customers express themselves. Joining the conversation on established social networks allows organizations to connect with their customers, whether it is Red Bull on its Facebook page, drug maker UCB on the PatientsLikeMe epilepsy community, or Kogi Korean BBQ's conversations on Twitter. Other businesses, such as Ford Motor Company and Bravo Media, host their own forums for passionate users to share opinions, start discussions, vote in polls, and connect with one another. By asking customers for ideas, platforms like My-StarbucksIdea.com and Dell's IdeaStorm help companies innovate valuable new products and services. In other cases, companies can integrate the customer's voice into their own, as in the March of Dimes "Every Baby Has a Story" social marketing campaign or the hit TV show *iCarly*, whose viewers upload their own videos and photos in hopes of becoming part of the next episode. Customer conversations can also add a layer of value to a business, as in Microsoft's customer-driven support forums, or the Epicurious.com recipe site, where users add creative variations to each posted recipe. By connecting with customers in their conversations online, businesses can build stronger relationships, gain valuable insights, and build their brands.

The COLLABORATE Strategy: Invite Your Customers to Help Build Your Enterprise

One of the most powerful ways to engage customer networks is to invite them to collaborate with your business on shared goals and projects. Collaboration can take many forms. Passive contribution systems, such as the Dash car navigation system or SETI@home, allow users to contribute things like real-time traffic information or computer scanning of images from space to assist in large-scale data projects. Active contribution systems allow customers to work on small parts of a collective effort, such as contributing news photos to CNN's iReport, adding details to an online tax guide for Intuit, or raising money for the next album by pop band Five Times August. In open competitions, customers compete to develop the best solutions to a challenge, whether it is a new T-shirt design for Threadless, a new venture business plan for Cisco, or the design for a hundred-mile-per-gallon car sponsored by Progressive Auto Insurance. By creating defined platforms for others to build their own businesses, companies like eBay, craigslist, and CD Baby can unleash tremendous creative and economic activity by users. With open platforms—such as open source code, software development kits, and Application Programming Interfaces—Apple has attracted thousands of programmers to develop applications for the iPhone and transform it into a category-defining product. Using open platforms, New York City's government enlisted citizens to develop apps that make its public data more open and useful for everyone. To collaborate with customer networks, businesses need to find the right balance of motivators for participants (love, glory, and money), to understand which large problems can be divided into smaller tasks, and to strike the right balance of bottom-up versus top-down control.

The Business Impact of Customer Network Strategy

As should be clear, these strategies are not just about creating goodwill on a few blogs or amorphous customer "buzz"; they can lead to real business impact. Customer network strategies can be used to achieve a variety of business objectives, including product differentiation, speed to market, more effective sales channels, reduced costs for customer service, customer loyalty and word of mouth, brand awareness among hard-to-reach target segments, customer insight, expanded innovation resources, and improved knowledge management.

Customer network strategy is not just for small start-up businesses. It can be effective for organizations of all sizes—midsize local businesses, Fortune 500 companies, and multinational giants.

Customer network strategy is not just for web and technology companies, either. It can be effective for a wide variety of categories—fashion, electronics, retailers, pharmaceuticals, business consulting, consumer packaged goods, nonprofits, rock bands, and political campaigns.

Nor is customer network strategy only useful in reaching out to end consumers. It is also effective in connecting with business customers, external partners, and an organization's own employees.

A few examples of the customer network strategies featured in this book, and their business impact, include:

- *Apple:* Which tapped a network of outside developers to design more than a hundred thousand apps to run on its second-generation iPhone, generating new revenue and transforming the smartphone category.

- *Author Stephenie Meyer:* Who reached out to early fans in online communities to build the cult following that propelled her *Twilight* series of vampire books into all four top slots of USA *Today*'s Best-Selling Books list.

- *Nike:* Which launched the world's largest running community, with more than a million members who use digital sensors to track, compare, and share their athletic performance and goals.

- *Dell:* Which gave voice to half a million customers on its Idea Storm site and generated more than ten thousand ideas for new product development.

- *Canadian toymaker Ganz:* Which reinvented the stuffed animal product category with its Webkinz toys that children play with in an online virtual world, an innovation that earned over a hundred million dollars in annual sales.

- *Kraft Foods:* Which created a branded iPhone application featuring thousands of recipes made with Kraft products and then charged customers for the app, selling more than a million copies.

- *Ford Motor Company:* Which, before the launch of the Ford Fiesta, generated an astonishing 38 percent awareness among Gen Y consumers, not with an ad campaign, but by selecting one hundred young people to spend six months with the car and share their unedited experiences online.

- *Cisco:* Which found what may be its next billion-dollar business through an online contest that yielded a plan for a new enterprise based on "smart grid" technology.

- *Kiva:* Which let donors choose the family businesses they want to fund around the world and attracted a network of more than half a million donors funding two hundred thousand projects worldwide.

- *The 2008 Obama presidential campaign:* Which gave millions of supporters the online tools to raise funds, register voters, and organize for caucuses across the country, propelling a long-shot candidate to the Democratic Party nomination and, ultimately, the White House.

The Rest of This Book

These cases and many more are presented in part II (chapters 3 to 7). These five central chapters explore the five customer network strategies: ACCESS, ENGAGE, CUSTOMIZE, CONNECT, and COLLABORATE.

Each chapter defines a customer network strategy and discusses its impact on key organizational objectives. In stories that stretch from Iowa to Tokyo, and from living rooms to war zones, the underlying customer network behavior is explored, along with social and technological factors which shape that behavior. Next, multiple approaches to that customer network strategy are presented. Each approach is illustrated by successful case studies of businesses from a variety of industries. Last, key lessons for implementing the strategy are presented, as well as emerging technologies that will continue to shape it in the future.

The over one hundred cases presented in part II draw on the many exceptional organizations I have met since launching the BRITE conference at Columbia Business School and at partner universities globally. Through BRITE (BRands, Innovation, and TEchnology), I have had the chance to interview, present onstage, and bring into the classroom a wide range of tech companies (including Google, craigslist, and MySpace), consumer brands (LEGO, P&G, Nike, Dove, Citibank), pharmaceutical companies (Eli Lilly), media businesses (MTV, NBC, NPR), and B2B firms (GE, SAP, Cisco), as well as advertising and public relations agencies (R/GA, Ogilvy, Edelman), political campaigns (Barack Obama, Mitt Romney), nonprofits (Soaringwords), and tech start-ups and entrepreneurs (Boxee, Maker-Bot, Sense Networks). The contribution of insights from their business cases has been invaluable in exploring the five strategies presented in part II.

Part III (chapters 8 and 9) focuses on the broader management and leadership of customer network strategy within an organization. Imagine that you are put in charge of developing an overall customer network strategy for your organization or for a division or a product line: Where do you begin? How do you decide which of the five core strategies to deploy and how to connect them? How do you sell your project to upper management, and if you move ahead, how do you know if your project is working? Chapter 8 presents a five-step process for the development of an overall customer network strategy for any brand, business unit, or organization (fig. 1.2). This process includes:

- *Setting Objectives:* Defining the most important business outcomes for your organization.

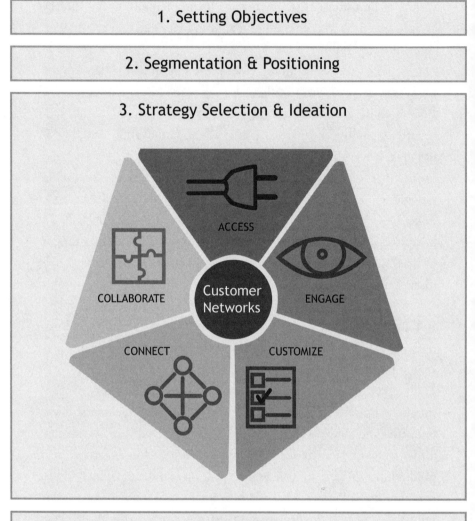

Figure 1.2 The Five-Step Customer Network Strategy Planning Process. *Illustration by Anna Fokina.*

- *Segmentation and Positioning:* Understanding who your customers are, how they are participating in networks, and what your brand positioning and value proposition are.

- *Strategy Selection and Ideation:* Choosing which strategies to pursue (A-E-C-C-C) and developing specific initiatives by mapping those strategies to your customers, your competitors, and your own business.

- *Execution:* Implementing your strategy using skills from traditional disciplines such as marketing, customer service, and operations, as well as developing new capabilities suited to customer networks.

- *Measurement:* Putting in place metrics to measure the results of your strategy against defined objectives and gathering feedback to continuously build and improve your strategy.

The final chapter (chapter 9) examines the nature of the customer network–focused organization. It describes three large organizations that have used customer network strategies broadly across customer segments and business domains. These and other cases point to how future organizations will operate in a networked world—by being borderless, collaborative, and pervasively connected. The likely impact on several industries is discussed, as well as the cultural traits that will be required of organizations and leaders. Such previously laudable attributes as transparency, responsiveness, and sharing social values are now essential to your success in a world of customer networks.

But before we examine the building blocks of an effective strategy for customer networks, we should answer a few questions regarding where we are and how we got here. What exactly is a network, and what can network science tell us about our digitally linked behavior? How has the Internet evolved, and what is so different about Web 2.0? How is the revolutionary rise of many-to-many communications tools changing our society? And if we truly are no longer in an era of broadcast messages and mass marketing, then what models should we now use for selling and for business? We will explore these and related questions in chapter 2.

Today, whatever your business, the network is your customer. To thrive in our interconnected world, every company needs a strategy designed for customer networks. Aligning businesses with the reality of customer networks will not be easy. But it offers enormous potential for organizations to deepen relationships with consumers, business partners, and employees. For long-standing organizations, this will require a shift from strategies and business processes of the industrial era. These processes aimed for mass economies, mass production, and mass marketing to an aggregate of thousands or millions of individual customers, each acting alone and in isolation. In the era of networks, customers are no longer alone. To succeed, businesses need to stop focusing on the bee and learn to unleash the power of the hive.

CHAPTER 2

Network Science and Lessons for Business

Putting on a comedy show for a hundred people in a Manhattan club may require months of effort and organizing. But for Charlie Todd, producing an Improv Everywhere event requires only a clever idea, an email to his network, and a video uploaded to YouTube to reach millions of followers.

In one such gambit, Todd sent an email to the list who had signed up at the comedian's improv shows and his blog. The email invited recipients who were men to meet him in Central Park on a fall Saturday: he stipulated only that they be willing to take off their shirts in public. With no further communication, 111 men showed up. They burst into laughter when Todd announced that they were going to perform a prank at the nearby Abercrombie & Fitch store. The hyper-trendy flagship store is known for employing shirtless male models to stand in its entryway and display their hairless, sculpted chests to in-coming customers and photo-snapping tourists. Inside the store, the dark clubby atmosphere (pulsing music, pinpoint product lighting) continues the fetishistic theme of strapping, shirtless men: images on product packaging, buff mannequins, the muscular bronze statue in the basement, and a four-story mural of ruddy, shirtless hunks labor-ing on shipboard. Todd's motley crew would present quite a contrast.

They entered the Fifth Avenue store separately, choosing locations on assigned floors. At exactly 4:37 pm, all 111 men removed
their T-shirts at the same time, stuffed them into their pockets, and
continued casually browsing, displaying their own versions of Abercrombie's bare-chested theme with widely varying body shapes, sizes,
and hairiness.

The stunt provoked shock, amusement, confusion, and an-
noyance among employees and shoppers; most laughed or took pictures of the bizarre scene. After fifteen minutes, the store's management requested that the half-dressed men leave, despite their protests
that they were only topless because they needed to buy a shirt. The
scene continued when the men exited to the street, with several of the
pranksters posing for pictures with the store's befuddled, then be-
mused, official model. Todd recorded the entire escapade with hid-
den video cameras and posted a video of the exploit on YouTube and
on his blog, where it attracted over a million views and press coverage
from New York to Belgium to Brazil.[1]

This was just one of more than a hundred improvisational
missions that Todd has organized, although the term *organized* may
be an exaggeration. Todd's theatrical events take some slight planning
on his part, but the crowd that performs them comes together in a
near-spontaneous fashion. A simple email, with scarcely any details,
spreads out to a network of curious volunteers who have signed up on
Todd's list. In a phenomenon akin to what Howard Rheingold has
called "smart mobs," they coalesce and disperse in rapid fashion, with
almost no formal organizing required.[2]

Abercrombie & Fitch's own sex-focused marketing message
was carefully planned, projected via an expensive set of tools (billboard ads, retail environment design, and staff training), and tightly
controlled by the company's employees. By contrast, Todd's parody of
that message was loosely planned, used free digital tools open to any-

one, and harnessed volunteers brought together on the slightest semblance of a relationship. Todd's success cleverly reveals how today's digital technologies have burst the barriers to organized action, linking us all into new kinds of human networks.

The Theory of Networks

The concept of a "network" first arose in a field of mathematics known as graph theory, pioneered by Swiss-born mathematician Leonhard Euler in 1736. In a seminal paper, Euler solved a long-standing puzzle of geography known as the Königsberg Bridge problem: Could someone cross each of the seven bridges of that Baltic seaport without repeating one?[3] Euler found the solution (No) by treating the city's islands and river banks as featureless *nodes* and Königsberg's bridges as *links* connecting them. By reducing urban geography to a simple mathematical graph, the puzzle was easily solved, and the mathematics of networks was born.[4]

At its most basic, a network is any system or structure of interconnected elements that can be represented by a graph of *nodes* (the elements) connected by some kind of *links* (whatever ties them together). The nodes of a network may be anything from landmasses to cells in a body, political institutions, or people. The links between the nodes might be physical connections, biochemical interactions, relationships of power and authority, or reciprocal social ties such as friendship (fig. 2.1).

In the midtwentieth century, the Hungarian mathematicians Paul Erdős and Alfréd Rényi greatly expanded the theory of nodes and links in eight papers exploring the topology and behavior of randomly generated networks.

In the late twentieth century, the mathematics of graph theory gave birth to a new interdisciplinary science of networks, devoted

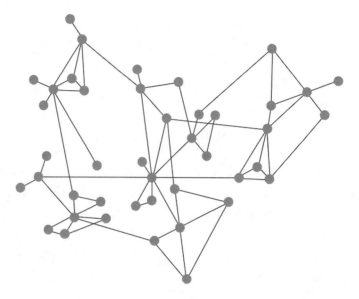

Figure 2.1 Diagram of a network of nodes and links with random clustering. *Illustration by Anna Fokina.*

to examining the common principles of network graphs that are found across domains ranging from engineering to information science to biology to sociology.

Transportation systems have been mapped as networks, starting with Euler's bridges of Königsberg, and continuing later as train networks, with stations (the nodes) linked by lines of track; road networks, with cities connected by interstate highways; and air traffic networks, with airports linked by the airline routes that crisscross our globe.

In the field of communications, networks were used to map telephone systems, with their wires (links) connecting phone lines and exchanges (the nodes). Later, these same phone networks began to link computers into the Internet. In terms of communications content (rather than communications hardware), the World Wide Web has been mapped as a network of interconnected Web pages linked together by hyperlinks.

In biology, network science has been used to map out the relationships of nerve cells connected by the dendrites and axons that transmit and receive their messages. Networks are used to map molecules in an organism by how they are linked through biochemical reactions. Network maps have also been applied to tracking the spread of infectious diseases, with patients representing the nodes and vectors of disease transmission being the links between them.

Decades before the arrival of Web sites like Facebook, sociologists attempted to map the social ties within groups via the field of social network analysis. Different typologies of networks were seen to represent varying organizational structures, from the hierarchical models of churches, companies, and traditional militaries to the more distributed, centerless topologies of terrorist organizations like Al Qaeda, whose numerous cells are only loosely connected to one another.

Just as disease may transmit through networks of people, so too do ideas. Social network analysis has often focused on how and why certain innovations spread rapidly, be they new technologies (use of the telegraph), new language (urban slang), or new ideas (the Christian teachings of the disciple Paul in the first century).[5]

In all these cases, a network model has allowed for new insights to be gained into the behavior and properties of extremely complex systems—insights that may not be visible by simply observing the actions of their individual constituent parts.

Customer Networks: A Definition

Today the model of networks can yield critical insights and understanding for another domain—understanding customers in our digital age.

In the past, a network model may have been less relevant to understanding the relationships of companies and customers. For the most part, advertising and products radiated out from large companies to customers via unidirectional mass production channels. Although a customer might buy from a company, purchase and sale was their only significant means of exchange. In terms of communication, companies advertised to customers but rarely listened to them (beyond responding to the occasional complaint letter).

Most important, customers had virtually no point of interaction with each other. If you were a regular customer of Ford Motor Company, that was a connection between you and the automaker, but the only connections you might have with other Ford customers would be extremely limited and local (perhaps the fellow patrons of a repair shop or dealership).

With the rise of an increasingly social Internet, however, this picture has changed dramatically. Any organization's customers are now quite easily connected to others around the world who share common experiences, interests, preferences, and purchasing behaviors; and the relationships of customers with organizations and with each other are reciprocal, dynamic, and participatory. For any organization looking at its customers today, the model of a network should appear very clearly and sharply relevant. Let me offer a more formal definition, then.

A *customer network is: the set of all current and potential customers of an organization, linked to the organization, and to each other, through a web of digital tools and interactions.*

Note that, being a strategic business model, a customer network is explicitly defined from the point of view of an organization and in terms of that organization's constituents. (Otherwise, it would simply be a model of "human networks," encompassing the entire universe of digitally connected people.) But the "customers" in a customer network may, in fact, be members of any key constituency of a business. Depending on the organization, its customers may be business clients, voters, music fans, students, or retail shoppers. Its "customers" may include internal constituencies as well (employees, volunteers, and so on).

Many organizations will have multiple types of customers to

consider in their networks. The customer network of a business software company may include client businesses, partners who develop complementary products, and even internal employees who must collaborate with outside innovators. The customer network for a literary agency could include both the publishers that it sells to and the authors it represents. A pharmaceutical company's customer network would likely include both doctors and patients, as well as regulators, insurance companies, and academic researchers, among others. For a philanthropic or political group, the customer network would include major supporters and small donors, as well as volunteers, grassroots activists, consultants, and other constituencies and partners.

What ties these customers together in a networked fashion are the "digital tools and interactions" in my definition above, which may range from sending an email to conducting a search to unleashing a malicious virus or editing a video in real time via the Web. They include tools for communication (such as email, cell phones, and social networking sites), for content creation and publication (blogging, microblogging, video sharing, and product review sites), for commerce and consumption (purchasing, downloading, streaming, and subscribing), or collaboration (file sharing and wikis). These interactions are carried today primarily over the Internet but also over cell phone networks and proprietary networks using Wi-Fi, Bluetooth, television cable, and other means of transmission.

What Network Science Tells Us about Customer Networks

Our understanding of customer networks will come primarily from investigating their patterns of behavior online and offline, and from examining case studies of customers' interactions with businesses in a variety of industries. This will be the focus of parts II and III of this book. But before we leave the hard science behind, it is worth understanding a few principles from the science and mathematics of network modeling and exploring what they reveal about the structure and nature of human networks.

Greater Connections = Much Greater Impact

From the field of telecommunications networks, we have a principle known as Metcalfe's Law. This principle states that as the number of nodes in a network increases, the value or impact of that network grows exponentially. An example can be seen in the invention of the fax machine. When the first fax machine was hooked up to a telephone network, its impact was nil. When a second fax machine was attached to the network, it now offered a private channel for communication between two parties. As the number of fax machines grew, their utility grew rapidly. In general, as you increase the number of nodes (n) in a communication network, the number of possible links between them increases exponentially, as $n(n-1)/2$. Two fax machines can make one connection; five fax machines can make ten connections; ten fax machines can make forty-five connections. Similarly, as the number of Facebook members grows, the number of potential links for each member rises.

The lesson of Metcalfe's Law for customer networks is this: as more of a business's customers adopt a new digital tool (be it smartphones or text messaging or Facebook), the potential impact of their networked behavior on that business increases dramatically. This holds particular significance for companies operating in markets where Internet usage is still growing (for example in India, where PC usage is low but growth is forecast for mobile Web usage by the country's half a billion mobile phone users).

Clusters, but No Centers

Human networks tend to be mathematically complex; they have no central plan like the hierarchy of a traditional organization or the street grid of a modern city. But human networks are not random like the graphs studied by Erdős and Rényi, in which any two nodes have an equal likelihood of being connected. Instead, human networks (whether the World Wide Web or a network of personal friendships) grow links spontaneously but shaped by underlying principles. One such principle for the Web is that once a page has several links from other pages, it is more easily found and is therefore more likely to attract additional links. A principle for social networks is that if you and I both share a friend, we are more likely to be friends with each other than with another random person. Networks shaped by these kinds of principles lack any definite center. They do, however, have *clusters* — groups of nodes that are more closely linked to each other (in a network of friendships, this might be a circle of friends, most of whom know each other).

One lesson for business is that customers will cluster with others around shared affinities and interests (like Charlie Todd's fans and their affinity for his sense of humor). Businesses should seek to understand and learn from the shared affinities of their own customer networks. Another lesson for business is that there will be no clear center to a customer network to be controlled; some customers will be more connected than others, but this may shift at any given time. Therefore, instead of trying to identify a few central customers ("influencers") in the network to market to, a business will do better to foster relationships with many different customers who are slightly more connected than the average — what Duncan Watts has called a "Big Seed" strategy.[6]

Six Degrees of Separation

In 1967, psychologist Stanley Milgram set out to prove what he called the Small World Hypothesis, which states that in a complex network, even with huge numbers of nodes, any two nodes are usually only a few links apart. In a famous experiment, Milgram set out to demonstrate this hypothesis through social ties. Milgram gave a set of letters to random people in Kansas and Nebraska and asked each of them to try to get their letter into the hands of a stock broker in Boston (whom none of the participants knew) by mailing the letter to whomever they knew who seemed most likely to know the broker; those recipients were then asked to do the same thing. The astonishing result: 42 out of 160 letters reached their target, with an average of 5.5 intermediate links between the Midwesterner and the Bostonian. This remarkable result was the inspiration for the title of the play (and later movie) by John Guare, which gave us the popular term "six degrees of separation." In fact, as the characters in Guare's play suggest, everyone is closely connected in today's networked world. A study of the early World Wide Web when it had only eight hundred million pages found that each page was, on average, only nineteen clicks away from any other.[7]

The importance of Milgram's hypothesis for business is that customers in networks are never more than a few links away from each other. This is why customer points of view can spread so quickly through customer networks—whether it is Dave Carroll's story of bad service on United or the enthusiasm of Threadless customers for a new competition. Given this speed of transmission, businesses need to be regularly monitoring online conversations and ready to leap in and respond where appropriate.

Power Laws and the 90–9–1 Rule

Another principle of complex, nonrandom networks is that they tend to follow what is called a "power law distribution." Many natural phenomena, such as the height of a species, follow the random distribution known as a bell curve: most animals grow to be quite close to the average height of their species, and those that deviate will be only slightly taller or shorter. (Even in a planet with six billion people, none of us is twice as tall as the average adult human.) But among phenom-

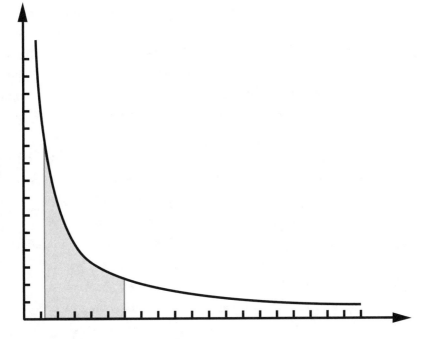

Figure 2.2 A power law distribution. *Illustration by Anna Fokina.*

ena that follow a power law curve, there is no clustering around the average; instead there are a few extremely high values and then many, many more increasingly small values (fig. 2.2). This distribution can be seen in the value of oil fields around the world: the total number of underground oil deposits is huge, but the vast majority of them are of insignificant value. A few deposits are very valuable, however, and a handful of those have extraordinarily high value. Power law distributions are seen in the size of grains of sand, the populations of cities, and even the distribution of wealth, as famously observed by Vilfredo Pareto's principle (later called the "80–20 rule") that 80 percent of the wealth is held by 20 percent of the population.

Customer networks follow this kind of power law distribution as well: some customers are much more or less connected or active within a customer network than the average customer. Jakob Nielsen described this in his "90–9–1 Rule," based on participation in online communities and forums such as Wikipedia. Nielsen's rule states that for every one hundred customers participating in an online network, roughly 1 percent will be highly active (posting regularly to blogs, writing detailed product reviews, or starting a new entry on Wikipedia); 9 percent will contribute somewhat actively (commenting on others' blogs, rating products with a single sentence or on a five-point scale, or making edits to an existing Wikipedia entry); and the remaining 90 percent will not contribute and therefore will be largely invisible. They remain important, however, because as they search, read, and observe, they are highly influenced by other network members.[8]

The lesson for businesses is to realize that the highly active customers in an online forum are only the tip of the iceberg. For every customer posting a detailed product review, hundreds more may be reading that review and shaping their opinions about a business based on it.

Easy Group Formation

A final lesson from network science is that networks allow for extremely quick and easy formation of groups and coordination of action without advanced planning. This can be seen in the synchronized chirping of crickets, the simultaneous flashing of millions of fireflies, or the ability of audiences at theater or sporting events to begin clapping in unison.[9] Today's digital tools and interactions allow us to congregate and coordinate over distances, too, and not just when we are in the same room. Charlie Todd's improv comedy mission to Abercrombie & Fitch, organized with a single cryptic email, is but one example of how human networks can take action with vastly less planning and investment of resources than in the past.

In his book *Here Comes Everybody*, Clay Shirky presents a case of customers organizing rapidly to lodge a protest against a business's practices. In 2007, the British division of HSBC bank had marketed its checking accounts to college students with a promise of no fees on overdrafts ("bounced" checks). The promotion was very successful in attracting customers during the school year, but over the summer HSBC changed its policy back to charging for overdrafts, no doubt assuming that the students, who had dispersed for the summer holidays, would have no easy way to organize a protest. Instead, Cambridge University student Wes Streeting set up a page on Facebook to decry "The Great HSBC Graduate Rip-Off," and it quickly attracted thousands of HSBC's customers who planned a public protest in front of the bank's London offices. HSBC caved in to the customers' demands before the protest could take place.[10]

The lessons from network science for customer networks are clear. Because of digital tools, it is now much easier for customers to connect and mobilize—for or against your business—without any formal or preexisting organization. Customer networks are inherently centerless, difficult to influence, and lack any consistent leaders (Wes Streeting was just another college kid with friends on Facebook). Customers are more closely and fluidly connected to one another today than ever before. As the use of digital tools spreads, the influence of customer networks will continue to grow.

The Roots of Revolution

Why now? What is different about today's digital tools, and why have they tied us closer together into networks of such growing power and influence?

For many years we have had tools for instantaneous communication over great distances, such as radio and television. Many of these tools have been widely available for individual communication— the telegraph and the telephone—and have been credited with shrinking the distances between us. There is one way in which today's tools are qualitatively different, however.

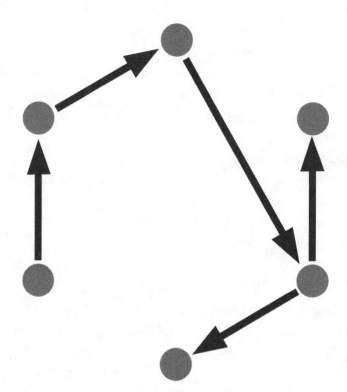

Figure 2.3 How ideas spread via one-to-one communications. *Illustration by Anna Fokina.*

Until recently, the vast majority of the world's population had access to tools that followed a *one-to-one communications* paradigm. These tools range from face-to-face speech to letter writing, telephone calls, faxes, pagers, cell phones, and instant messaging. With one-to-one communication tools, an individual can communicate his or her own message or point of view, but only to one or a few recipients at a time (fig. 2.3). With access to only these tools, customers in the past behaved very much as individuals, sharing limited amounts of information with limited numbers of people. If a customer had a bad experience with a company, he or she might write a letter to the company, might tell friends at work, and might tell some family members by phone, but the customer's point of view could not spread far.

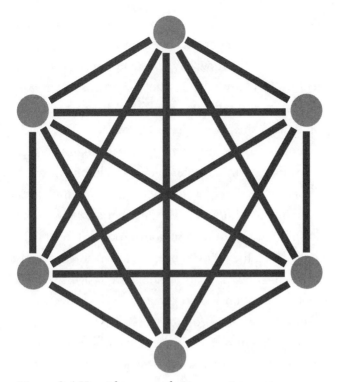

Figure 2.4 How ideas spread via many-to-many communications. *Illustration by Anna Fokina.*

At the same time, a small group of large organizations have had access to tools following a different paradigm: *one-to-many communications.* These included broadcast radio and television, cable, and the printing press for books, newspapers, magazines, and other print materials. These tools have allowed large organizations to project their own message instantly to large audiences, up to the millions. The resulting power imbalance allowed organizations to dominate and assume a central role in interactions with customers.

What is qualitatively different about many of today's digital tools for communication is that they follow a new, third paradigm: *many-to-many communications* (fig. 2.4). Tools such as email (which can be sent almost as easily to a thousand people as to one), blogs (which allow publishing on the Web with virtually no technical skills), online comments, product review sites, social networking sites, video sites, wikis, and Twitter allow any user to communicate any message simultaneously to many others, who can in turn communicate to many others. As a result, the voices of a customer can easily multiply through a network, just as musician Dave Carroll's did on YouTube when he complained about United Airlines breaking his guitar.

The origins of these many-to-many technologies can be found in the history of the Internet, the network of interlinking networks through which they all operate. The Internet has grown dramatically since its birth. In the 1970s it arose from a specialist tool for academics and the military. In the 1990s it became a mass medium for sending messages, ordering products, and reading Web pages. Today, it allows seamless communication and integration in every aspect of our lives.

The Internet has also grown increasingly dynamic. At first, the pages and content of the World Wide Web were all created by professionals or highly skilled amateurs with a knowledge of programming languages like HTML. In the new century, a new generation of tools makes it easy for anyone with some curiosity and a mouse to post their own photos, videos, blog posts, social networking profiles, and other media to the Web. The explosive growth of brand-name Web services such as Flickr, YouTube, Blogger, Wikipedia, Facebook, and Twitter make anyone and everyone a Web publisher. Even Web users who have never penned a blog post or uploaded a baby video have consumed from the sea of "user-generated content." They may have added their own voice to the social web without even realizing it, by renting a movie on Netflix, commenting on a product or vendor on eBay, or updating friends on their whereabouts or mood via Facebook. By 2009, most U.S. Internet users were not just reading and consuming content on the Web but creating it themselves.[11]

Today's Internet, then, is increasingly omnipresent and social. It is this maturing of the Internet, and its spread of many-to-many tools to everyone, that has given a worldwide platform for the voices of aggrieved folk musicians on YouTube, enthusiastic Coca-Cola fans on Facebook, and outraged protesters in the streets of Iran. These are the tools that have given rise to today's customer networks.

Lessons from History

In many ways, the rise of many-to-many communication tools via the Internet parallels the broad social changes brought on by Johannes Gutenberg's invention of movable type printing in 1439. The history of the printing press may offer lessons as we explore the forces at work in the rise of customer networks.

Before the printing press, all printing was done by hand by a professional class of scribes. The tremendous effort required meant that there was basically only one book in wide circulation in Europe, the Bible. The Bible was written in Latin and controlled by the Catholic Church, Europe's preeminent political power.

Much like the Internet, Gutenberg's invention was revolutionary because it removed the barriers to the distribution of information. Suddenly, texts could be printed much more quickly and cheaply. As a result, all sorts of publishers began to arise and produce texts for a broad range of purposes. Not only were Bibles printed in vernacular languages (over the protest of the Church), but secular writings of all kinds (political, scientific, even erotic) became available to a population in which the rapid growth of literacy became an immense source of empowerment.

The printing press, like the Internet, also posed profound challenges to prevailing institutions and authority. Differing points of view on religion, government, and society could reach a much vaster audience than ever before. As Clay Shirky has observed: "Martin Luther's 95 *Theses*, reproduced widely, were the first mass media event."[12] There were big winners and losers. Vocations vanished, including the profession of scribes, among others. The Church lost its preeminent hold on the flow of information and, with it, political control of the Continent. Raging debates about government were unleashed and rose to inspire revolutions and topple governments in Europe and around the world.

We have yet to see the full fruit of the Internet revolution in our own age, and as we look to the future, we should expect the unexpected. As Elizabeth Eisenstein describes in *The Printing Press in Early Modern Europe,* the transition from a scribal society to a literate society of the printed book was slow and messy. Decades after Gutenberg's invention, many were still passionately arguing for the defense of the scribes, ironically using printed treatises to spread their point more quickly.[13] Although we can identify a few of the early losers in our current revolution (print newspapers and major record labels, to name just two), we still have yet to see the full impact of our digital tools and the ways they connect us.

From Mass Market to Customer Network

One area where we do not need to wait to see if society will be changed is in how businesses relate to their customers. As the examples we have already seen indicate, the revolution of customer networks demands a transformation in some of our core models for business. Businesses today need to reorient themselves from a mass-market model to a customer network model.

The old mass-market model arose in the early twentieth century and came to its peak with the spread of television as a mass medium. In this model, the company is central, and customers can be treated as isolated and passive individuals (fig. 2.5). A mass-market strategy focuses on the mass production of similar products and services and the use of mass communication to broadcast messages out to as large an audience as possible. In this model, targeting specific

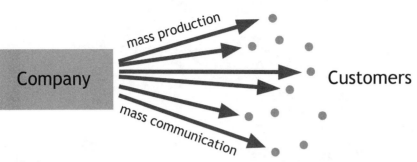

Figure 2.5 Mass market strategy model. *Illustration by Anna Fokina.*

people for whom your message or product is relevant is desirable, but not as important as using broadcast tools to maximize the range and frequency of your messages.

In a customer network model, things look quite different (fig. 2.6). Companies are no longer the only ones able to produce or to communicate. Individual customers also have a voice, whether inter-acting directly with each other or using powerful platforms like product reviews, videos, blogs, and forums. Rather than simply receiving messages and products from the company, customers both receive and create. In a customer network strategy, companies recognize that they exist within a network, sending and receiving messages, content, and value to and from their customers. This leads to a shift in orienta-tion. Before, businesses tried to *control* the relationship via outputs that were entirely from the organization (products, advertising, and so on). Now, businesses try to *manage, influence, and nurture* relationships, and expand connections within their network, via a mix of outputs and in-puts that originate both from the company and from external parties.

The Purchase Funnel Revisited

How this plays out in marketing to customers can be seen by examin-ing the model known commonly as the "purchase funnel," which

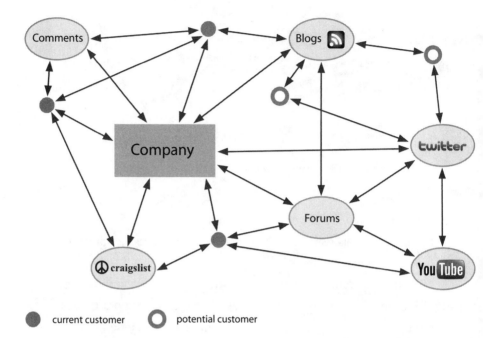

Figure 2.6 Customer network strategy model. *Illustration by Anna Fokina.*

arose out of consumer research into the "hierarchy of effects" of marketing (fig. 2.7).[14]

In the traditional purchase funnel, potential customers proceed through a staged process. This typically begins with *awareness* of a product or product category, followed by *consideration* of purchase, then *preference* for a particular product or brand, and finally *action*, which may include purchasing a product, casting a vote, or becoming a member.[15] At each stage of the process, there are fewer customers (only some customers who have *awareness* will move on to *consideration*, and so on), hence the funnel shape. Traditionally, customers are nudged along this path through a series of outbound, company-controlled marketing tools, such as television, out-of-home advertising, and direct mail. A fifth stage, *loyalty*, was added to the purchase

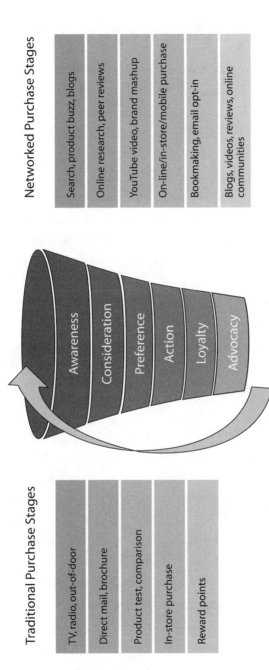

Traditional Purchase Stages

TV, radio, out-of-door

Direct mail, brochure

Product test, comparison

In-store purchase

Reward points

Networked Purchase Stages

Search, product buzz, blogs

Online research, peer reviews

YouTube video, brand mashup

On-line/in-store/mobile purchase

Bookmaking, email opt-in

Blogs, videos, reviews, online communities

Awareness

Consideration

Preference

Action

Loyalty

Advocacy

Figure 2.7 Traditional versus networked stages in a purchase funnel. *Illustration by Anna Fokina.*

funnel to represent that subset of purchasing customers who go on to become repeat customers.

Today, a similar path can still be traced in customers' decision-making process. And yet, at each stage, the customer is influenced much less by the outbound tactics of the company. Instead, networked customers use tools like search and social networking to find a much broader range of information, including information from other customers on blogs, product review sites, and even videos that may mash up and distort the company's original vision of their brand. The stages of "action" and "loyalty" often take place in a digital space as well, with mobile shopping, online bookmarking, and a digital opt-in for further communications. Most significant, in a customer network model, the purchase funnel adds an additional stage beyond loyalty. This final stage represents those customers who not only become repeat purchasers but who advocate within customer networks on the company's behalf—feeding back into the information sources at the top of the funnel with their own buzz, product reviews, and commentary, which spread awareness, consideration, and preference among other consumers.

This revamped purchase funnel, then, demands a new orientation toward the discipline of marketing. Business must move past the old mass-marketing approach.

In the old approach, the company broadcasted one-size-fits-all messages and products, drove sales by advertising, and attempted to interrupt customers and persuade them to buy. The dominant tools were brand awareness, differentiation, and messaging.

The new approach to marketing for customer networks is different. Companies recognize that niche customers will seek out or create distinctive products or services. Companies connect with customers by both sending *and* receiving communications, and they earn customer attention by providing relevant and useful content. Companies realize that customer advocacy is the strongest tool for selling and

Table 2.1 Mass-market versus customer network approaches to marketing

Mass-market approach to marketing	Customer network approach to marketing
• Mass (market/manufacture/message): one size fits all	• Niche: each will choose, create, or modify to suit his or her needs
• Broadcast out	• Send out and receive; connect with the customer
• Interrupt attention	• Earn attention by providing good content, utility, and experience
• Most effective selling is by the company (advertising)	• Most effective selling is by customers (advocacy, reviews, and word of mouth)
• Goal of marketing is to persuade	• Goal of marketing is to inspire (confidence, trust, loyalty)
• Dominant tools: awareness, differentiation, and messaging	• Dominant tools: innovation, collaboration, and values

aim to inspire confidence and loyalty. The dominant tools of this approach are innovation, collaboration, and shared values (table 2.1).

A New Imperative for Business

In our digitally networked world, customers are dynamically connected. Where they used to be isolated, they are now linked to others. Where they used to be individual, they are now self-organizing. Where they used to be passive, they are now active, dynamic participants. Where they used to have little individual impact beyond the reach of their own pocketbook, they now wield power and influence.

For organizations to succeed in the future, they must create value by putting their network of interconnected customers at the center of their business. This begins with a focus on providing the kinds of value that customer networks seek in the new digital age. These kinds of value correspond to five core behaviors that continually shape customer networks. The five core customer network behaviors are: *accessing, engaging, customizing, connecting,* and *collaborating.*

As explained in chapter 1, each core behavior forms the basis for a core customer network strategy: the ACCESS strategy, the ENGAGE strategy, the CUSTOMIZE strategy, the CONNECT strategy, and the COL-LABORATE strategy.

In part II of this book, each chapter will take a detailed look at one strategy. We will examine specific approaches that work using numerous case studies and analyses of technological and social factors. By examining the five strategies in greater detail, we can begin to understand in depth what it means for an organization to embrace the future of customer networks.

PART II

Five Strategies to Thrive with Customer Networks

CHAPTER 3

ACCESS
Be Faster, Be Easier, Be Everywhere, Be Always On

On the day of his inauguration as the forty-fourth American president, Barack Obama received a gift from the Secret Service: a specially encrypted BlackBerry. For weeks, behind closed doors and in the light of the press, the president-elect had been waging a battle with the national security and legal offices of the federal government. Obama was determined to hold onto his favorite digital device as he transitioned into the presidency. While aides complained of his obsession with keeping it, the president-elect complained to reporters, "They're going to try to pry it out of my hands."[1]

For Obama, the BlackBerry was not just a convenience. It was the digital tool he used to keep in contact with a broad and important personal network. That network ranged from political advisers to family, personal friends in Chicago, and the experts whose advice he had sought. During the campaign, Obama had eschewed the traditional small circle of foreign policy experts and instead relied on a network of three hundred leading thinkers around the world. He also used his BlackBerry to keep up on Chicago White Sox scores.

After the election was won, Obama did not want to be confined in the "bubble" of the American presidency. At his insistence, his national security team developed the specially encrypted Black-Berry, whose messages could not be forwarded and which could receive email only from a list of approved contacts. As the first American president born after the Baby Boom of the late 1940s, Obama had a more networked approach to his work and communications than any of his predecessors. Access to that network, at his fingertips, at any time, was not something he was willing to give up.

Mullah Abdul Sallam Zaeef was a senior member of the Taliban when it ruled Afghanistan, serving as its ambassador to Pakistan. Until forced from power in 2001, the conservative Islamist regime banned all modern technology in Afghanistan, including television, the Internet, and cell phones. So Al Jazeera reporter Hamish McDonald was understandably shocked to see Mullah Zaeef clutching an iPhone when he interviewed him in Kabul in early 2009, after Zaeef's release from Guantanamo Bay.

"I'm addicted," confessed Zaeef, in a thick beard, black turban, and traditional clothing as his fingers slid across the iPhone's glowing touchscreen, scanning Web sites. "The Internet is great on this, very fast."[2] Having left the Taliban, Zaeef had reconciled both with Afghanistan's new government and with the new role of digital technology. "It's easy and modern, and I love it. . . . This is necessary in the world today. People want to progress."[3]

When the Taliban held power in Afghanistan, there were only a few hundred cell phone users in a country of thirty-two million people. Eight years later, more than eight million cell phones were in use. In a country racked by war and extreme poverty, shops based in roadside shacks sold mobile connection to the world. The Afghan population was eager to access music and movies, to play virtual chess games, and to vote by text message in the *American Idol*–like TV show *Afghan Star*. Female lawmaker Shukria Barakzai told a reporter that the youth were no longer so caught up in a culture of war. "They are engaging with the rest of the world. That's why technology is so important for Afghanistan."[4]

The ACCESS Strategy

Like Barack Obama with his customized BlackBerry and the ex-diplomat of the Taliban with his iPhone, we all share a powerful desire to access digital data, content, and interactions as quickly, easily, and flexibly as possible. The pursuit of access is one of the core behaviors of customer networks.

Sixty percent of American adults report they would abstain from alcohol for a week before giving up their mobile phone; 15 percent would sooner have their teeth drilled by a dentist.[5] Internet access is no longer something customers are content to have at their office and when logging in to a home computer late at night. Instead, frequent travelers are using tiny EV-DO modems that plug into their laptops and create a Wi-Fi connection over their phone networks, or pocket routers like the MiFi that allow them to carry a "hot spot" in their pocket, giving access to anyone sitting nearby. Virgin America was the first airline to introduce in-flight Wi-Fi throughout its fleet (videochat with the kids at thirty-five thousand feet!). Passengers, not surprisingly, are delighted. In fact, 76 percent reported that they would change airlines to have in-flight Internet access.[6] Access to networks is no longer a premium experience; it is becoming like the air we breathe, something that customers expect everywhere.

Imagine that you are traveling on business and arrive to check into a premium hotel with a grand lobby and striking views of the city. When you enter your posh room and put down your bags, you discover that the water is not running from your faucet or shower. "No problem," the front desk informs you when you call down. "We will provide you with an ID and password. You can select from our range of options for how many hours you would like your water to be on, pay the required fee, click through a few screens, and you'll have water running in no time. If the pressure happens to falter, just let us know if it lasts more than a few minutes."

As outrageous as this scenario might sound, this is precisely the treatment that most premium hotels offer their digitally connected customers when they try to access the Internet. Many upscale hotel chains fail to recognize that Internet access is the most pressing need travelers have when they check in. Savvier midprice hotels attract loyal customers by offering instant Wi-Fi access throughout their building with no logins, no firewalls, and no extra fees.

Network access has transformed not just where and when we work but how we work as well. Even during downsizing and layoffs, companies continue to pay for their employees' BlackBerry service because they know that their entire workstyle is now based on always-on access. The trend has helped spur a new style of worker: the "digital nomad." These laptop-toting road warriors of the networked age are able to take their work with them wherever they go. Their office is everywhere and anywhere. All they need is a Wi-Fi connection—at home, in a hotel lobby, at a coffee shop, or in a shared space in any of their company's offices. Email is by BlackBerry, calling is by Skype, communicating is on social networks, and meetings are scheduled on Google calendars. Digital nomads may be independent agents or corporate employees. The ability to access data and work anywhere is especially valuable for knowledge workers, for whom mobility is productivity. For some, the idea of a "desk job" is becoming obsolete, as they forgo any designated desk and work always on the move.

The desire for better access—to digital data, content, and interactions—is the first core behavior of customer networks. It provides a critical opportunity for businesses and organizations of all kinds to innovate, deliver value, and build closer relationships with their customers, be they busy travelers, online shoppers, or employees in the field.

The first core strategy for customer networks, then, is the ACCESS strategy—to provide your customers an easier, faster, always-on connection to the digital world. A business can provide customers better access to its digital services, products, and communications, or it can provide customers better access to their own digital content and interactions with others. Either approach can create a competitive advantage for business by delivering experiences that networked customers keenly value.

By improving the digital experience for customer networks and employees, an ACCESS strategy can help an organization to achieve such key business objectives as: differentiating its products and services, optimizing communications with customers, increasing efficiency in sales channels, increasing the speed of business decision-making, and improving data transparency within the organization.

Developing an ACCESS strategy requires an understanding of the changing ways that customers access digital networks. What new technologies are they using? When, where, and how are they connecting to their online world? What are the key issues, problems, or pain points that determine where they spend their online time, attention, and money? And how are your own employees accessing the data and processes they need within your organizations at all times and in real time?

Seven Approaches to ACCESS Strategy

A decade ago, the imperatives of digital access were basic: have a Web site, make sure it can be found by search engines, and design it so users can easily find products and information.

By now, most organizations of any kind have an established Web presence. But evolving technologies, and evolving behaviors online, have opened up a variety of new ways to provide digital access. These include mobile phones and other newly connected devices, networks that are aware of our location, and data that is accessible anywhere and in real time.

These and other new elements of digital access pose challenges for organizations—just as creating a first Web site did in the past. But they also provide exciting new opportunities for businesses to innovate, to distinguish themselves, and to better relate to their customers. Each new technology offers new ways for an organization to provide better, easier, more flexible access to digital data, content, and interactions.

Together these technologies point to a set of complementary approaches to ACCESS strategy:

- *Be On-Demand:* Offer your services and content to customers whenever and wherever they want them, on their schedule, not yours.

- *Harness the Cloud:* Make your customers' data accessible to them from any device they use through cloud computing.

- *Go Mobile:* Take advantage of how smartphones and devices allow us to be fully networked wherever we go.

- *Find Your Location:* Use location awareness to improve communication and target your customers with more relevant interactions.

- *Be Real-Time:* Provide instant feeds of the most critical information to customers through real-time data services.

- *Embed the Network:* Provide access through the network connections that are becoming embedded in objects all around us.

- *Keep It Simple:* Focus on simplicity and ease of digital access, as software and hardware grow increasingly powerful and complex.

These seven approaches are not exclusive: an ACCESS strategy can combine on-demand service with location awareness or go mobile with real-time data. But it is helpful to examine each approach separately at first, to understand the technology and behaviors that are behind them and how businesses have successfully used them with their customers.

Be On-Demand

In the 1970s, when Sony chief executive Akio Morita first ordered his engineers to develop a cassette player that could be worn on a belt with earphones, it was a radical product idea. "Why can't I listen to music when I am playing tennis?" Morita reportedly asked. When the Sony Walkman arrived in 1979, it offered a totally new experience — the ability to access your music whenever and wherever you wanted. Although many Sony employees were skeptical (the initial product cost over two hundred dollars), the player became an international sensation, eventually selling more than two hundred million units worldwide. The Walkman became a cultural icon, eagerly adopted by young consumers and entering the *Oxford English Dictionary* as a new word in 1986. (In those days, dictionaries were not yet edited by readers online as a wiki.) People loved or hated the way the Walkman helped users tune out and disengage from others around them, but there was no disputing the demand for the new experience it offered, of listening to music on demand.

Today, digital networks allow for an on-demand experience of any media we consume. Digital video recorders, since the original TiVo box, have put television programming on the schedule of consumers, rather than the networks. For gadget-loving consumers, the Slingbox allows them to watch that same programming on a computer or mobile phone, anywhere in the world. Movie rentals have quickly shifted from a retail offering to mail order to an on-demand stream served up by cable companies and the Web-based services of Netflix, iTunes, and Amazon.

Even radio broadcast has shifted to on-demand service to meet the appetites of networked customers. Not long ago, to hear NPR's *All Things Considered,* you had to turn on a radio at 5:00 pm. Missed a segment? You had to ask a coworker about it in the morning. Now customers can receive NPR programming at their own timing and via a host of options: streaming audio, podcast, text articles on the

Web, Twitter, email alerts, newsletters, RSS feeds, mobile Web sites and phone apps, and, of course, satellite and terrestrial radio.

This may sound like a lot of distribution channels to manage for their content, and it is. But today's customer networks make use of a diverse media landscape. Whether you are a radio programmer or a business looking to communicate about your products, you can no longer reach a broad range of customers simply by broadcasting during a single block of time and in a single mass medium. You need to be able to reach customers on whatever medium they choose, on their schedule, and on demand.

Digital networks allow us to turn more than just media content into on-demand experiences, though. Many other services are leveraging networks to offer the on-demand access customers seek.

Banks have found that they can save significantly on customer service costs when customers bank online or via text message rather than by calling toll-free numbers or visiting retail branches. Bank of America began closing 10 percent of its retail branches nationwide in 2009, due to customers' broad shift to on-demand banking. USAA, a privately held bank serving members of the U.S. military and their families, has only one branch, in San Antonio, Texas; otherwise it relies entirely on an on-demand model. An innovator in digital access, USAA was the first American bank to allow customers to deposit a check by uploading a digital photograph of it through their phone. Banks save money and customers save time when banking is on demand.

Zipcar has built a new business model by turning car rentals into an on-demand service. Every car in its fleet is equipped with a network-connected box that sends data back to the company regarding the car's location, miles driven, engine performance, amount of gas in the tank, and battery charge (for plug-in electric cars). Networking these cars over the Internet allows the company to offer uniquely responsive service to customers. To rent one of Zipcar's Mini Coopers, VW Jettas, and other cool models, the customer has no wait in line, no insurance paperwork, no sales pitches to upgrade, in fact, no face-to-face registration at all. Customers simply log in to a Web site, choose a preferred car parked nearby, then walk out to the car and swipe their pass card over the windshield to unlock the door and start driving. With its seamless on-demand experience and 275,000 members in North America, Zipcar has become the dominant player in the new car-share market. As its next step, Zipcar has begun to lease its dashboard boxes and network software to companies and municipalities to manage their own car fleets more efficiently.

As networks increasingly facilitate interaction on the customer's schedule (and not just the company's), other types of service business may be transformed as well, from conferences, to healthcare and education. Salman Khan is reinventing the experience of student tutoring with an on-demand library of video tutorials in basic subjects like arithmetic, algebra, and biology. His free "Khan Academy" started as a way to tutor his young cousins long distance when their schedules did not match his own, but it quickly began attracting students from Uganda to Dubai to his YouTube channel. Students loved that they could watch the lessons at any time, and pause and rewind until they mastered each one. By the time Khan had quit his job at a hedge fund in 2010 to focus on his nonprofit, Khan Academy's fourteen hundred videos were attracting two hundred thousand unique visitors per month and had been watched fourteen million times on YouTube. Khan, who had never been a professional teacher, had transformed the model of tutoring by making it available to students anywhere with a Web connection, at anytime, on their own schedule. [7]

Harness the Cloud

BMX bike rider Cameron Muilenburg is always on the lookout for great spots to ride and practice stunts — ramps to race, embankments to leap, even stairs with long handrails that he can ride his bike down.

To keep track of the best locations he finds, Cameron uses Evernote—an application that bills itself as "your external brain." Using his phone, Cameron takes a photo, adds a few notes or tags ("ramp" "bikeable" or "rail"), and uploads it over the air to the database on Evernote's remote Web servers. From there, he can remember, search, and find his notes anytime—via his phone, desktop PC, or the Web browser of any computer in the world. Cameron's phone adds geo-location tags to his photos, too. So the next time he returns on a bike tour to Joplin, Missouri, he can simply open up Evernote's map view on his phone to see all the photos and notes he had posted on previous trips and find Joplin's best spots for BMX riding.

I used Evernote to clip and organize more than two thousand articles, images, blogs, case studies, and my own topical notes on customer networks as I wrote this book. Evernote synchronizes my data to multiple local versions so that I can access my notes on my phone or my laptop even when I don't have an Internet connection. And if an idea comes to me in conversation or on the walk home from my train, I can use Evernote's voice memo function to capture and file it. Because all the data is stored in a server cloud, my research team at Columbia University can continually feed new sources into my Evernote notebooks for me to review, tag, and file. I even use Evernote to remember which wines I like from my local wine shop. Each time I go into the store, I can revisit varietals and vineyards by opening Evernote on my phone and flipping through my annotated snapshots of wine labels. "This wine was great with shrimp last time—do you have that in stock?" I love having an external brain.

Evernote is an example of cloud computing—the practice of storing data and running computing applications on remote servers located in the "cloud" of the Internet rather than on our own computers located at home or work. Increasingly, cloud-computing technologies like Evernote will define how customer networks access their data. Customers are already familiar with Web mail services like Hotmail and Gmail, which keep their email inbox in the cloud. Calendars and personal contacts are likewise stored online by programs like Microsoft's Outlook and Apple's MobileMe. Services like Flickr and Snapfish keep photo collections in the cloud for easy sharing. But what if every file on your desktop or laptop computer was saved on the Web? You could access them all from any Web-enabled machine in the world or from a simple lightweight netbook or smartphone. Cloud-based storage has become popular for emergency backup of data. But new Web applications by companies including Zoho, Adobe, Google, and Microsoft allow users to do much more: create documents and spreadsheets, edit photos, and even query databases, all through the Web, with the files stored remotely.

When Marc Benioff left his job at enterprise software giant Oracle to start his own company, he saw an opportunity to use cloud computing to reinvent the business of corporate databases. His new company, salesforce.com, offered small businesses a way to buy powerful database and customer relationship management (CRM) capabilities without a large price tag. It did this by keeping the entire database in the cloud and offering a suite of Web applications that his customers could use to access the data through a simple Web browser. Using the "software as a service" model (SaaS), salesforce.com charges companies a simple monthly fee for use of the data and applications. Customers no longer pay for software licenses, data servers on their own property, or salaries for an IT team of their own to take care of their databases. Salesforce.com began by serving small and medium-size business. As its capabilities grew and awareness spread of the power of cloud computing, salesforce.com quickly grew into a billion-dollar business with companies like Siemens, Motorola, Allianz Insurance, and the American Red Cross among its seventy-seven thousand customers. More recently, salesforce.com launched a platform called Force.com, which allows users to build and run custom applications on top of its computing platform. Whenever a custom application is upgraded, the update is distributed automatically to all users, avoiding the usual delays for deployment and licensing that you would experience with traditional software.

The market for cloud-computing services is expected to surpass $150 billion by 2013. Moving data and processing into the cloud is redefining how businesses not only access information but communicate within their own networks of employees. Coca-Cola Enterprises, which distributes Coke beverages in North America, uses a mobile cloud-computing platform to keep in touch with the twelve thousand merchandisers who deliver its products in the field to retailers every day. The platform allows merchandisers to enter data on their deliveries at each stop and tracks their progress via GPS in their phones. The resulting information allows the company to better allocate merchandisers, reduce their driving time, and keep them in closer contact with fewer trips back to the central office.[8]

In *The Big Switch*, author Nicholas Carr predicts that cloud computing will turn computing power into a utility service, like electricity or running water, as broadband access becomes more powerful and ubiquitous. As data processing increasingly moves to servers run by enterprise providers like Google and Amazon (both of which provide cloud-computing services to companies), everyone else will save on overhead cost, as they access all their data in the cloud. In this scenario, companies will have to own much less and maintain much less; they will simply "turn on the switch" and pay a usage fee to connect to the digital world.[9]

Go Mobile

When I was a kid watching television episodes of *Star Trek*, the technology I was most amazed by was not the phaser guns, the USS *Enterprise*'s warp-drive engines, or the transporter that beamed crew members to the surface of alien planets. What most amazed me was the ship's computer, which the captain could effortlessly address by a simple voice command, as if speaking to the air. "Computer!" he would bark out, with no need for a keyboard, a touch screen, or even that strange eyepiece that Spock would gaze into on the bridge. "What are the coordinates of Gamma Centurion??" And miraculously, a seemingly disembodied computer would calculate and respond to the captain's question.

Today, we are surprisingly close to life on the deck of the *USS Enterprise*. Mobile access to digital networks has brought us to a rough approximation of that ability to pose any question, wherever we stand, and retrieve a near-instant answer. Just watch anyone with a smartphone and its browser pointed at Google.

In fact, "smartphone" is probably a misnomer for the new generation of computing devices that fit in our pockets and are revolutionizing where, when, and how we access digital networks. My "phone" is, first and foremost, a mobile computer that connects me to the power of the Internet at virtually any moment: walking on the street, waiting in line for lunch, riding in a taxi. Smartphones now offer full-fledged operating systems for sophisticated applications that range from social networking to games to business tools. My mobile computer has even replaced the magazine at my bedside for an idle moment's reading while my wife slips into something more comfortable.

Friends and colleagues have similarly described the freedom of using a mobile computer. "It used to be, if I was at home and wanted to email or go online, I had to go somewhere—stop what I was doing and walk into the room where my computer was," says innovation and experience guru Bernd Schmitt. "Now, I can just stay on the sofa, or in front of the refrigerator, or wherever I am. It's always with me." One survey found that 25 percent of iPhone users felt as if the phone was an extension of their brain or body. [10]

We are just beginning to understand the lifestyle implications of carrying our network connection with us everywhere we go. Blogger Steve Rubel proclaimed the death of boredom thanks to his iPhone. How could he be bored during any idle moment when in his pocket was a device that contained "a rented movie, three video and audio podcasts, two thousand songs, five Amazon Kindle ebooks, 10 games, 125 unread RSS items in NetNewswire plus dozens of cached articles in Instapaper, the New York Times, and WSJ apps"?[11] This was the downloaded content he could access during the temporary downtime of an airline flight without Wi-Fi. When he landed, the whole online universe would return as well.

By 2011, smartphones (such as iPhones, BlackBerries, and Android devices) are expected to outnumber standard mobile phones in the United States.[12] Every business can expect to see a large and growing share of its customers using these mobile devices for network access. Whatever a business's Web sites, Web services, or online products, it will need to ensure that they are customized to work optimally on the small screens and interfaces of these pocket computers.

But the network in our pocket opens up more opportunities for completely new products and services as well. Companies can now innovate software and services that would make no sense on a deskbound computer, or even a laptop. Think of Evernote's photo-taking function that Cameron Muilenburg uses to snap memories of biking ramps. Or the iBird Explorer—a field guide on the iPhone, complete with bird calls that you can use to attract feathered friends to your feeder or identify their species. Or Shazam, an application that can listen to a song playing from a radio and search an online database to identify the song title and artist. These mobile applications demonstrate the potential for new products and services for customers with mobile access.

Mobile applications are also being used to give employees better access to company data and to each other. Pharmaceutical company Genentech uses a mobile application to support its sales reps when they visit doctor's offices to discuss the company's cancer drugs. If a technical question comes up that a rep cannot answer (for example, a particular drug-to-drug interaction), the rep can use his or her smartphone to search Genentech's employee social network for a colleague with the appropriate expertise. Genentech offers sales reps more than a dozen phone applications in an app store modeled after Apple's; offerings include the social network, Google apps, and salesforce.com.[13]

Mobile commerce (or "m-commerce") will provide a range of new options for interacting with customers via their phones and mobile computers. Increasing numbers of consumers are making purchases of physical goods via their phones, through mobile Web pages (entering a credit card, as on any Web browser), SMS text messages (after creating an account, with billing information), or new smartphone apps and accessories. Retailers including American Eagle Outfitters and Amazon.com have started using SMS shortcodes (numbers you "call" with a text message) that allow customers to purchase by phone or request information on a product. Magazines such as *Cosmopolitan* include shortcodes in advertisements that readers can text to receive free product samples or enter advertiser sweepstakes. Sears's ShopYourWay initiative links mobile commerce, Web sites, and retail stores to provide networked customers with a wider range of purchasing options. Customers who can't find the product they want while shopping in a store can order it at an in-store Web kiosk. Customers who order a product by phone can arrange to pick it up in-store with easy curbside pickup.

The future of mobile commerce can be better seen in Asian countries like Japan, where 90 percent of cellphone subscribers use the mobile Web. As early as 2005, more Japanese used mobile phones to access the Internet than used personal computers. Today, Japanese consumers use their phones to place orders at fast-food restaurants; purchase products via credit card, bank transfer, or debit to their mobile phone bill; check in for flights at airports; open car doors via electronic key; and scan bar codes on products to check prices and download product information. Emerging markets such as India and China will create huge markets for mobile products, services, and purchasing experiences, as the affordability of mobile phones ensures that they are much more widespread than personal computers.

Find Your Location

Because mobile computers include geo-positioning capability (via GPS satellite and other technologies), they also open up the possibility for what are called location-based services (LBS). These services include geo-tagging (tagging by location) for photos and other documents created on a mobile computer. But many other kinds of services can take advantage of location awareness as well.

Apps such as the popular Urbanspoon, Yelp, and iFood Assistant help users search for restaurants, supermarkets, or wine stores within their immediate vicinity. As computing becomes increasingly mobile, location-based results may become the standard in search engines, rather than a special feature. LBS apps allow much more specialized and in-depth information on what is nearby. With Urbanspoon, users can search for nearby restaurants while setting parameters on type of cuisine, specific neighborhood (Soho yes, Tribeca no), popularity, and price range. They can pull up a menu for the nearest bistro and read customer reviews as well. After dining, they can give their own thumbs-up or down within the app, post a photo, write a review, and share it all with their Facebook friends with one click. Other specialized apps will allow users to search nearby wine stores (what's in stock? who liked it? what was *Wine Spectator's* score for that *cahors?*), subway lines (what's my shortest route from here to Carroll Gardens?), or nightclubs (what's the new popular spot this week here in Haight-Ashbury?).

Location awareness also allows companies to communicate with customers in a more targeted way, often at the point of purchase. Location-based apps may include discounts and promotions offered by local businesses to customers in their vicinity. Services like 8coupons.com aggregate discounts of all kinds by location and neighborhood—so that you can see which bar is offering a two-for-one happy hour as you get off work or which dentist is offering a free initial checkup when you move into a new town. LBS opens up the potential for marketers to target advertising directly to customers nearby a point of purchase, with just the right incentives and communications that are welcome and unobtrusive.

Be Real-Time

The data we access on networks is increasingly shifting toward real-time flows of information. The growth of the microblogging service Twitter first demonstrated the power of real-time information and real-time search on the Web. By 2008, enough users around the world were posting short status updates on Twitter to make it *the* source of breaking news and information on earthquakes, plane crashes, and political uprisings—for general users and professional journalists alike. Previously, users of search engines like Google could not even sort Web sources by date (a year-old article on "IBM profits" might appear before the latest quarterly report). The ability to search Twitter by topical keyword or by hashtag (used to indicate a topic, such as "#iranelection") opened up an entirely new kind of search: real-time search.

Twitter's search offers a true real-time window into conversations on customer networks. With third-party dashboard applications like Tweetdeck and Seesmic, companies can follow trending topics of interest, as well as user comments on their own products and brands.

Search engines such as Google and Bing have quickly responded, incorporating real-time data from sources like Twitter and Facebook into their results. By 2010, six hundred million real-time searches were being conducted each day on Twitter.[14]

Real-time data can be applied to specific information needs of customer networks as well. A weather forecast that is updated hourly may be fine for choosing what coat to wear as you head out the door. But in choosing which route to drive on a commute, customers would prefer traffic information that is analyzed in real time (you're about to come to a bridge: should you get in the lane that will cross on the upper level or lower level?). Mapping and traffic services like Israel's Waze will offer real-time traffic analysis that can feed into driver navigation systems.

Real-time data is likely to become important for data shared within businesses as well. Serena Software's Jeremy Burton transformed his management style, acting as both CEO and head of sales, by maintaining constant access to real-time business data on his smartphone or computer. Burton uses an iGoogle home page with a variety of widgets to display up-to-date sales data, as well as news feeds, social networking updates, email, and instant chat.[15]

Start-ups like Notify.me are developing platforms so that companies can create customized real-time data feeds that are sent out to computers like the "push" email feature on a BlackBerry. Although customers may not want to "put their mouth on the firehose" of a real-time stream of alerts from a business, the possibilities for internal use are compelling. Medical firms see the potential for doctors to receive real-time lab results and critical patient updates on drug conflicts or allergies without having to log in to a Web service to request them. Manufacturing businesses could use real-time order and production information to improve efficiency and streamline supply chains. Real-time inventory analysis may lead, in turn, to greater sales efficiency through flexible, real-time pricing.

Embed the Network

Network access is not only moving into the devices we used to call phones. Thanks to the power of tiny chips and short-range broadcasting, it is becoming embedded in nearly every object that technology touches.

A running shoe might seem like an odd place to insert a link to digital networks, but that is precisely what Nike did with its Nike+ running platform. Customers insert a small device the size of a rubber eraser into their shoe. As they run, the device measures their speed and the distance traveled and transmits the data to a receiver plugged into their iPod. Runners set a goal before starting, and voice prompts interrupt their iPod's music to update their progress ("one mile finished; two miles to go"). When they return home and plug their iPod into its computer dock, the data from their run is automatically uploaded to their account on Nike's online running community, Nikeplus.com. Runners have long enjoyed tracking their mileage while running; Nike created a device that allows them to connect that data to the cloud and access and share it digitally. Nike has found that once a customer tracks and uploads his or her performance on five runs, the habit becomes irresistible. In fact, most customers who purchase Nike+ use it at least four times a week.

Access to Nike+ also provides customers with a regular and powerful experience of the Nike brand. Rather than visiting a Nike Web site only when they are shopping for a new pair of shoes, customers interact with the brand online several times a week, giving Nike natural opportunities to showcase new products. Just as important, Nike's site is designed to be social. Customers form small running groups with their friends to share their goals and accomplishments, motivate each other, and pose competitive challenges (first to run a hundred miles, fastest five-mile time, and so on). In the first two years of Nike+, more than a million runners bought the device and joined this network, logging over a hundred million miles of running data, and making it the largest community of runners ever assembled. Over the same period, Nike's global running-shoe sales rose $1.7 billion, and its U.S. share of the category grew from 48 percent to 61 percent. Industry analysts have attributed a significant amount of that growth to Nike+.[16]

Others are following suit by embedding Internet access in a variety of devices. Since the introduction of the iPhone's operating system 3.0, any developer can create applications that allow iPhones to talk to external accessories, such as shoes, televisions, and even medical devices. LifeScan was quick to introduce an application for diabetes management. With it, patients who need to test their blood sugar level and inject insulin throughout the day can transmit glucose readings automatically to their phone, easily track their diet, calculate how much insulin to take, and even choose to transmit their progress to their physician or family. Operating systems for other smartphones are likely to soon offer similar compatibility, linking embedded sensors in our physical world to our data and networks in the virtual world.

Other products are quickly incorporating their own embedded access to the Internet. E-book readers like the Kindle and the Nook download and synch books and magazine content over a wireless Internet connection. Game consoles, televisions, printers, and cameras are all using Wi-Fi connections to download, upload, and share data and content without needing a computer connection. Our increasingly connected cars will look more like the Zipcar that transmits data on location, performance, and safety to servers in the cloud. By 2015, it is predicted that there will be fifteen billion devices with chips inside connecting them to the Web—in what has been dubbed the "Internet of Things."[17]

Our networks will even be embedded in our own bodies soon, thanks to innovations in the new field of "intelligent medicine." Companies such as Proteus Biomedical have developed tiny sensors made of food ingredients, which are activated on swallowing and transmit an ultra-low-power digital signal before being digested in the body. This signal transmits data to a receiver on the body (such as a digital wristband), which tracks the patient's medication (dose, type, and time taken), as well as the body's response, including heart rate, activity, and respiratory rate. For only a few cents per sensor, these devices may soon allow for much more personalized and effective medication.

Keep It Simple

One more feature has been critical to the success of every new breakthrough in network access, whether it is Nike+, Twitter, the iPhone, or salesforce.com. Each of these services is simple to use. By focusing on their core functionality, each one sacrificed or avoided some of the countless additional features that engineers could have easily crammed into them (imagine the temptation to add a heart-rate monitor and GPS into Nike+). Instead of overwhelming complexity or a steep learning curve that would hinder customer adoption, each of these services is built with an interface that is intuitive for new users. As a result, each one provides customers a compelling simplicity.

Customers demand that network access be made simple. After years of "feature creep" in technologies from word-processing programs to digital cameras, customers are turning away from anything new that requires a [Your brand] for Dummies book. No one wants to pay for difficult experiences any more. Our digital world is already so complex, with so many platforms and devices to wade through, that customers gravitate toward any product or service with fewer features and an easier, more intuitive access to the digital world.

Think of the mobile computing market. Microsoft invested heavily in its initial Windows Mobile platform, which tried to cram in the entire functionality of Microsoft Office into a mobile phone screen. "Look, you can edit Excel spreadsheets, PowerPoints, and Word documents!" said Microsoft. But users just saw a tiny screen filled with drop-down menus and unreadably small icons. By contrast, the BlackBerry focused on doing a few things really well—email and phone—and created an incredibly simple and efficient design for them. Apple's iPhone offered another equally easy operating system, with an intuitive touch interface focused on browsing the Web, music, and media. Like most Apple products, it came with an instruction guide the size of a cocktail napkin. Unsurprisingly, the iPhone and the BlackBerry won the hearts of customers and reviewers alike.

The Flip pocket video camera is another product that succeeded by offering simpler network access. When the Flip arrived, the few customers who were already shooting digital video largely derided the camcorder for its lack of features and its low resolution. Why would anyone buy a video recorder whose image was not much better than what you could shoot with a digital camera? But the radical value of the Flip was its simplicity. Small enough to fit in a shirt pocket, the Flip featured one-push recording and a flip-out USB key on the side. All you had to do was push to record, push to stop, then plug the USB key into the side of your computer, and . . . *voila!* The footage was automatically uploaded to your YouTube account and the world.

YouTube had already made online video incredibly popular by making access simple. Its strategy was to lower the bar somewhat on image quality and focus on making video incredibly simple to create, embed, and share in networks. No more worries about codecs, compression rates, and incompatible player formats. Suddenly, anyone with digital video footage piling up unused on their computer could easily share it online. The Flip camera applied the same strategy to solve the last remaining hurdles for mass users: shooting that video and moving it off the camera. Together, YouTube and the Flip revolutionized online video, turning millions of users into videographers for the first time—just as, more than a century ago, Eastman Kodak's simple and inexpensive Brownie box camera turned millions of amateurs into first-time photographers after its launch in 1900.

Simplicity of access is critical for any organization as it examines how to conduct business and communicate with constituents digitally. How easy is it for customer to access your digital content and services? How easy is it for them to do business with you? To pay you?

Retail giant Amazon.com has built its business with a relentless focus on optimizing the online customer experience—making it easier to find, evaluate, purchase, track, and receive products from Amazon than from any other e-tailer. Amazon Web designers constantly tweak, test, and modify every icon, purchase link, and information display. Amazon's metrics team uses A/B tests to compare the impact of each proposed modification against a previous control. One of Amazon's early differentiators, the "1-Click" purchase option, was widely regarded as likely to fail, even by employees. This was back in the 1990s when customers were still afraid to enter a credit card on a Web site, let alone commit to a purchase without multiple confirmation screens. But when 1-Click went live, the results were clear: customers bought more, and they even took the time to write Amazon and tell them how much they loved its simplicity.

Amazon's innovations have continued since then, all focused on making products easier to find, evaluate, and purchase. Amenities include: the ability to locate your previous orders (forgot what exact type of printer ink you need? Just click on what you ordered six months ago), save prior shipping addresses (need it sent to your Chicago office? No need to type it in; you sent something there last year), or display arrival dates next to each shipping choice ("2-day shipping costs $11.99—will ship Dec 19 and arrive Dec 21"). When Amazon began selling digital music downloads, it knew that stealing market share from Apple's iTunes would require making its interface easy for iPod users. Amazon developed a download interface so that the first time you paid for an MP3 song, it could seamlessly download the music into your preexisting iTunes music library, without even requiring users to browse and select the appropriate file folder. Amazon's relentless focus on simplicity and ease of access has made it one of the top-converting retail Web sites and recipient of consistently high scores in the American Customer Satisfaction Index.

The Future of ACCESS

Even as customers' desire to access digital data and interactions stays constant, the technologies available to help them achieve that continue to evolve. As network access becomes more ubiquitous and embedded in more devices around us, your customers' online and offline experiences will continue to merge.

This is already visible at conferences, where the live experience of speakers, panels, trade booths, and face-to-face networking are today juxtaposed with "backchannel" conversations and search on digital media. Danah Boyd relates a typical experience of listening to a speaker at a Modernity 2.0 conference in Urbino, Italy, with laptop in hand: "During the talk, I had looked up six different concepts he had introduced (thank you Wikipedia), scanned two of the speakers' papers to try to grok what on earth he was talking about, and used Babelfish to translate the Italian conversations taking place on Twitter and FriendFeed. . . . Of course, I had also looked up half the people in the room . . . and posted a tweet of my own."[18]

For some of the older attendees at the conference, the behavior of Boyd and others was perplexing, but for her cohort of digitally networked scholars, access to the Internet during presentations is a tool to enrich their understanding and participation. Readers on her blog chimed in with comments describing how they, too, access the mobile Web in the classroom, in museum galleries, and at dinner parties to expand on and enliven their daily experiences.[19]

As more data shifts to real time on the Web, our network experiences will focus less on searches of relatively static content and more on live interactions. New hardware for self-charging phones (for example, magnetic coils that recharge as you walk) will allow us to stay online at all times. As sensors and network connections become embedded in more of our world, our pocket computers will be constantly talking and learning from the things around us—scanning bar codes on the pedestals of public statues, picking up Bluetooth signals from passing stores, or receiving the expected arrival time of the next train as you approach a station.

Our new experience of "augmented reality" (AR) will allow us to literally juxtapose the online and offline worlds and see network data as we look at the world around us. The start-up Layar was one of the first to bring AR to mobile phones that have both location awareness (where you are) and a compass (which direction you are facing). Using the Layar app, users can hold up their phone and on the screen see the city streets in front of them (coming through the phone's camera lens) overlaid with floating markers and digital information about their surroundings. In Layar's first iteration, this information included arrows to nearby subway entrances and hovering real estate listings of apartments for rent or sale. Soon users had the option of accessing other layers of information—reviews for that bar you are looking at, historical information from Wikipedia about the park you are visiting, or sale prices on the items in the store you are passing by. In the next generation of AR ("true AR"), live video input from your phone will allow it to respond to dynamic information on people, vehicles, and other nonstationary items around you.

Keys to an ACCESS Strategy

The desire to access digital data, content, and interactions is at the heart of today's customer networks. Whatever your type of business, an ACCESS strategy can add value to customers who are increasingly spending their lives in digital networks.

This can be done by innovating new products and services that help your customers access their own data and interactions more easily and flexibly, or by making it easier for your customers to access your business's digital products, services, and communications.

Successful approaches to an ACCESS strategy include: offering on-demand services and content; using cloud computing to make data accessible from any device; offering mobile access for phones and portable devices; using location awareness to better target and communicate; providing real-time feeds of critical data; embedding network connections in new products; and focusing on simplicity and ease of digital interfaces.

Whatever the approach, digital access is largely about speed: you want to offer the most findable, flexible, speedy choice among competitors. On-demand car rentals, real-time Twitter feeds, and mobile-phone payment systems are a part of our lives, and the speed of service has become increasingly critical to business and mass customers alike. "I can get that for you tomorrow" is fast becoming a reason for your customer to look somewhere else. Faster access to shared data within a business is increasingly critical as well. Can you, like Jeremy Burton, find up-to-the-minute information on your critical business metrics, wherever you are, throughout the day?

If your business is focused on better digital access both within and outside your organization, you are well on your way to delivering value to customer networks and earning their business and their loyalty.

But as customers connect with you more easily, quickly, flexibly, and ubiquitously, what will they find? What information are you providing? Are you simply using the new tools of our networked age to blast out the same broadcast messages: "Our brand is best! We deliver innovative, global, best-in-class products! Buy now!"? Or do you recognize that the best way to communicate with customer networks is to provide valued content and information, so that they will engage and spread the word virally among others?

What is the content that people want? In a world of amazing network access, we all seem to suffer from information overload and attention deficit. So how do you get customers to pay attention to you? To find the answer, we first need to understand which content customer networks seek out and engage with, and why.

CHAPTER 4

ENGAGE
Become a Source of Valued Content

Mone was just the kind of young woman whom Japanese pundits decried as evidence of the death of reading; her generation seemed to spend all their time on cell phones, while book lovers of any kind were a vanishing breed. Mone was twenty-one, a college dropout and newlywed, when she went home from Tokyo to her parents' house in the country for a visit. Melancholy and reflecting on her life, she began to while the hours composing a story of a girl not unlike herself, written in short screens of Japanese characters on her cell phone. Mone (the pseudonym she picked to write) was posting to a Web site called Maho i-Land where users can post media of various kinds, including on a "let's make novels" template. Mone posted about twenty screens of text each day. After three days, readers on the site started asking her to post more, eager to hear what happened next to her characters. Within nineteen days, Mone had finished writing "Eternal Dream." This *keitai shosetsu* (cell phone novel), written on a lark by its first-time author, was read nearly three million times online and went on to become a successful movie and printed book.

Keitai shosetsu may be the first new literary genre of the digital age. It first appeared when Japanese phone companies started offering unlimited data plans for Web-enabled phones. The genre is dominated by romantic fiction like "Eternal Dream" where young love is foiled by tragedy and drama at nearly every turn. But the story of the genre has been anything but a tragedy. In a country where readership of books was bemoaned for being in decline, the genre has proven explosively popular with young readers. Maho-i-Land receives a staggering three and a half billion visits to its site per month. Keitai shosetsu have had a profound impact on the sagging business of printed books as well. As the most popular works have started to be released in print copies, keitai shosetsu have dominated Japan's bestseller lists for fiction, and been a boon to publishers struggling to make a profit.

Written on the screen, these novels read left to right, rather than the standard top-to-bottom sequence for Japanese characters. They make heavy use of *hiragana* script, because *kanji* (an important script in literary writing) can only be typed indirectly on a phone. The resulting style is breezy and slangy, with copious line breaks to rest the eyes of a small-screen reader. When the best-selling keitai shosetsu were first released in print, publishers kept the unorthodox printing style, which had never before been seen in a Japanese book. They not only succeeded, they began to influence other print books. The Goma publishing house has begun releasing traditional literary classics in new editions for the youth market, formatted on the page to mimic the distinctive scripts and left-to-right format of cell phone writing. Goma's marketing describes them as "Masterpieces in your pocket! Read horizontally!"[1]

Mone was an accidental author, more comfortable composing on her phone than with a pen in her hand. Yet her readers point to the fact that even a generation weaned on digital networks still continues to seek out engaging content. It may simply take new and unexpected forms.

The Engage Strategy

Customer networks seek to engage with content: cell phone novels, Wikipedia entries, breaking news updates, sports scores, or video clips from *Saturday Night Live*. The content may be trivial or complex, useful or entertaining, a momentary glance in a multitasking flow, or completely absorbing. The media that embody our content are changing, though, as are our habits of engaging with it.

Contrary to the wailings of doomsayers, we are not becoming a nation of nonreaders. The readership of print newspapers in the United States continues to decline sharply, and yet at the same time, the *New York Times* (via its Web site, mobile site, RSS feeds, online video, blogs, and phone apps) has millions more readers than ever before. A few short years ago, when you rode the New Jersey Transit trains into New York City during commuting hours, you would see passengers reading newspapers and magazines; now they are still reading, but on their phones.

The average age of Americans who watch television programming via broadcast (rather than time shifted, or over the Internet) is now fifty.[2] Coincidentally, the customer age at which most television advertisers stop paying for viewers is also fifty years old. So by the standards of mass-media marketing, half the audience for TV is literally too old to count. At the same time, consumption of TV content on the Web continues to rise, with Hulu.com (the joint venture showing programming from NBC, Fox, and ABC) having become one of the most watched sites for video on the Web. The top-ranked site, YouTube, receives more than one hundred million unique visitors every month from the United States alone.[3] Niche video content draws audiences as well, such as the TEDTalks series, which showcases speeches by innovators and scientists on new ideas from their fields. TEDTalks have been viewed online more than 150 million times. Online video has exploded as a mass-creator medium (as opposed to simply a mass-audience medium); it is being produced not just by television networks but by amateur musicians, movie mash-up artists, and corporate communications departments.

Other digital media like gaming are quickly becoming mainstream as customer networks seek out interactive content. Nintendo's Wii game console, with its interactive physical style (swing the controller to swing your virtual bat) and easily shared group play, helped bring younger and older audiences into a gaming world that was once dominated by eighteen-to-twenty-four-year-old men. New technologies like augmented reality are poised to provide even more interactive digital experiences for customers, blending the online and offline worlds. In 2009, U.S. Internet users spent fifteen billion hours on online content sites, more than any other category (including social networking sites), and 40 percent of their total time online.[4]

Engaging with digital content—interactive, sensory, and relevant to our desires or needs—is the second core behavior of customer networks. It provides a powerful opportunity for businesses and organizations of all kinds to attract, connect, and strengthen relationships with customers by providing content that those customers seek.

The second customer network strategy for business is the ENGAGE strategy—to become a valued source of content and information for customers. This content can be funny, entertaining, or highly useful. It may be content the business produces, curates, or sponsors.

By creating engaging content for customer networks, an ENGAGE strategy can help an organization achieve key business objectives, including: breaking through media clutter, earning permission to market to customers directly, communicating to hard-to-reach customers, driving direct marketing sales, and generating customer leads.

The road map of how to engage customers with content has shifted dramatically in the age of customer networks. In the broadcast marketing era, companies would simply piggyback advertising messages onto mass-media content, interrupting customers to force them to watch marketing pitches in an era when customers had no way to avoid them and few media choices. Today's customer networks face no such limitations, and engaging them with content requires a dramatically different approach.

Who is producing content that attracts audiences? How are customers consuming, sharing, and repurposing it? And what formats do they find engaging in new digital media? To understand how businesses can use content to engage customer networks, we must first better understand the new landscape of media.

Age of Abundance

Google's CEO Eric Schmidt estimates that by the year 2019, the digital devices in our pockets will be able to carry more hours of video than we could watch in a lifetime. "Start watching when you're born. Maybe you'll see the final credits in old age."[5] There will be no trouble filling up these devices, thanks to the ubiquity of content in our digital age.

The first challenge for an ENGAGE strategy is the abundance of content today. In an earlier era of industrial information, the distribution of media required large capital investments in infrastructure, such as printing presses, delivery trucks, radio transponders, local television stations, and movie theaters. Creating content for newspapers, radio, television, film, and other mass media was expensive, too (think of those professional copywriters, camera operators, and editors). But most of all, it was the cost of distributing that set limits. Only a small number of players ever got air time on mass-media broadcast channels.

Today, anyone with Internet access and a consumer device like a digital camera or a mobile phone is empowered to create video, audio, text, and photos and share them with the world via online networks. And create it they do. The result has been described as a glut, or an "information overload." More accurately, what we are experiencing is a dramatic reversal of abundance and scarcity in our economy of information.

In the past, that economy was marked by a scarcity of content (two local newspapers and three national television channels were the only options for most of us) and an abundance of attention (an advertiser could reach the attentive eyeballs of tens of millions of viewers by advertising on a single television program). Today, the situation is reversed. We face an overwhelming abundance of content and a scarcity of attention. We have moved from three national TV networks to hundreds of cable channels to the near infinitude of the Internet. As customer attention fragments between all these options, advertisers are rushing to buy ever smaller and smaller slices of it.

Which is not to say that attention cannot be won. Compelling content continues to draw large audiences online. New opportunities have arisen, such as search advertising, to buy the attention of customers. Most important, as the mass media decline in reach and power, more opportunities are opening up for companies to reach their customers directly without the intermediary of a television program, radio show, or other media from a third party. But the challenge of standing out in the ocean of content, of capturing customers' attention directly, is intense. The ability to engage customer networks with content is simultaneously more difficult and more valuable.

Malleable Bits

Another challenge for content in the digital age is the difficulty of controlling how it is distributed or distorted within digital networks.

When content existed only in analog formats—newspapers, music records, television broadcasts, and the like—it came in a whole piece, uneditable to the customer. But digital content is inherently more malleable. By design, the Internet is a giant "copy machine," in the words of futurist Kevin Kelly, capable of producing and distributing infinite copies of any information for free.[6] It is also radically easy to parse that content into ever smaller pieces. Anyone who has used a mouse to point and click can grab the text content of any Web site, select portions, rearrange it, and share it with others via email, blog, or social network. Even our less malleable digital media, such as audio and video, can be easily captured and edited by many users.

The result has been the atomization of content on digital networks. That is, any content in networks can be, and will be, reduced by users to its most elemental unit—its "atom." With the shift to online distribution, music quickly reverted from a medium of albums to a marketplace of individual songs (the atom of music), downloaded or streamed from sites like iTunes or Rhapsody. The atom of news journalism is the article, and although the *New York Times* has many readers online, they frequently arrive via hyperlink to read a single article—without needing to enter through the site's home page or purchase an entire day's newspaper.

As a result of this atomization, media producers have lost much of their ability to bundle content. It used to be, if you wanted to read the classified advertisements in your city, you had to pay to buy the national news, sports, fashion, and politics, too—a whole newspaper that was financed, in large part, by the classified ads. Now, of course, classified ads exist as a separate service (mostly free on craigslist), and each section of the local paper must attract its audience on its own merits.

This unbundling of media also poses a stark challenge for advertisers. Once upon a time, television could force huge audiences to watch advertisements bundled in with its programs. Now viewers skip many of these ads by using digital video recorders or watching TV content online. New formats and technologies offer some opportunities to foist unskippable advertising on customers, but the tide has shifted. Customers are increasingly disinterested in having their lives interrupted by advertising. They have more options to engage content without it. So they are less willing to give their attention to the media that continue to insist on interruption.

Advertising agencies have talked for years about how to measure how "engaging" their ads are for customers. But if broadcast advertising was truly engaging, we would have no need for television programming, and a lot of money could be saved on producing all those comedies, sci-fi dramas, and reality show contests. But the fact is, no one has ever turned on the television at 7:00 pm because he or she wanted to watch a beer commercial.

Engaging Formats

The formats of content that customers find engaging are also changing, so content needs to adapt. These new formats are much more dynamic than in the broadcast age, or in the first era of the mass consumer Web, with its static HTML pages and reliance on text and low-resolution images. Instead, networked customers are drawn to content that is:

- *Sensory*: Customers seek out the rich media that a broadband Internet is now able to provide, including video, audio, maps to navigate, and plentiful images. Even newspaper Web sites have become multimedia platforms, incorporating original video, audio interviews, and photo slideshows, to bring stories to life for customers.

- *Interactive*: Customers seek content they can interact with, rather than just consume passively. They want to search for keywords, follow hyperlinks to pursue related information, rewind or skip forward within audio and video, and scan across maps or diagrams while zooming in and out. They want to navigate through virtual space, whether steering an avatar in an online game, exploring panoramic views of the planet at all angles and resolutions in Google Earth, or strolling through a virtual conference as they network with professional contacts and explore diverse presentations and content online.

Five Strategies to Thrive

- *Shareable:* Customers don't just want to experience content on their own, they want to share it with others in their networks by emailing a link, posting a video to their blog, or embedding a widget in their Web page. When customers share your content in networks, it extends the impact and creates the opportunity for a "viral" effect, carrying content to many more customers than you could reach on your own. Your content comes with much more credibility when it arrives from a known colleague or friend rather than directly from your business. But sharing is not just good for your business, it's an experience that customers enjoy. The content becomes more engaging *because* they can share it with others who they think will enjoy it as well.

- *Mashable:* Some of the more sophisticated customers in your network will enjoy doing more than just passing along your content; they will want to "mash it up." Mash-ups are the collages of a digital age. Just as Georges Braque and Pablo Picasso cut out and combined pieces of paper, fabric, and images to create painterly collages, today's digital artists create new works out of editing and remixing what came before—like the critically acclaimed *Grey Album* by Danger Mouse, which mashed up musical elements from the Beatles' *White Album* and *The Black Album* by Jay-Z.

- *Portable:* Customers prefer content that is accessible and portable. If they can download it for later viewing, subscribe to it on a podcast or videocast, or access it through their phone, this increases their opportunities and likelihood to engage with it. Increasingly, content is not just consumed during dedicated moments sitting before a television, desktop computer, or movie screen. It is engaged on the go, through mobile devices.

- *Varied in Size and Length:* It used to be that rich media content over the Internet was greatly limited in length. With limited broadband access and file compression, it was not feasible to deliver videos longer than three minutes. As those limits on delivery have vanished, platforms like Hulu.com and Netflix's streaming service have proven that there is an audience for thirty-minute and even ninety-minute content on the Internet. Length now should be determined by the content itself and how the customer seeks to consume it—be it in short serial form or in longer in-depth pieces.

Five Approaches to ENGAGE Strategy

With the broadcast advertising model turned on its head, businesses face a remarkable new imperative: to create or provide content that engages customers directly. *We are all media companies now.*

If brands and businesses hope to foster awareness and relationships with customers, they must create content and experiences that customer networks will value, seek out, engage with, and share with others. The emerging model for marketers is to create content that actually engages the customer with your brand—rather than engaging them with something else and then shoving ads at them at regular intervals.

To engage, a business may become a media producer itself. Or it may become a curator, pulling together content from the overwhelming abundance of the Web that is selected to be particularly relevant to the customer and the company. Businesses may become sponsors, reinventing the model of early television programs and integrating their brand into content in new ways. Whatever roles businesses take, they need to understand the dimensions of engagement in a digital age.

By looking at businesses that have successfully created content that both engages customer networks *and* increases their connection to the business and its brands, we can see five approaches to an ENGAGE strategy:

- *Try Branding, Not Selling:* Offer a story, entertainment, or a compelling idea that you can link convincingly to your brand, rather than trying to sell products or services directly.

- *Offer Utility*: Provide content and interaction that helps solve a problem or answers a critical information need for your audience.

- *Show a Personal Face*: Engage customers by showing a personal side and an authentic voice in digital content rather than the objective and authoritative voice of an institution.

- *Focus on the Particular*: Focus on niche audiences and their specific needs and interests, rather than trying to engage every possible customer with the same content.

- *Make It a Game*: Use the interactive, goal-based play of online games to engage customers for fun, education, and relationship-building.

By examining these five approaches and how they have been used successfully by a wide range of organizations, we can gain insights into how to create engaging content for customer networks.

Try Branding, Not Selling

When California pop-punk band Blink-182 reunited after a four-year hiatus, fans of the band got their first chance to see them together on the back of a bag of "Late Night" flavored Doritos. The band's musical performance came to life for consumers using augmented reality, one of the newest forms of interactive digital media. A special marker was printed on the back of select bags of chips; when the customer visited Doritos' Web site and held up the bag to the webcam of their computer, a 3-D image of the band seemed to burst out of the chips bag and perform a song on a holographic stage. Users could manipulate the concert by shaking and moving their Doritos bag in front of their webcam, and if they made enough noise at the end of the song, the virtual band would come back onstage and play an encore, which was followed by an opportunity to enter a Doritos contest to win tickets to the band's non-virtual summer tour. Ann Mukherjee, marketing vice president of Frito-Lay North America, said the experience gave Doritos lovers a chance to enjoy their favorite music in an unprecedented way. It also gave them an unprecedented experience of the Doritos brand.[7]

One of the biggest success stories in promoting a small business with online content is the Blendtec video channel on YouTube. In its now-famous "Will It Blend?" videos, filmed with cheesy music in a retro 1970s style, company founder Tom Dickinson shows off his high-powered blenders. He puts them to the test by pulverizing everything from glow sticks to golf clubs to an iPad. The small, specialty food manufacturer built huge awareness of its blenders as the short videos attracted more than eighty million views. Not bad visibility for a brand that never bought a television spot.

Like the Doritos virtual concert in a bag, the Blendtec blender videos give the customer an extremely entertaining experience. They put the company's brand front and center in that experience. And they create positive associations for the brand, linking it to an idea ("powerful blending" or "cool late night entertainment") and a memorable musical or visual story.

In neither case, however, was the digital content a traditional advertisement focused on selling. The Doritos virtual concert was a high-tech reward for customers, with a chance to enter a sweepstakes (and, no doubt, enter a database for follow-up communications from the company). The Blendtec videos keep the focus on the comedy and make no mention of the product model or where to purchase it.

"The thing about all these things that go viral on the Web," says digital marketer Stephen Voltz, "is that the brand is very small. It's there, but sort of down in the corner. It's not trying to push you with any hard sell to buy."[8]

Voltz should know. He was the customer who, along with Fritz Grobe, created a set of videos in the woods of Maine showing how to turn Diet Coke bottles and Mentos candies into exploding fountains. Their videos, created completely independently of the companies, have been seen more than forty million times and spurred millions of dollars of additional sales for Mentos and Diet Coke.[9] Customers are seeking entertainment, not hard-sell advertising. Businesses need to understand that.

Offer Utility

For many companies, the most effective way to create content that their audience will seek out is not to be creative, funny, or entertaining but simply to be useful. By providing content that solves a problem or answers critical questions for the audience, organizations can create extremely engaging experiences for networked customers.

That was the goal for American Express when it launched its OPEN Forum site for small business owners—the target customers for its American Express OPEN accounts. The OPEN Forum's Idea Hub features articles on such topics as money, marketing, management, technology, innovation, and entrepreneurship that are written by well-known business writers including Henry Blodget, Guy Kawasaki, and Adam Ostrow, thanks to media partners that include *BusinessWeek* and *Wired* magazines. Additional contributors write articles for entrepreneurs focusing on "in-the-trenches" topics such as franchise management or taking a small business global. The forum includes a video series that features entrepreneurs ranging from Susie and George Kirchhoffer of Moravian Florist in Staten Island, New York, to Richard Branson, chairman of the multibillion-dollar Virgin Group. The forum's calendar highlights upcoming events and conferences for small business owners around the country. Its "Pulse" feature pulls Twitter updates that are relevant to small business owners, sortable by industry. Altogether, these features make the OPEN Forum a powerful resource for small business owners seeking useful content on the Web, whether commissioned, produced, or curated by American Express. It's a strategy that matches Amex's focus on building its OPEN business by becoming a strategic partner for small business owners. The Forum grew from 20,000 to 160,000 monthly unique visitors in just one year.[10]

Computer maker Dell has pursued a similar strategy with its Web site digitalnomads.com. The site targets the mobile workforce of "digital nomads" who are prime customers for Dell's laptop computing products. The Digital Nomads site sponsors blog and video content from independent thought leaders focusing on the lifestyle and work trends of today's mobile workforce. Content includes tips for working remotely, data security in the cloud, the best airline Wi-Fi service, work-life balance, keeping in touch with the office when working from home, smartphone product reviews, software links and downloads, and even listings of the best cafés to work in. Instead of creating a site to advertise Dell's laptops, Dell engages the most ardent and influential laptop users with useful and relevant content, sponsored by Dell, and with a few Dell product videos in the sidebars.

Content that aims to engage by being useful can also take forms that are more interactive than articles, videos, and news. One such form is branded apps for smartphones. Kraft created its iFood Assistant phone app with the goal of forging deeper relationships with its customer network, particularly women age twenty-five to fifty-four who shop for family meals with their smartphone in hand. The iFood Assistant offers seven thousand recipes that can be browsed by meal type, key ingredient, or length of preparation time. Users can add them to a mobile recipe box that feeds into "smart shopping lists" on the phone and sorts the ingredients from all the recipes by shopping category (dairy aisle versus produce versus meat). With their digital shopping list in hand, customers can search for nearby grocery stores via GPS. Back at home, step-by-step instructions and instructional videos aid in preparing the recipes—which happen to include a healthy sampling of Kraft-manufactured ingredients.

The iFood Assistant quickly became the second most popular

app on the iPhone in the "lifestyle" category, with more than a million downloads despite a cost of $0.99 to consumers. Besides being able to charge customers for its marketing, Kraft sees the app as a way to gather data on when and how customers are shopping and which ingredients and recipes they prefer. The app encourages purchase of Kraft's products via its recipes and displays advertisements during some videos and searches. Most important, it provides useful content that builds affinity between the customer and the brand by engaging in an intimate experience with the customer. One customer reviewed the app thus: "I've never really cooked a lot but these recipes make me feel like Rachael Ray in the kitchen! Thanks Kraft!"

Opportunities to engage customers with genuinely useful content can be found in almost any industry. Home Depot has built a popular YouTube video channel featuring how-to instructional videos with tips on mowing your lawn, starting a container garden, and saving money with home insulation. The video channel positions Home Depot as a trusted adviser to customers. Fidelity Investments offers customers podcasts with insights on market trends, widgets for monitoring your investments on your computer desktop, and market commentary throughout the day on Twitter. Like Kraft, grill maker Weber has a cooking app for the iPhone. Weber's all-purpose grilling companion lets you set a timer for your specific cut of meat (strip steak versus porterhouse) and its thickness (measured to the quarter inch). One reviewer exclaimed, "A man, a grill, and an iPhone. What could be better?" As customers continue to tune out advertising, offering utility can be an effective approach to getting customers to experience your brand and tune in to the voice of your business.

"Are you making something better for your customer or intruding on an experience they are having?" asks Claire Bennett, senior vice president of advertising, marketing, and media at American Express. "We want to be invited in by the consumer: from transaction to relationship; from disrupting to empowering."[11]

Show a Personal Face

After taking office, President Barack Obama continued posting online videos to reach his constituents, but now he used both the "White-House" YouTube channel and his "BarackObamaDotCom" channel. Both featured the same star brand, yet the personal channel had more than twice as many subscribers during his first six months in office and received ten times as many views.[12] What was the difference? Both sites covered the same topics: the president's agenda, legislative goals, and Supreme Court appointment. But while the White House channel offered official-feeling videos of public speeches, bill signings, and press conferences, the Barack Obama channel featured intimate video chats by the president and the stories of individual Americans facing the challenges his agenda aimed to address. The most viewed of all the videos: candidate Obama dancing as he came onstage for Ellen Degeneres's talk show.

Content that is more personal, that shows the authentic stories and perspectives of individuals, and not just the talking points of a press release, is far more engaging to customers and more likely to be embraced and shared within customer networks. This is why the best corporate blogs have a personal point of view—they are clearly written not by a nameless communications officer but by an executive, CEO, or business manager with a particular interest, specialty, and personality.

An authentic persona comes across loud and clear in the online videos created by wine seller Gary Vaynerchuk for his Wine Library TV channel. When Gary took over his father's wine distributorship in Springfield, New Jersey, it had annual revenues of about five million dollars. Within three years, he had grown the business to ten times that size, in large measure due to the runaway success of his online video channel.[13]

Every weekday, Gary sits down in his office wearing a New

York Jets T-shirt to sample a few wines by swishing them in his mouth and spitting into a large metal bucket. In spontaneous, unscripted, and unedited monologues, Gary reviews his wines of the day, offers thoughts on wine appreciation, and answers questions that fans have sent him on Facebook. Gary has tested wine outdoors during a snowstorm. He has tasted kosher wines for Passover with his dad. In an episode devoted to developing your flavor profile, he tasted kiwi, currants, buttered popcorn, Cinnamon Toast Crunch cereal, sage, paprika, a sweaty sock off his own right foot, and a mouthful of New Jersey dirt. Through it all, Gary's offbeat personality emerges. His natural lack of pretension complements his intense passion about his subject and his eagerness to engage his audience. That audience has steadily grown, to include countless thousands of "Vayniacs." Included among these are celebrity guests on his show: British wine guru Jancis Robinson, hockey star Wayne Gretzky, and tech entrepreneur Kevin Rose, to name just a few. The growth of Vaynerchuk's intensely loyal audience, and the impact on his business, show the power of an authentic personal voice to engage customer networks.

A similarly devoted video following can be found among a different customer group: musical theater fans. More than two hundred thousand people have tuned into the YouTube channel featuring the touring production of the Broadway musical *Spring Awakening*. (By way of comparison, this is nearly ten times the number of views for the very active YouTube channels of three landmark consumer brands: Kodak, Toys "R" Us, and Southwest Airlines.)[14] The musical's channel, dubbed "Totally Trucked," eschews carefully edited interviews and opening shots of well-lit performances before applauding crowds. Instead, its camera focuses on the real faces of the cast and the not-quite-glamorous tales of their life on the road: rehearsing songs in the dressing rooms, chatting on the tour bus during an eight-hour ride, strolling the streets of Louisville, tasting juices at a vegan bar in Baltimore, or performing a song at an Apple Store in

Boston. This is not a site to slickly promote the show to a mass audience. It is clearly an online haven for musical theater geeks who fill up the comment sections with questions and praise for the show and linger to watch the cast's back-stage confessionals about opening night nervousness.

Personal stories can also engage customers in more conservative business categories, such as health care. Like hundreds of other hospitals, Methodist University Hospital in Memphis has begun using digital media including blogs, Twitter, Facebook, and YouTube to communicate with its constituents. One of the most effective approaches it has found is letting Methodist's patients share their stories and even their procedures. Shila Renee Mullins, for example, participated in a live Webcast of her surgery during an awake craniotomy. The video showed Mullins speaking while surgeons cut into portions of her brain and praising the hospital's work afterward. More than twenty thousand people watched a preview of the surgery on YouTube; thousands more saw the Webcast live; the hospital's marketing department even knows which viewers followed up to request appointments of their own. At other hospitals like Henry Ford Hospital in Detroit, doctors blog their proceedings on Twitter after or even during an operation (dictating to a tweeting assistant, of course). By spotlighting real patient stories and experiences, hospitals like Methodist University find that they are better able to demystify medical care, locate patients for clinical trials, attract recognition and donors, and recruit top doctors.

Focus on the Particular

The Internet is a mass medium in terms of whom you could possibly reach, but in terms of whom you are *likely* to reach, it is often as local as a small-town newspaper. Organizations that are trying to create content that engages customers often succeed by choosing a segment of potential customers and creating the content that they will find most compelling. Instead of thinking like a television producer, companies should think of themselves as niche publishers, creating content for a very particular audience.

In many cases, this means creating content that is not intended for end consumers at all. Business-to-business (B2B) companies may want to focus on creating content that engages business customers, suppliers and partners, investors, or regulators. General Electric uses its Web site GE Reports to communicate with precisely these kinds of constituents, particularly investors. The site's blogs, videos, and Twitter account provide in-depth news at a moderately technical level focused on technology, innovation, and social responsibility. For example, it highlights GE's "healthymagination" projects, supporting such goals as broader access to medical technologies in India. Amazon Web Services (the division that provides cloud computing and hosting to companies such as Linden Lab, 37signals, and Virgin Atlantic) has its own blog, aws.typepad.com. Content for its highly tech-oriented audience focuses on such subjects as "secure test and dev environments," "scaling to the stars," and "elastic load balancing." (No, I have not the faintest guess what that is about.) Rather than relying on one overarching blog, many large enterprises opt for a profusion of channels and voices, so that different business customers can pick what they wish to learn about. IBM, one of the first large companies to embrace blogging by employees, hosts over a hundred designated topical blogs. The content on these B2B channels is quite different from what you would see in an advertisement, even in a vertical industry publication. The content is highly topical and extremely focused on information that is relevant to the customers' interests. These businesses are acting not like advertisers but like media companies.

Businesses that create content for end consumers benefit from the same focus on particular audiences and interests. In many cases, they do best by finding a core audience of customers who have the greatest affinity and interest in the brand. Coca-colaconversations. com is targeted at the kind of fans who collect Coke memorabilia and attend or are curious about events for collectors. The site is managed by Phil Mooney, who has served for three decades as Coca-Cola's historian and archivist. Blog posts and videos chart his visits to conventions worldwide, offer information about commemorative bottles, and showcase personal stories of the brand's many collectors. Masi, a premier bicycle manufacturer with a devoted following, keeps in touch with bike enthusiasts via the Masi Guy blog. The author, Tim Jackson, writes about his trips to trade shows around the world and posts links on vintage Masi bike restorations, along with photos of street art, his personal Pandora music channels (with eclectic artists like Madeleine Peyroux, Daft Punk, and M.I.A.), links to "bike stuff for bike nerds," and tips about his favorite brand of socks for riding. Tim self-identifies on the blog as: "Devoted father. Lifelong recovering bicycle addict. A tool of corporate oppression—well, Marketing/ P.R., anyway."

Even when a business is trying to increase its appeal to a broader consumer audience, it may want to focus on creating content that engages a small but influential subgroup. When Mercedes-Benz wanted to increase the appeal of its brand among younger audiences (its future customers), it focused on creating content for a specific group: musical tastemakers. Mercedes-Benz's long-running "Mixed Tape" music Web site attracted over two million users and became one of the most popular sites for in-the-know music lovers, because it consistently discovered exciting emerging artists in the independent music scene. The brand's bimonthly program offers ten free downloads of new music, and rising acts in Europe and the United States vie to gain extra credibility by inclusion in Mercedes-Benz's mix.

Toyota has taken an even narrower focus in curating music culture for its own Scion car brand. The Internet radio station Scion

Radio 17 focuses specifically on DJ subculture, highlighting artists like British Underground blue-collar hip-hopper Reach, and Amp Live, producer and DJ of Zion-I. By programming specifically for DJs and not for a general audience, this automotive brand creates a much more cutting-edge music magazine than a media company like MTV. The Scion Radio app for the iPhone allows users to tap along to a track with their thumb on the screen to measure its BPM (beats per minute) and use this to mix together shareable playlists of songs at the same tempo. BPM-based song mixes are an important part of DJ culture, and Scion clearly understands its audience. Like Mercedes-Benz, Scion is building its brand with its next generation of customers by creating content for a particular and influential customer segment.

Make It a Game

The growth of digital gaming offers important opportunities to think about how businesses can engage customer networks. Gaming has shifted from an industry catering to a young male audience to one that reaches men and women across a wide age range. Two-thirds of U.S. households include gamers, and 40 percent of them are women.[15] Popular game platforms range from graphic-intensive consoles, including the Sony Playstation, Microsoft Xbox, and Nintendo Wii, to apps on smartphones and handheld gaming devices, to Web-based games that may be played individually or by huge numbers of simultaneous users interacting with each other from around the world (massively multiplayer online games, or MMOG).

Companies in all kinds of industries use branded games to produce engaging content for customers. Games are found on the Web sites of consumer brands from beverage (Mountain Dew) to automotive (Mini Cooper). Apps for smartphones like the iPhone have created another market for spreading free branded games. Nissan's well-rated Cube Party Roundup for the iPhone allows the user to drive the streets in the taxilike Cube car, picking up friends in multi-player mode, adding music, and finding their way to the evening hot spot just in time. Others, like the Coca-Cola Happiness Factory app, have won praise from customers for innovative game play that beats many paid games for excitement. Expectations are high, however, in the competitive market of smartphone games. Any business seeking to create an engaging game experience linked to its brand will do best to hire a designer with a proven track record in the medium.

Other brands are seamlessly integrating themselves into gaming experiences as a sponsor. A gamer is driving through an American landscape in a virtual race—what should be placed on billboards as the car passes? On Xbox Live, brands placed in these and other background settings can be interactive, with links to video clips or more information if the player clicks on one. In some cases, brands are integrated directly into the gameplay (a shampoo brand appearing in the online game of *The Price Is Right*) or into storylines (a credit card brand as part of the fraud in a mystery in the *CSI* game). In games where brands had this kind of prolonged attention, aided customer recall of the brands has approached 80 percent.[16] As huge brand owners like Unilever shift money into brand integration, corporate spending on in-game videogame advertising is expected to reach $650 million by 2012.[17]

Gaming experiences can even help revive an established product category. With its Webkinz "pets," introduced in 2007, Canadian toy company Ganz transformed the product category of stuffed animals by linking offline toys to an online gaming experience. For eleven dollars, customers get an adorable stuffed animal, such as a Clydesdale horse, a hedgehog, or a koala. But they also get a code that provides entry to a virtual online world where their animal comes to life as an online character (an avatar). Once there, kids can play games, feed their pets, start a garden, or decorate their room with themed furniture. They can also meet and visit actual friends in Webkinz World, compete with them in games, or mail them virtual presents. The toys became a breakaway hit in their first year, with sales estimated well above a hundred million dollars[18] and over six million unique visitors to the site per month.[19] With many users purchasing several Webkinz, some gift stores were forced to take advance orders, and discontinued product lines have sold for hundreds of dollars on eBay. Webkinz's success has inspired a host of knock-offs, including Beanie Baby 2.0, an online world for Barbie dolls, and virtual worlds for kids of various ages developed by Disney and Nickelodeon.

Gaming is more than just a platform for race cars, avatars, and cute animals, however. It offers a unique class of experiences for engaging customers based on interaction, goals, and, frequently, competition (against other players, oneself, or the game). Gaming technology is being used to bring greater interactivity to other media that are not strictly "games"—the Wii, for example, has already been mashed up to work with Google Earth, creating a gamelike flight simulator that harnesses the Wii to fly over the globe.

Gamelike experiences may be a growing part of education, journalism, and even lead generation for marketers. IBM's number-one software is Websphere, a product that helps customers improve business process management (BPM of a different kind than the beats per minute of Scion Radio's music DJs). When the division in charge of marketing Websphere wanted to generate new leads, it built a video game called Innov8. Its goals were to educate the marketplace on the topic of BPM—an overlapping discipline of business management and information technology—and to demonstrate IBM's leadership in the field.

The first generation of the game aimed to educate and grow IBM's potential market. Targeted to universities, it used familiar elements of gameplay (joystick, villain, team members, and scavenger hunts for critical data) to let players explore how different business model processes succeed or fail when faced with changing business scenarios. The second generation of Innov8 was designed for business leaders, from fresh MBAs to C-level executives. It featured shorter play time to suit this audience, and it added more process-focused game modules: call centers, supply chains, green scenarios, traffic management, and order processing. In Innov8's third generation, the game moved to the Web and allowed users to post their scores on Facebook and MySpace. If users wanted their initials on the scoreboard, they needed to provide information about who they were to IBM.

"Innov8 has become our number one marketing tool for lead generation," says Sandy Carter, IBM's vice president in charge of strategy for Websphere. By targeting potential customers, educating and exposing them to IBM's thinking on BPM, and capturing voluntary user information, Innov8 has proven a new model of marketing for IBM.

Carter has also catered to a variety of customer types by focusing gaming options on their particular needs. Users from the business management side use some modules (for example, the traffic management or green scenarios), while the tech people make more use of the tech-focused modules. In its newest iteration, IBM is opening up parts of Innov8 as open source code, so that companies can modify it to focus on the key performance indicators (KPIs) used by their own organization.[20]

The Future of Engage

As digital media continue to evolve, content will rapidly change to match them. New media lead to new messages. Books, for example, will likely undergo dramatic change in the next few years. Shorter works, in particular, will transfer well to reading on phones and other devices that are less book-centric than the Kindle e-reader. Books as phone apps may be shorter, more link-based, and less linear. Already, travel books by Lonely Planet and a Klingon dictionary for *Star Trek* fans have been launched successfully as phone apps. These and other types of books have been printed for years but are better suited for a smartphone than a bound set of pages with no search function.

New digital interfaces will allow for increasingly interactive ways to engage with content. Large touch-screen interfaces will greet customers as part of retail displays. Cheap 3-D chips from companies like Canesta will allow the cameras in devices such as PCs and cell phones to recognize a user's gestures in space. As a result, turning on a TV or playing a videogame may soon require little more than a wave of one's hand.

Currently, Web content faces a trade-off between interactivity and rich media. Text and simple images can incorporate significant interactivity for users, but richer media experiences such as video are much more taxing to edit and manipulate. The viewer of an online video cannot interact with it with the same speed and dexterity as with a map or discussion forum. These limits are changing quickly, however, as Internet bandwidth increases and innovative new tools are developed for on-the-fly editing and manipulation of rich media.

Start-ups like Innovid are pioneering technologies that will make online video far more dynamic. Imagine a speaker in the foreground (Stephen Colbert delivering a monologue from *The Colbert Report*) with a video background that can be redesigned on the fly, including dynamic elements that the user can click on to move, alter, or learn more from.

These and other emerging technologies will provide new opportunities to include brands in engaging digital content and to create experiences that customers will participate in and share with others in their networks.

Keys to an ENGAGE Strategy

The desire to engage with relevant, sensory, and interactive content is at the heart of customer networks. Whether your organization is an automaker, a hospital, or a financial services firm, an ENGAGE strategy can help you cut through the clutter of media messages and build powerful relationships with your target audience. This can be done, not by piggybacking advertising onto other content, but by creating content that your customer networks will seek out themselves.

By thinking of yourself as a media company, and not an advertiser, your business can use an ENGAGE strategy to communicate with hard-to-reach customers, earn permission to market to customers directly, and drive lead generation and direct marketing.

Successful approaches to an ENGAGE strategy include: offering a powerful story or idea linked to the brand, rather than selling directly; providing utility to customers by helping solve their problems or information needs; showing a personal face and authentic voice in digital content; focusing on niche audiences and their particular needs and interests; and using gaming to engage customers in an interactive, goal-based experience.

Whatever the approach, to capture the scarce attention of customers, your business must focus first and foremost on what is relevant to them. Too often, businesses start with the message they want to transmit to customers. Instead, businesses should ask themselves: What do customers want? What do they care about? What content will they be most interested to see, to hear, to interact with, and to share?

By helping customers engage with content that is relevant to their particular needs and interests, businesses can effectively communicate and market to customers no longer living in an age of mass media and mass consumption.

But how narrow can your niche focus go? And if one message or type of content will not work for all your customers, can you still offer all of them the same product or service? Just as the Internet has splintered attention into a million channels, it has fostered a million customer niches, each of which value and seek different things. To innovate for all of the niches in their customer network, businesses must find ways to help each customer find or create the unique products and services he or she is looking for.

CHAPTER 5

CUSTOMIZE
Make Your Offering Adaptable to Your Customers' Needs

I have seen the future of television, and it looks good. No longer will the flat screen in the living room, the most expansive screen in our increasingly multiscreen homes, be confined to showing cable and television broadcasts. In keeping with our networked lives, our TV, too, will be networked, allowing us to view our choice of digital media.

Video from across the Web will appear in large-screen glory from sites like MLB.com, ComedyCentral, and Howcast.com. Movies from Netflix, television shows from Hulu.com, and music from sites including Pandora and Last.fm will all stream live to the big screen. The TV will pull in news and blog feeds from Digg and Tumblr. Videos on YouTube and photo albums on Flickr will enrich our couch-potato experience. You will be able to screen any media file stored on your hard drive—your downloaded movies and TV shows, family digital photo albums, and MP3 music libraries—when and where you want.

If all those choices seem like too much to navigate, don't worry. The television experience of the future will be nothing like the cable experience of today. Instead of scrolling through long vertical programming lists in day-glow text, you will be able to search and jump directly to the media you want. The awkward and time-consuming menus of today's "on-demand" video will be replaced by simple icon-based navigation. And if you are unsure where to start with so many choices, you'll be able to get ideas from your friends using a social recommendation system to see what they are watching and listening to and which media are their favorites.

The choice-rich television of the future is already here, in the form of an open-source software platform called Boxee. Started by the quietly enterprising Avner Ronen, an Israeli transplant to New York, this small start-up has shaken up the television business by giving us our first taste of its future. For years entrenched players in the television business have dragged their feet, claiming that "consumers don't really want an Internet-like experience with their TVs."[1] These luddites have left the field wide open to early innovators like Boxee, and soon others like GoogleTV, to offer integrated TV and Web. By opening up its source code, Boxee even invites outside developers to create additional applications for its platform, bringing more content, increased design options, and added choice to the Boxee experience.

The result is television as it should (and soon broadly will) be—not a mass medium for broadcasting limited choices but a customizable medium for the age of customer networks.

The CUSTOMIZE Strategy

Customer networks share a desire to customize their digital and physical experiences—the content that they watch, listen to, and read; and the products and services they use and enjoy. In an era when digital networks provide access to seemingly endless choice, the options for customers are irresistible.

Consumer choice has been growing for decades. Supermarket aisles are filled with ever greater varieties of cereals and toothpastes. Where we once could choose from one color (black) of one automobile (the Model T Ford), we now have cars in every size, shape, style, and detailing. Marketers have known for years that we do not all want the same thing, and even in a mass-market economy they found it valuable to offer brand extensions and niche products. Where we once might have drunk a Coca-Cola, we now choose between Diet Coke, Coke Zero, Caffeine Free Coke, and Coca-Cola Blāk— not to mention the array of juices, energy drinks, bottled teas, and branded waters offered by the same parent company.

For customer networks, though, customization is about much more than picking from a dozen bottles in the beverage aisle. The new tools of our digital age allow us vast choice and vast options for personalization—of not just digital products and services but physical ones. With centralized inventories, distributed selling partners, and dynamic Web interfaces, online retailers such as Amazon.com are able to offer far more products than even the largest big-box store could ever carry. Netflix.com can offer more than a hundred thousand DVDs for rental by mail, more than ten times what a retail video store could carry. As customers go online, they find themselves exposed to vastly more options—not just today's best-selling new books and movies (*Spiderman I, II,* and *III*), but niche products and offerings (a documentary on jazz bassist Charles Mingus) that simply were not available to most customers a few years ago. The Web itself is the ultimate customizable medium. Its endless pages, with options to find just what we are looking for, epitomize the rise of niches and of niche audiences. There are well over ten thousand Web sites that regularly draw a hundred thousand different visitors every month. The profusion of smaller niches online is even more pronounced: the number of sites with over two thousand monthly visitors (comparable to that small-town college radio station you love) is nearly half a million.[2] Meanwhile, new technologies for finding and remixing media allow us to easily "mash up" our content just the way we want it. And new digital prototyping tools mean that we can easily modify physical products as well.

CUSTOMIZE

Customers have always sought choice and control of individualized experiences. Welsh sociologist Raymond Williams famously observed that "there are, in fact, no masses; there are only ways of seeing people as masses."[3] During the age of mass media, it was convenient and cost-effective to lump customers together in vast swaths of demography: eighteen-to-twenty-four-year-old female, urban Hispanic voter, baby boomer. But each one of us is, in reality, an individual, not a demographic. Today's customer networks do not behave like demographic categories. Our digital choices and tools have rekindled our desire to satisfy our individuality in consumer choice.

The pursuit of customized content, products, and services— with the help of digital tools for choice and personalization—is the third core behavior of customer networks. It provides a powerful opportunity for businesses and organizations of all kinds to develop stronger and more valuable relationships with customers.

The third customer network strategy for business is the CUSTOMIZE strategy—to provide services and products that are adaptable to the unique needs of each customer. This can be done by offering a variety of options and ways to choose among them. Or it may be done by offering tools to modify products and services to suit individual desires. Either approach can deliver value to customers and competitive advantage to businesses.

By creating an offering that is flexible and adaptable to customer needs, a CUSTOMIZE strategy can help an organization achieve key business objectives, including: achieving greater sales in online channels, differentiating products and services, reaching customers with diverse habits of media consumption, and marketing to high-value niche audiences.

But offering choices does raise issues as well. Which choices will you offer? How much choice do customers really want? Some of the first attempts at customization in the early days of the Internet were failures. Psychologists have demonstrated what is dubbed "the paradox of choice": the fact that too many options may shut down consumers and reduce the likelihood of their making any choice at all.[4] To carry out a CUSTOMIZE strategy successfully, business needs to understand what makes choice valuable and meaningful to their customers, rather than overwhelming.

The Quest for 10 Percent Better

Why do we like what we like? Can human taste be predicted? If I loved the film *Michael Clayton,* will I like *A Few Good Men?* For nearly three years, more than fifty thousand contestants from 186 countries puzzled over those questions as they grappled with the largest set of customer ratings data ever released to the public. The contestants were statisticians, engineers, and computer scientists specializing in machine learning. The data set was one hundred million movie rankings by Netflix customers, scored on a scale of 1 to 5 stars. The goal of the contest was to improve Netflix's Cinematch recommendation engine, which attempts to predict a customer's preference for an unseen movie based on that customer's previous preferences. To gain the million-dollar Netflix Prize, the winning team had to improve the accuracy of Cinematch's mathematical algorithm by 10 percent.

This may seem a rather modest improvement, but the challenge of the Netflix Prize was exceedingly hard. Although some factors of human taste can be fairly easily mapped with mathematics (a penchant for courtroom dramas or a dislike of historical war movies), others proved baffling for the contestants. Customers' tastes change over time. Some days they may simply rate movies lower because they are in a bad mood. And certain quirky independent films—like the cult hit *Napoleon Dynamite*—just seem to defy categories or predictable customer reactions. The "*Napoleon Dynamite* Problem" was one of the biggest sources of Cinematch error.

For years, the task remained out of reach for scientists like

Bob Bell (a scientist at AT&T working on the puzzle), Len Bertoni (trading ideas with his teenagers and running computations on the family computer), and Martin Piotte (working at night in Montreal after putting his four kids to sleep). Every time a solution was submitted, it would appear on a live leaderboard, showing its ranking. But the closer each team got to a 10 percent improvement on Cinematch, the more their progress slowed. Netflix had to give out "progress prizes" of fifty thousand dollars each year to the leading team just to ensure that they would stay in the game. Eventually, some of the highest-ranked competitors formed super teams, and two of them broke the 10 percent threshold thirty-three months after the contest was announced.

But why was a small improvement in Cinematch worth a million dollars to the company? For Netflix, 70 percent of rentals come from the "backlist"—smaller, independent films, as well as major studio films that are no longer recent. (By contrast, traditional retail stores make only 20 percent of their business from backlist; but they don't have the voluminous backlist catalog that Netflix does.) Cinematch recommendations drive fully 60 percent of all Netflix rentals, especially the discovery and rental of backlist movies. Because customers pay a flat monthly fee even if they watch no movies, Netflix needs to keep mining the backlist and finding them well-suited films to rent in order to retain them as happy, paying customers.[5]

Without tools like Cinematch, finding the right movie out of a hundred thousand is like pulling the proverbial needle from a haystack. Digital networks give us an alluring range of choices. But they have also replaced the glazed-over eyes of the customer wandering the aisles of a video store with the glazed-over eyes of the customer staring at a computer screen, clicking through endless lists. Netflix is not the only business that has discovered the urgency of providing assistance to customers seeking to make the most of their choices in a networked world.

The Paradox of Choice and Six Filters to Fix It

For years, access to more choice was seen as an unqualified plus for human happiness. Psychologists and economists alike found that greater choice corresponded with greater intrinsic motivation, sense of control, and life satisfaction. But a groundbreaking series of experiments by Sheena Iyengar and Mark Lepper revealed that offering too many choices can sometimes have the opposite effect.

In their first experiment, shoppers in a grocery store were offered a discount on gourmet jams. One group of shoppers was offered free samples of six different flavors, and the other group was offered twenty-four. Amazingly, the shoppers given more flavors to consider were *one tenth* as likely to make a decision and use the coupon to buy one of the jams. A similar experiment with chocolates found that students allowed to choose a free chocolate from thirty selections were less satisfied with their choice than those offered only six to choose from. In a final experiment with homework assignments, students were offered a chance to write a short essay for extra credit. Students given a longer list of writing topics to choose from were less likely to complete the assignment.[6]

The more choices you give a customer, the harder it may become to make a choice. Like the customers faced with two dozen flavors of free jam, many may simply throw up their hands and leave without choosing anything. This phenomenon was dubbed "the paradox of choice" in a popular book of the same name by psychologist Barry Schwartz.[7]

The paradox of choice points to the critical need for filters to help customers choose from a vast array of options. While many see the Internet age as creating a problem of information overload, it is perhaps more accurate to see our predicament as a problem of "filter failure." As Clay Shirky has observed, the old media barons filtered our options because they could offer only a limited range of media through the old expensive distribution systems, such as broadcast television and radio. Once the price of distribution dropped, everyone become a broadcaster, and no one held the editorial role of filtering options for the consumer.[8]

Today, to make choice work for customer networks, we need to be sure to offer the right kinds of filtering tools, including recommendations, ratings, and choice schemas. Following are six approaches to help you help customers to choose. Many of these filters are quite familiar to anyone who has browsed a site like Netflix or Amazon, but understanding each one is helpful to learn how they can combine to help customers avoid the paradox of choice.

Taxonomies

Sorting through a hundred thousand types of toothpaste would certainly be overwhelming, yet choosing from a hundred thousand books or movies is not. One reason for this is that we carry around in our heads a shared system for classifying books and movies: what we call genres. Comedy, romantic comedy, British comedy, political comedy, spoofs and satires, African-American comedies . . . these are all categories used by Netflix. A taxonomy is any system of subdividing a group into subcategories. Netflix could subdivide its movie library in countless ways, but most would be of no use to customers searching for something to watch: Sort the films by year of release? Alphabetically by title? Date of birth of the director? The key to making taxonomies a useful filtering tool is to use a system that is intuitively meaningful to most users. Traditionally, taxonomies were hierarchical, with only one option at each level of categorization (an animal can be a mammal or a bird but not both). Tagging systems allow for overlapping categorizations, so that a movie may appear under comedies as a "romantic comedy" and under foreign films as "Italian." This allows more dynamic filtering, such as an option to see "all Italian romantic comedies."

Ratings

Sometimes simply knowing what others have liked can be a valuable filtering tool. In its most basic form, ratings can be a "top sellers" list, like the list of top-selling iPhone apps in the iTunes store. To be more useful, ratings can be combined with taxonomies ("20 top-selling paid apps in the Medical category"). Ratings can be based on popularity in purchasing or on user satisfaction, such as the 1-to-5-star ratings on Netflix. Other kinds of ratings may include objective product criteria that can be measured by the seller. When considering a long list of airline tickets, we sort by price, airline, departure time, and length of travel in making a choice. Combining user ratings with objective ratings can allow for very dynamic filtering.

Text Reviews

Text reviews, either by designated experts or open to all customers, are a valuable filtering tool. Although the data in text reviews is not quantifiable (you can't sort a list for "movies with the most glowing text reviews"), it can be extremely helpful in evaluating choices. When choosing between two espresso machines on Amazon.com, it is only moderately helpful to know that one model averaged 3.4 stars among eighteen reviewers while another model scored 3.2 stars among nine reviewers. It is far more useful to read the reasoning behind each reviewer's rating (speed of brewing, ease of cleaning, attractive visual design, whether it fit beneath custom cabinets in the kitchen). Traditionally, product reviews were the exclusive domain of professional critics and testers, and many businesses still offer "staff picks." But companies like Amazon.com are able to offer much more help to customers by encouraging them to post their own product reviews, thereby allowing many more voices to evaluate. Customers are often more inclined to trust each other's reviews, perhaps because they are seen as more authentic and less biased.

Collaborative Filtering

Amazon is also famous for another kind of filtering tool: the messages that show up on its Web pages declaring "Customers who bought this, also bought . . . ." By tracking the aggregate behavior of millions of customers, Amazon is able to make surprisingly useful recommendations based on as little information as the last two books you looked at on its Web site. This technique, called "collaborative filtering," was pioneered by MIT professor Pattie Maes in 1994, when she created the first Web site where users listed songs and bands that they liked and received recommendations based on the preferences of other users. Collaborative filtering does not require a great deal of information to work—rather than needing to know a great deal about one person's tastes and choices, it relies on knowing a little bit about the behavior of a great many people. At its simplest, collaborative filtering uses only one-to-one correspondences: how many people who bought product 37 also bought product 96. Research from the Netflix Prize has introduced such mathematical techniques as singular value decomposition, which can look at the data of millions of customer choices and group products that share some common quality (like "lighthearted female-driven comedy") that tends to predict customer preference.[9] As new techniques such as these are incorporated and more data is captured—on what we browse, purchase, and enjoy— collaborative filtering systems will develop increasingly sophisticated recommendations.

Choice Schemas

A choice schema is any step-by-step process that a customer can use to reduce the number of potential choices (and arrive at the most relevant ones) without having to consider them all. This often takes the form of a series of questions that successively narrow the range of options. An online guide for choosing a digital videocamera

(I used one by David Pogue of the *New York Times*) may start by asking usage questions, such as "Are you filming for home use or professional?" or "How long do you want to shoot without having to download your footage?" With a handful of careful questions, hundreds of product options can be narrowed down to a short list of appropriate ones for the customer to compare. Retailer Sears lets its online customers create an avatar (an online persona) and use preference-matching software to view a personalized selection of products from Sears's countless departments (clothing, kitchen appliances, furniture, and so on). This choice schema allows customers to find what they are looking for from a much narrower range of products. Some Sears business units that use the choice schema have seen double-digit increases in their average order value.[10]

Social Filters

Friends and family were always a crucial source of recommendations in the predigital world. With the rise of social networking services online, they help customers make choices in virtual space as well. Facebook Connect is a service that allows third-party Web services to access the network of friends that a customer has on Facebook (unless the customer opts out). This allows companies to add a social layer to recommendations. Not sure which book to read? See a list of the latest nonfiction titles purchased by friends in your social network. In essence, your own friends become the "experts" whose reviews and ratings may be given more weight in your own personalized recommendation engine. Early efforts at social filters, such as Netflix's "Friends" feature, were not used much because they relied on creating a list of your friends at each retail site. By allowing customers to carry their existing friends list across many sites, services like Facebook Connect may make social filtering a seamless, effortless tool for customers.

Five Approaches to CUSTOMIZE Strategy

A successful CUSTOMIZE strategy requires both tools for choice and tools for filtering. It is the combination of the two that allows business to avoid the "paradox of choice" and create compelling value for customers.

The motivations to customize may vary. Customers may customize your business offerings to suit their interests, to fit specific functional needs, to match their aesthetic sensibilities, or to express themselves to others.

What they customize may be physical or digital; it may be products or services. When they do customize, it may be a single choice or an ongoing and iterative process. They may make a choice from a set of options or start with a basic template and modify it at will.

By looking at businesses that have successfully used digital tools to help customers adapt their own products, services, and content, we can see five approaches to a CUSTOMIZE strategy:

- *Offer a Vast Menu:* Take advantage of the Web to offer a huge range of products, but pair them with a useful set of filters to help customers find what they are looking for.

- *Customize Your Playlist:* Provide a steady stream of content that adapts to the preferences and feedback of your customers.

- *Mash Up Your Products:* Let customers modify your products or services to express their individuality or match their interests.

- *Make the Choice Personal:* Put a human face on the choice you offer customers, so that by choosing, they connect with real people.

- *Create a Platform for Choice:* Find or build a platform that allows others to create more products or content for your customers to choose between.

By examining these five approaches and how organizations have used them successfully, we will learn how to add value to any business by helping customer networks customize their experiences.

Offer a Vast Menu

One approach to helping customers customize is to offer them a vast range of options among the types of products, services, or content that you offer. As we have seen with companies like Netflix and Amazon, the Internet allows businesses to offer customers a vast menu of options far beyond what could be provided in a traditional retail store or catalog.

Of course, that vast menu will need to be paired with appropriate choice filters in order to be useful to customers. In Netflix's case, its vast catalog of movies is made navigable thanks to taxonomies (like movie genres), ratings, text reviews, and the collaborative filtering by its Cinematch software. For every movie a customer sees listed, Netflix provides a personalized score ("Our best guess for you: 3.2 stars"), but the user can also see a raw score (the unweighted average of all reviewers).

The menu of products on Amazon.com is much larger and seems to grow by the minute. Although the site began as an online bookstore, it has expanded partnerships with others to allow it to sell everything from books to music, movies, toys, electronics, office supplies, home furnishings, groceries, clothing, sporting equipment, and even automotive parts and accessories. When searching within a category, customers can sort their results by the most popular items (in terms of sales), the best customer reviews, or the price. As users visit specific product pages, Amazon uses its own collaborative filtering tools to make constant recommendations ("Customers Who Bought This Item Also Bought . . ." and "Customers Who Viewed This Item Also Viewed . . .").

The open-source television software Boxee expands customer choice in a similar way. Boxee's value is that it offers customers a much vaster menu of media options when they sit down in front of their television set: Web video, music, photos, and all the media stored on their hard drives, along with their traditional television programming. Boxee's simple visual interface makes moving among all these choices easy. Its social filters allow customers to see what their friends are watching as well as how they are rating it.

The My Virtual Model Web service lets users create an avatar to try on clothing and other products from such online retailers as Adidas, Levi's, Land's End, Best Buy, and Sears. As customers use it, the system narrows the full assortment of products to specific options and recommendations that match their needs. Retailer Land's End has seen a 45 percent jump in its conversion rates and 15 percent increases in the average order value of customers using this choice schema. Adidas has used My Virtual Model with its retail business partners, letting merchandisers see and give feedback on virtual prototypes of shoes Adidas is developing, thereby saving the manufacturer millions of dollars each season.[11]

Customize Your Playlist

As we saw in the previous chapter, engaging content is critical not just for media businesses but for any business seeking to build a relationship between its brand and customers. Yet not all customers want to engage with identical content, not even a narrow target group. Instead, businesses can succeed by offering a customized "playlist" of content that fits the individual interests of each customer.

The Pandora digital music service does this by offering customers a personal radio station playing a mix of songs suited specifically to their tastes. The user simply picks a favorite song, and Pandora uses collaborative filtering to start generating a radio playlist of other songs with similar musical qualities that it thinks the user will enjoy. Rather than relying purely on mathematical algorithms, Pandora uses a team of fifty employees to map what it calls a "music genome" for each song—assigning values on up to five hundred attributes, such as "aggressive female vocalist," "Brazilian jazz influences," and "varying tempo and time signatures." The result is a vector profile on each of the seven hundred thousand songs in Pandora's database that allows the service to recommend songs that may not yet be well known by users (and therefore would not show up in simple collaborative filtering) but have similar musical qualities to their favorite songs.[12] Pandora's filtering is iterative as well. Once the service starts playing recommended songs, the user can vote on each one with a thumbs-up or down and skip over those songs that don't interest them. This data is also collected and feeds into Pandora's database so that it can continually improve its recommendations and provide an ever-more customized playlist. The results have drawn forty million listeners to Pandora to listen to 361 million custom radio stations and have made Pandora the number-one music app on the iPhone.[13]

Another kind of customized playlist is used by followers of the microblogging service Twitter. Many users, like myself, use Twitter to create a real-time filter for news, commentary, and articles on topics of interest to them. By choosing a list of twitterers to "follow," the user can quickly and easily generate a twenty-four-hour mix of news articles, blog links, and discussion. If a user is interested in trends and news on digital media, marketing, and technology, they could subscribe to twitterers such as Edelman analyst Steve Rubel (@steverubel), venture capitalist Fred Wilson (@fredwilson), and myself (@david_rogers). They could generate a celebrity magazine mix by following the likes of Ashton Kutcher (@aplusk), Diddy (@iamdiddy), and TMZ (@tmzaol). To generate a feed of up-to-the-minute news headlines, they could follow accounts like CNN (@cnnbrk), the *New York Times* (@nytimes), and the BBC (@bbcbreaking). Or to get new thinking on book publishing, they could follow such writers as Joanna Penn (@thecreative penn), Shelley Lieber (@wordywoman), and Dana Lynn Smith (@Book Marketer).

Used this way, Twitter becomes an extremely powerful social

filter. Unlike Facebook Connect, though, the user is appointing whomever they find most knowledgeable or interesting on a given topic to be their "filter" for news, rather than the assorted mix of family, high school friends, and work colleagues who populate their Facebook friend list. RSS readers can be used in much the same way to generate a customized mix of daily reading from blogs on specific topics and interests. But although they offered this capability to users much earlier than Twitter, RSS readers were always somewhat complicated to set up and lacked a simple interface, so they never gained broad user adoption. The simplicity of Twitter has made the same type of filtering much easier and helped millions more customers discover the value of a custom mix of content.

Customized mixes can also be offered by a single media channel or even a single brand providing content for its customers. NPR's podcast service allows users not only to choose from a list of topical podcasts (with popular programs like *Science Fridays* and *Car Talk*). The NPR "Mix Your Own Podcast" tool allows customers to create a customized podcast mix. Customers can enter keywords for topics they are interested in ("technology" or "swine flu"), as well as names of programs, favorite reporters, and musicians. The tool then creates a custom podcast just for them, pulling in all the day's stories that are tagged with any of the search terms they have chosen.

Nike has also shown the value of custom content mixes for brands that sell products instead of media. As part of Nike's Sparq program for athletic training, the company created more than sixty training videos for sports including football, basketball, and soccer. Customers can use an online tool to mix the videos into a customized training program. Custom mixes can be downloaded to mobile video players and act as virtual trainers for customers.

When Nissan created the urban-guide.co.uk content Web site for its Quashqai car brand in Britain, it wanted to connect with a young, urban audience by offering in-the-know advice on the best things to do and see in such cities as London, Birmingham, and Liverpool. Rather than create a single urban guide to fit all users, Nissan recognized their individual tastes by creating a customizable Web site for each city. Using a library of widgets, the site allows visitors to customize which cool bloggers (Rob Ellis or Graeme O'Callaghan), video news streams ("100 percent London" or "Urban Undiscovered"), and topics ("art & music" or "pubs & bars") will fill up the page with constantly updating content and blog posts. For a target audience that would not be likely to accept any one vision of what's cool in their home town, Nissan's site offered a customizable experience that users could make their own.

Mash Up Your Products

Networked customers are familiar with a wide range of tools for finding and adapting content, products, and services to fit their particular needs. But customization also enables self-expression and affirms identity. This can be seen in the phenomenon of media mash-ups that flood the Web. Mash-ups are created by remixing, editing, and combining existing media, content, or software to create something new and distinctive. It is the digital age's answer to collage—the early twentieth-century art form based on pasting together fragments of existing photographs, fabrics, drawings, and painting.

Many of the most popular videos on YouTube are video mash-ups that combine existing audio or video—the soundtrack from Budweiser's famous "Wassup?" commercial, scenes from an episode of *The Simpsons*, or footage of a political candidate. Comedian Stephen Colbert is famous for his "green screen challenges," where he asks television viewers to mash up footage of himself (or, once, presidential candidate John McCain making a particularly uninspired speech) with whatever other sources they choose to create a humorous new video. Fans of Japanese anime enjoy creating new music videos by mashing up scenes from Japanese cartoons with soundtracks of pop music and unrelated dialogue. There is even a contest—the Iron Editor contest, modeled after the *Iron Chef* TV show—in which contestants must remix video in real time, in front of judges and a live audience.

Likewise, businesses can offer customers the digital tools to create personalized versions of their products and services, inviting the customers to express their identity, style, and taste.

The NikeID platform allows customers to create unique designs for Nike running shoes. On a Web site or in the NikeID Studio at NikeTown stores, customers use a digital interface to mash up a variety of color options for the laces, trim, swoosh, collar, and other elements of the shoe design. The result combines the functional features of a Nike training shoe with the opportunity to wear a one-of-a-kind design that shows off the customer's unique sense of style. Customers can share their designs with friends online and purchase their one-of-a-kind shoes for a premium price. Nike has engaged customers with other design interfaces, too, such as a touch screen that lets window shoppers play with the NikeID experience before entering the store. An interactive billboard in Times Square allowed passersby to customize a pair of shoes on a seven-thousand-square-foot public billboard; they would then receive an SMS message to their phone with links to download a wallpaper image and order the shoes online. The PhotoID interface allows European customers to send any photo from their mobile phone to Nike and receive back a sample NikeID shoe design combining the color elements of that photo into a shoe. In Britain, Nike has extended this mash-up concept to football (soccer) uniforms, with a digital kiosk that allows customers to create uniform designs in the store.

BMW's Mini Cooper has linked its brand closely to the self-expression of drivers who can customize their cars. The Roof Studio online tool allows customers to create unique roof designs—a leopard skin print, Brazilian flag, or multicolored racing stripes. Customers can also choose from hundreds of options among the car's components because of BMW's flexible production cells, which enable it to manufacture the vehicles on demand.

The LEGO brand has always been about creativity and making your own designs. But what if you don't have just the right LEGO bricks to build your vision? At LegoFactory.com, customers can design their own models in virtual 3-D space with the LEGO Digital Designer. After finishing a design, they can purchase it as a real-world LEGO kit that arrives by mail with printed instructions, all the bricks needed to assemble it, and custom packaging with the customer's own name and model number. They can also share their designs with other users on the site (who can adapt them by adding and subtracting their own parts). More than three hundred thousand customers have participated in LEGO Factory worldwide.

Businesses can help customers mash up services to suit their personal style, too. Affinia Hotels, a boutique chain in New York, Chicago, and Washington, DC, allows customers to design a personalized hotel experience through its MyAffinia.com online tool. Guests can choose from six types of pillows for their bed, including a natural buckwheat pillow, a self-molding Swedish "Memory Pillow," and a "Sound Pillow" with ultrathin speakers inside that play music from an MP3 player. Travelers can choose the grooming options that will await them in their room, as well as electric chargers and adapters to suit their laptop and mobile phone. For more distinctive fun, guests can request cupcakes, a rubber ducky, or an Ibanez acoustic guitar to greet them. To make choosing easier, Affinia uses a choice schema to bundle some of its options into themes, such as the StayFit Kit (yoga mat, weights, and workout bands), the Walking Kit (pedometer, city walking guide, and a preloaded iPod shuffle), and the BYOB Kit (wine carrier, picnic blanket, and guide to the best local picnic spots).

By offering choices to personalize products and services, businesses can provide a niche experience that allows customers to express their personality and connect more deeply to the brand.

Make the Choice Personal

Digital tools for customization do more than just tap into a customer's creativity and sense of style, however. Choice can also allow for a much stronger and personal connection to a business or organization. This is particularly true for nonprofits, where the customer is motivated by the impact of contributing time and money rather than the desire to consume goods or services.

Matt and Jessica Flannery are two young Americans who were living in Uganda when they first got the idea to start an online microcredit service. "My wife got really excited about living in Africa," says Matt, "and I was really excited about living in San Francisco. So we had this marriage dilemma."[14] They solved the dilemma by starting Kiva, a Web start-up based in San Francisco that funds small loans to entrepreneurial families and individuals in Uganda and 183 other countries around the world.

Kiva is a new kind of philanthropy, one based on individual donors (lenders) and individual recipients (entrepreneurs). With Kiva, anyone with twenty-five dollars, a credit card, and an Internet connection can choose his or her own way to better the world.

Rather than donating money to a giant collective fund managed by a large charitable organization, Kiva lenders make loans directly to individuals who have been prescreened by microfinance institutions in their home country. Lenders may choose to contribute to a farmer in Peru seeking to buy a cow, to a seamstress in Lebanon seeking to buy a new sewing machine to employ her sister in her shop, or to a barbecue stand owner in Samoa needing money for a stove, pot, and materials to build a roadside stand. On Kiva's Web site, lenders can view hundreds of loan requests and sort by the recipient's gender, geographical region, type of business, or fundraising status. By clicking on a recipient, lenders see a photo and profile of the family, business, and terms of the loan. By bringing lenders face to face with borrowers, Kiva makes giving loans to those in need far more personal, and compelling to users. As Mother Theresa said, "If I look at the mass I will never act. If I look at the one, I will."[15]

By turning loans into a personal choice—which entrepreneur will you support with your twenty-five dollars?—Kiva has unleashed a groundswell of participation among networked donors. Within its first four years, more than half a million lenders loaned eighty million dollars to two hundred thousand recipients around the world. The average loan request waits only four days to be filled. With a repayment rate of over 98 percent, loan funds are constantly being redirected by their lenders to new businesses and families in need around the world.

Other charities, such as GlobalGiving and DonorsChoose, have similarly found that giving choice to customers increases their involvement in the process of helping others. Pierre Omidyar, founder of eBay, had already made his fortune creating a Web auctioning service that served the niche markets of customer networks when he turned his attention to philanthropy and the support of organizations like DonorsChoose. Started by public school teacher Charles Best, DonorsChoose lets users pick specific projects to fund at local schools around the corner or around the country. On the Web site, donors can search for projects by state, by school subject, or by keyword topics such as "flash cards," "gardening," and "autism needs." The charity has attracted more than a hundred thousand donors for whom choosing whom to support makes giving all the more meaningful.

Create a Platform for Choice

There are limits to how many product options and choices one company can generate for customers on its own. While LEGO building blocks easily generate endless iterations, a hotel like Affinia must create and source each new feature, service, or option itself.

One extremely powerful way to generate options for a CUSTOMIZE strategy is to use or build a platform for choice. A platform for choice is a technology, service, or protocol that encourages other people or organizations to develop options for your customers. Businesses may create their own platform for choice, or they can tap into an existing platform to find a broad range of niche offerings.

The RSS protocol for Web publishing is one popular platform for choice. RSS established a standard format for anyone publishing content online (text articles, videos, and audio) to make it available in public "feeds" to attract more viewers. RSS is what allows Web sites such as Nissan's Urban Guide to pick from millions of Web publishers and bloggers and assemble a targeted menu of content options for its customers (while directing profitable traffic back to the original publishers).

When Amazon.com moved beyond selling books, it also developed a platform that allows independent retailers to sell their products through Amazon's site. Large specialty retailers like J&R Music and Computer World offer an expanded range of products that show up in Amazon's standard product listings. The Amazon Marketplace allows much smaller businesses to sell used, discounted, and hard-to-find books and music. By providing a platform for other businesses to sell online, Amazon is able to greatly increase the huge range of product options it offers. Similarly, when Amazon introduced its Kindle e-book reader, its success hinged on Amazon's ability to offer more than three hundred thousand popular books, newspapers, magazines, and blogs, already suited to the Kindle's reading format.

New digital technologies continue to create more platforms for choice. HP's MagCloud service allows micropublishers, from corporations to individuals, to create customized and microniche print magazines and books. This new print-on-demand technology allows anyone to upload the publications as PDF files and have HP take care of the printing (through one of a network of print shops that have purchased the MagCloud printers). MagCloud can print one copy of a hundred different magazines for the same price as a hundred copies of one magazine. Publishers, who pay twenty cents a page, have started to create niche magazines on topics such as paintings by Mormon artists or for industries such as the Arizona cactus business. On-demand printing for books is also allowing niche publications to aim at specific valuable audiences with a particular interest. For example, Lexus produced a custom book on its environmental practices and published it for eighteen hundred specially selected customers. On-demand books have soared in recent years: in 2008, for the first time, the number of on-demand titles surpassed the number of traditional books published.[16]

An even greater impact on the book industry may come from the arrival of custom-printing kiosks, such as the Espresso. This "ATM for books" can print a hundred pages a minute and bind the pages into a finished book on a machine that will fit in the corner of a local bookstore. The first Espresso in Europe appeared in the famed Blackwell's bookshop in central London, where it expanded the bookstore's famously large selection with an additional half-million titles, ready to print from digital files. A customer coming in to find Charles Darwin's out-of-print book on earthworms was able to print a copy in minutes for about twenty dollars (instead of paying a thousand dollars on the secondhand market for rare books). The first Espresso in the United States was in the homey Northshire Bookstore in Manchester, Vermont. The store found that many aspiring authors came in to print short runs of their own unpublished books once they found out they no longer needed an established publisher to accept their manuscript. As its digital library expands, the Espresso will allow small, local bookstores like Northshire to offer just as many niche books as an online powerhouse like Amazon.

On-demand manufacturing services can produce more than just books. Services like Zazzle allow businesses large and small to offer customizable products for customers. These personalized designs can be printed on T-shirts, mugs, and stationery, of course, but also on skateboards, postage stamps, and even canvas shoes. Customers of Flip Video can use the Café Press customization platform to buy a pocket camcorder emblazoned with their own cover design, just like they can design the roof of their Mini Cooper.

On-demand manufacturing is much more than just decals and graphic designs added to finished products, however. New platforms allow small designers, or even individual customers, to order products built to their own physical design specifications. London custom clothier Styleshake allows customers to customize dresses, tops, skirts, and accessories. Users select a fabric, create a custom design using the online studio (or select from those already created), and order the clothing tailored to their measurements. In its first three months, the site received twenty-five thousand customer designs and glowing reviews in the fashion press.

New Zealand firm Ponoko lets designers around the world custom manufacture furniture, jewelry, toys, housewares, and even electronics. An independent designer creates a design using such tools as the open-source Blender 3-D or Google's free Sketchup software. Next, he or she uploads the digital design to Ponoko's Web site. Then, at one of a network of fabrication shops, laser cutters are used to automatically trim wood, acrylic, bamboo, cardboard, leather, or felt to bring the design to life. The result (some assembly may be required) is shipped to a consumer anywhere in the world. For anyone with a big idea and no design skills, there is an option to commission a product to be designed by one of the community of designers on Ponoko.

The Future of CUSTOMIZE

New platforms and new technologies will continue to expand the ways businesses can use CUSTOMIZE strategies.

New, better, and easier design tools will enable more people to create their own designs for some products and to tweak and modify others with a personal touch (think of your Garage Band software, but for editing furniture instead of music). The ProFORMA modeling tool by Cambridge University student Qi Pan already shows how a full 3-D scan of an object can be made by rotating the object in front of a simple webcam on any computer.

After customizing the design, a new generation of 3-D printers will give customers the power to fabricate their own unique physical products right on their tabletop. Bre Pettis's Brooklyn-based Makerbot Industries has already pioneered a 3-D printer that can fabricate any shape you upload into it out of layered ABS plastic. Need a plastic cup? A plastic bust of your own head? Just print it. At a thousand dollars, the Makerbot offers the power of 3-D printing in your own home for less than the cost of many laptops. As the next generation of design and prototyping tools becomes easier to use and more flexible, an ever wider range of products will be customizable to suit the niche needs and creative expressions of customers.

Customers may also begin to develop more detailed digital profiles of their tastes, interests, and purchasing behavior. Sharing these profiles with organizations could allow for much more targeted and helpful products, services, and communications. Detailed profiles would allow us to receive advertising that is more suited to our own interests, to automatically subscribe to newsletters or blogs in the format and frequency we prefer, and to integrate a personalized social element into the results we find on search engines like Google. Journalist and author Stephen Baker predicts that if magazines like *BusinessWeek* are to survive online, they will need to grow more dynamic, so that article topics, and even their length and level of detail, will be matched to the preferences of each reader.[17]

Keys to a CUSTOMIZE Strategy

Whether your business is selling products or services, digital or physical, a CUSTOMIZE strategy can offer your customer network the chance to choose from, or modify, a diverse range of products, services, and content. This can be done by offering a wide array of products and the tools to sort through them or by offering digital tools that let customers design and modify to suit their own needs and taste.

While too much choice without structure or guidance can be off-putting for customers, the right filters can assist customers in making decisions that add value for them. A CUSTOMIZE strategy can increase sales, differentiate from competitors, and build closer relationships with networked customers.

Successful approaches to a CUSTOMIZE strategy include: offering a vast menu of products, services, or content; providing a playlist of streaming content that adapts to customer preferences; letting customers modify or mash-up your products or services; using choice to help customers connect with real people; and finding or building a choice platform that allows third parties to continually create new products or content for your customers to choose.

Whatever the approach, it is critical to offer choices that people care most about. Not many customers would choose to customize their stapler, yet everyone has an opinion about what movie they want to see next weekend. Figure out where your customers' desires diverge and what matters most to them. They may customize to make a statement or express themselves, to match their specific interests, or to answer a particular functional need. If it matters to them, it should matter to you.

By helping customer networks customize their products, services, and communications, businesses can enhance their value, deepen their relationships, and learn more about how to innovate for their customers' needs.

But let's go further. Networked customers want more than just to create, purchase, consume or enjoy what is personal and reflects their individuality. They want to share their unique selves with others in their networks. They want to share their ideas in words, sound, and images and to share their relationships in network links to others. One of the most powerful drivers of customer networks is the desire to connect with others. But how do businesses facilitate and participate in all this connection? Do customers even want them to, or would they prefer that businesses butt out of online conversations? If business is going to tap into the personal connections within customer networks, they will need to first understand how and why customers share and connect with one another.

CHAPTER 6

CONNECT
Become a Part of Your Customers' Conversations

When U.S. Army soldier Jeff Taylor was considering the difficult decision of whether to reenlist for another tour of duty in Iraq, he discussed it with his wife, Sarah. She was back in their home in Fort Riley, Kansas, but could see Jeff in his room in Baghdad, thanks to an Internet connection and the video webcams connected to their laptop computers. Sarah would leave the video connection on much of the day, her own laptop propped on a coffee table so that Jeff could watch their infant daughter and young son. With grainy video streaming from Iraq, Sarah would watch Jeff come home in the evening and get ready for bed. Across thousands of miles, it felt a little like having him in the same room.[1]

GIs like Taylor serving in Iraq and Afghanistan use a variety of network technologies to stay connected to loved ones back home. On battlefront blogs, soldiers share their day-to-day experiences of war in a way that no television footage or news article can capture. Other soldiers share photos online at Flickr.com, write short text updates to Twitter, or share links with friends on MySpace and Facebook, in each case using digital technology to connect with others in their personal and professional networks.

Or at least they do so when they're not being banned from these sites by superior officers. Throughout the wars, the U.S. military leadership has wrestled with itself back and forth on whether, when, and how to allow personnel access to these communication tools. At one point, the army announced that all blog posts, and even personal emails, needed to be cleared by a superior officer. Then they issued a "clarification" that suggested soldiers could write at their own discretion. Policies varied: in the summer of 2009 alone, the army ordered that all bases provide free access to Facebook, the Marines issued a ban of all major social networking sites, and the Department of Defense mulled a blanket Web 2.0 prohibition for all the armed services. The reasons given for prohibition were frequently nonsensical (for example, to save bandwidth for mission critical activities, despite the modest bandwidth used by many of these sites).

Many within the military loudly decried the restrictions, arguing that allowing soldiers to honestly share their experiences online was the best way for the armed forces to represent themselves to civilians back home. They also saw digital media as a critical tool for soldiers to share insights among themselves. That had been the goal of army majors Nate Allen and Tony Burgess when they started the online forum CompanyCommand.com on their own dime.

Inspired by a discussion forum for outdoors hunters, Allen and Burgess's unsanctioned site invited officers (with a password) to ask questions, share advice, and pose topics for discussion. After the army entered Iraq in 2003, the site became an invaluable tool for new officers arriving with little training in local customs or counterinsurgency warfare. CompanyCommand gave them crucial real-time learning from their more experienced peers already on the ground in the war zone. Participants shared leadership advice on such topics as coping with fear and handling the pregnancy of a subordinate; practical advice on how to kick in a door, holster a gun in a Humvee, or protect a convoy; insight on local customs such as tea sharing and funeral mourning; and recommendations on equipment including simple tourniquets and the best sunglasses for sandstorms.[2]

CompanyCommand was greeted with wariness by more senior officers, but after the site grew to include more than a third of all army captains, it was made official and moved onto the military's Web servers. Allen and Burgess were brought home to teach at West Point, and they continue to run the site. By 2009, the top commander in Iraq, General Ray Odierno, had set up his own Facebook page, and the top commanders in Afghanistan had set up MySpace and Facebook pages, a YouTube channel, and multiple Twitter feeds to represent the campaign in that country. The army was even experimenting with a wiki to allow soldiers of any rank to add their anecdotes and experiences to many of the field manuals used for troop training, just as one might contribute to an article on Wikipedia.

The uncertainty with which the army's leadership has responded to the spread of new media and their adoption from junior officers up to senior brass, mirrors the reaction of many large, established businesses. These traditional organizations, built upon hierarchies of command and control, are understandably uncomfortable with the increasingly democratic and unmanaged flow of information within and outside the organization. Yet both traditional businesses and militaries realize that they face the threat of disruptive competitors (start-up innovators or loosely organized combatants) who will use networks to organize and communicate. To compete, large, established organizations will have to adapt to a world where not all communications are controlled from the top.

The CONNECT Strategy

Today's networked customers seek to connect with one another by sharing ideas, opinions, and feelings through digital media. Like the general, the soldier, and the military family back home, they use a variety of tools for creating and sharing text, images, videos, votes, and social links with others around the world.

Much of this connecting is happening on social networking sites like Facebook, MySpace, and Twitter. By linking to other users on these services (becoming someone's "friend" or "follower" in their parlance), hundreds of millions of people worldwide have connected to each other in the digital realm, instantiating a web of personal ties. The prevalence of social networking sites is hard to overestimate. The global population of active Facebook users surpassed four hundred million in 2010.[3] But other social networking sites dominated in some regions: QZone in China, Orkut in Brazil, and VKontakte and LiveJournal in Russia.[4] Although participation in social networking sites was initially driven by young users, their demographic reach quickly broadened. By 2009, most Facebook users were over twenty-six years old, and the fastest-growing segment was fifty-to-sixty-five-year-old females.[5]

On these and a variety of other types of Web sites, customers are producing an avalanche of "user-generated content" that they use to share ideas with one another. By 2009, nearly a quarter of online adults in the United States wrote their own blogs, uploaded original audio or video, or posted stories online.[6] Others express themselves in smaller contributions, such as voting, posting short comments, or sharing links to what they find interesting online. The total outpouring of customer opinions and ideas takes many forms and is produced at an incredible rate:

- *Videos:* Twenty hours of new footage are posted every minute to YouTube.[7]
- *Status Updates:* Twenty-one million short texts are posted each day on Twitter, or as many words as are in a Harry Potter book per minute.[8]
- *Blog Posts:* Two hundred million people blog; most of them blog or tweet every day.[9]

- *Wiki Entries:* Fifteen million encyclopedia entries in 262 languages can be found on Wikipedia.[10]
- *Photos:* Four billion user photos are shared on Flickr.[11]
- *Combinations of the Above:* Five billion pieces of content are shared every week on Facebook, including messages, links, photos, videos, and more. [12]

Other popular media for sharing ideas online include customer product reviews (on sites like Yelp), reader comments (on blogs), votes for news content (on Digg), user ad postings (on craigslist and eBay), and tags and social bookmarks (on Deli.cio.us). New tools continue to emerge for sharing ideas, opinions, and messages within customer networks.

The desire to connect with others—by sharing and communicating our ideas in a range of media—is the fourth core behavior of customer networks. It provides a powerful opportunity for businesses and organizations of all kinds to learn from and build relationships with customers by participating in these conversations.

The fourth customer network strategy for business is the CONNECT strategy—to become a part of their customers' conversations. They can do so by joining the conversations already happening in popular forums like Facebook and Twitter or by creating their own forums where customers express themselves and have a voice.

By participating in the conversations going on in customer networks, a CONNECT strategy can help an organization achieve key business objectives, including: gaining customer insights, building brand image, capturing and evaluating customer input and ideas, nurturing and amplifying positive customer word of mouth, lowering customer service costs, and aiding reputation management and crisis response.

Developing an effective CONNECT strategy requires an understanding of the conversations already taking place in customer networks. What media are customers using, and what is it that makes these media so "social"? Who are your customers connecting with, what are they sharing, and what is motivating them? And what is the impact of their conversations on brands and businesses? Answering these questions will be required before beginning to develop a CONNECT strategy.

All Media Are Social Media

Taken together, social networking sites and our various tools for user-generated content are collectively referred to as "social media."

Unlike the traditional media that preceded them, social media allow users a voice of their own. With traditional media—newspapers, magazines, television, radio—customers merely consume the content provided by reading, watching, or listening. By contrast, in social media, customers still consume content, but they also connect with one another, either by contributing their own content or by linking, voting, and commenting on the content created by others.

But is "social media" even a distinct category anymore? Or is it just a description of what all media are becoming in the digital age?

Today, even traditional broadcast media companies are incorporating social elements. Most American newspapers, for example, now incorporate user-generated content in their online editions, including user photos, videos, and even articles. Nearly all allow reader comments—the first step in a two-way communication pattern that gives readers a voice of their own. In fact, many newspapers like the *New York Times* have stopped referring to their audience as "readers" and describe them instead as "users."

Broadcast television is getting social as well. Viewers of *American Idol* help shape the content of that hit program by casting votes for the performers they like. In the United States, 57 percent of Internet users watch at least some of their television while simultaneously using the Web.[13]

News broadcasters have started not only to accept questions and comments via Web sites and services like Twitter but to rely on viewers to provide them with breaking news content—particularly for global news of disasters, terrorist attacks, or political upheaval, when reporters are unable to be on the ground at the scene. In 2010, one of the prestigious George Polk Awards for journalism was awarded to the unnamed citizens who filmed and posted the online video of the death of Iranian student Neda Agha-Soltan during Iran's 2009 election protests.

Books may be the oldest traditional medium still in widespread publication today. Readers can write notes in their margins, but the printed page still does not allow these comments to be easily shared with other readers or the author (perhaps the next e-reader will improve this). And yet, many books are now published alongside author blogs, MySpace pages, or other platforms that allow readers to contribute their point of view. In many cases, the author's blog builds the audience that lands them their publishing deal before the book is ever written.

Even advertising billboards—perhaps the ultimate example of one-way traditional media—have started getting "social" around the edges. This trend first appeared with the inclusion of SMS short codes on signs ("Send a text to 55522 to get a free ringtone"). More recently businesses have begun to adorn their billboards and roadside signs with their Twitter addresses. The Naked Pizza restaurant in New Orleans turned its roadside billboard into an invitation to follow the restaurant on Twitter. Restaurant cofounder Jeff Leach says that 20 percent of Naked Pizza's sales stem now from its Twitter presence.[14]

Whether powered by WordPress or a printing press, all of our media are increasingly including ways for customers to comment, contribute, and connect. Given the tremendous popularity of social media among today's customer networks, this should come as no surprise. In ways large and small, customers are seeking to connect with one another and share their point of view at every opportunity.

Why We Connect

The motivations for customers to connect via networks are many. A single medium such as Twitter may be used for business advertising, for a personal interchange like email, for discussion of a technical topic with an audience whom the author has never met face to face, or for sharing the trivial minutiae of one's day with their close friends ("Rainy outside, taking the dog for a walk").

This mix of motivations can be confusing to social media newcomers. They may see one person posting on Twitter about their morning dog walk and ask, "Why on earth should my business use Twitter?" But it would be a mistake to think that a communications tool like YouTube or blogging or Twitter is used for only one purpose — any more than telephone calls are used for only one type of conversation. Customer networks connect via these tools to share an incredibly wide variety of ideas, opinions, and feelings.

Some of these expressions are intended for a few close relationships — such as sharing news of a death in the family with friends on Facebook or making a marriage proposal to a beloved via Twitter (several have been offered and accepted via the Twitter @ message format). In other cases, our digital expressions are intentionally sent out to the whole world. When American graduate student James Karl Buck tweeted that he had been arrested in Egypt while covering an antigovernment protest, he notified a host of online "followers" who helped to alert his university and assist in his release the next day. Countless others have used social media to share eyewitness updates and photos of important events with the whole world. In 2008 alone, these included testimony of the massive earthquake in China's

Sichuan province, photos of US Airways flight 1549 landing safely in New York's Hudson River, and news of the terrorist attacks on hotels in Mumbai, India. In each of these dramatic events, personal messages via social media broke the news before the traditional media of television or radio.

We connect online to express our opinions and discuss the things that matter most to our lives. For some, these may be matters of faith or spirituality. Ireland's Cardinal Sean Brady asked the Catholics of that country to "Make someone the gift of a prayer through text, Twitter or e-mail every day. Such a sea of prayer is sure to strengthen our sense of solidarity with one another."[15] *Church Solutions*, a magazine for pastors, recommends that they use Twitter or Facebook regularly to keep in closer touch with their congregation and the challenges they are dealing with, so that pastors can make their sermons more relevant to parishioners and pray for those in need. On networks like Twitter and specialty sites like Gospelr.com, believers share a mix of personal experiences, Bible quotations, and spiritual votives such as this one tweeted by @twitturgies: "Move into my neighborhood, God. Come sing in these suburban streets. Love the loveless. Laugh with the lonely. Spray the walls into beauty."[16]

For others, connecting through networks is a way to cope with intense challenges. The site PatientsLikeMe hosts online communities for those suffering from chronic illnesses such as ALS, Parkinson's, HIV/AIDS, multiple sclerosis, and mood disorders. Using a search function similar to those found on online dating sites, members can find and meet others with medical profiles that closely match their own. With easy-to-use charts and health tracking tools, users share some of their most private medical information (symptoms, medications, and health outcomes) in minute detail, often adding personal photos and their real names. Users can also share any drug side effects they are experiencing and report them directly to government regulators. But mostly, members are driven to connect with one another, finding companionship among others who share the burden of living with an incurable illness.

Others use social media to connect around more joyous occasions. Rebecca Sloan turned online for the wisdom of others when she was approaching the birth of her first child. A thirty-five-year-old biologist, Sloan had already completed childbirth classes, read the standard books on "what to expect," and logged on to the mommy chat rooms when she turned to YouTube to watch some of the real birth experiences of other mothers. She found thousands of videos there, like Sarah Griffith's nine-part video of the birth of her son Bastian, from moans and contractions to the baby's crowning head and first cries. Bastian's birth has been viewed online more than three million times. In the nineteenth century, women regularly observed the birth experiences of family and neighbors in their homes before their own pregnancies. In the twentieth century, childbirth was mostly sequestered from view within hospital maternity wards. But social media has given mothers a chance to demystify birth and once again share their experiences with each other.[17]

Expectant mothers are just one of the many groups that connect online around shared experiences. People with shared affinities and values, "tribes," as author Seth Godin calls them, are using the tools of social media to form niche networks that connect far fewer members than a general service like Facebook, but their members are held together by unique bonds.[18]

More than forty thousand firefighters around the world meet online at Fire Fighter Nation, a niche social networking site that was built using the Ning platform. On this network, members read news articles related to their profession (news of forest fires, hiring and retirement of chiefs, successful rescues, firefighter injuries or fatalities). They read and post to discussion forums on topics relevant to them (fire suppression tactics, safety rules, vehicles and equipment, education and outreach). They create profiles of themselves, introduce themselves to other members, and join smaller subgroups (fire engine drivers, volunteer firefighters, the "Officer's Club," the "Firefighter Saloon," fans of the TV show *Rescue Me*). They organize and publicize offline events in the real world (golf outings, memorial services, firefighting conferences, field days for volunteers). They share their personal points of view and experiences in blog posts, photos, and videos.

In more than a million niche networks of this kind, your customers are joining together to connect in similar ways: by sharing content, reading topical news, meeting others, discussing online, and organizing activities that happen offline. These groups form around a variety of affiliations. Some coalesce around ethnic identity, like 360pars.com, a global social network of forty-four thousand Persians around the world. Others share a common geography, such as the dating site Singles En Barcelona or Why Leave Astoria?, a site where residents of that outer-borough New York neighborhood plan events and meet neighbors. Some networks form around professional vocations, such as the niche dating site Farmers Only (care to meet a bachelor dairy man?) or the GovLoop network for professionals in U.S. federal, state, and local government. Some of the most passionate networks form around amateur passions: Classical Lounge (classical music aficionados blog and share music), Kicks On Fire (avid sneaker collectors show off their latest footwear), and Chainlink (a one-stop resource for Chicago bicyclists to find rides and routes). For popular sports teams, authors, or musicians, a social network can provide a place to nurture an ardent fan community with insider news, artist videos and blogs, special offers, and, of course, opportunities for users to comment, discuss, and post their own content. Rapper 50 Cent's social network ThisIs50 provides an online hub for nearly half a million fans to connect with one another.

How Brands Are Shaped by Conversations

The vibrant online fan community of 50 Cent is, of course, a boon for his brand and sales of his recordings. But conversations in customer networks reach far beyond music artists and popular entertainment brands. Customer word of mouth is hugely influential for all kinds of business, and customer networks have greatly expanded its impact and reach.

Research has found that recommendations from personal acquaintances are trusted by 90 percent of global online consumers in evaluating products, far more than any other source of product information.[19] This is not a new phenomenon: word of mouth and referrals have always been critical to business, especially for small and medium-size businesses who could not easily reach their audiences with broadcast advertising on mass media. What is new is that the word of mouth of today's customers is reaching far larger audiences as they connect and share opinions online. Rather than sharing a comment about a product or company with three friends over lunch, a customer today may post it on their Facebook page, and a hundred friends could see it in their news feed the same day. If the customer posts on a more public online forum, such as Twitter, their comment may be passed along and seen by thousands of people outside of their direct circle of friends.

When customer word of mouth reaches those farther afield, does it lose its credibility and impact? Who would pay attention to an online product review posted by someone they have never met? Lots of people. The same research found that the second most trusted form of information on products was "consumer opinions posted online." With 70 percent trusting them "somewhat" or "completely," online opinions edged out newspaper articles (the traditional goal of public relations) as a source of trusted information, as well as surpassing brand sponsorships and all types of advertising: television, print, radio, billboards, banner ads, and search engines.[20] With so much influence, it's no surprise that opinions shared in customer networks have begun to have a powerful effect on companies' reputations and brands.

In chapter 1, we read about musician Dave Carroll, who, after terrible customer service from United Airlines, posted a comical music video called "United Breaks Guitars" that attracted millions of views and a firestorm of bad publicity for the airline. Other infamous examples include the "Comcast Technician Sleeping" video, seen a million times on YouTube, in which a repairman arrived for a service call and proceeded to fall asleep on the customer's sofa while waiting on hold for an hour to speak with Comcast's central office. Even more notorious was the story of blogger (now author and professor) Jeff Jarvis and his campaign against Dell. In 2005, Jarvis received terrible customer service for a new laptop, despite having bought the gold-plated service plan. He posted a complaint on his blog. Dell's policy at the time was to not respond to customer complaints on blogs, but Jarvis's post, titled "Dell Sucks," was seen by other customers who recognized his experience as their own, linked to his post, commented on it, and created sarcastic Web sites about the truth of "Dell Hell." Soon, Jarvis's original complaint had become a focal point of so many links that it was appearing on the first page of Google results for any search on "Dell." By the time mainstream press outlets like *Business-Week* and the *Houston Chronicle* were covering the story, Dell's rating in the American Consumer Satisfaction Index was down 5 percent and its stock price was sliding in a year when competitors were experiencing rapid growth.[21] (To his credit, Dell founder Michael Dell used this experience to help spur a broad effort to improve service and focus on customer networks.)

Bad buzz travels faster now, too. For movies, it used to be that customer word of mouth would take at least a week to sink a film that failed to live up to its marketing hype. Now many moviegoers use mobile devices to post their opinion of a new movie from their seats while the credits are still rolling. In a 2009 Web poll, 12 percent of respondents told Movietickets.com that Twitter influenced their movie choices. Add in Facebook, MySpace, and other social media, and you start to see a significant portion of the movie audience.[22] When the shock comedy *Bruno* received scathing opening night reviews on Twitter, the film suffered a 39 percent drop in ticket sales from Friday to Saturday.[23] *Bruno* had arrived with much anticipation as a follow-up to the cult hit *Borat,* but many movie industry watchers guessed that its quick box office demise was accelerated by what was dubbed "The Twitter Effect."

But customers' word of mouth can also have remarkably positive impact on brands online. We read the story, in chapter 1, of L.A. actor Dusty Sorg and his friend Michael Jedrzejewski, who created a Facebook fan page for Coca-Cola. What began as a simple online expression of love for their favorite soda blossomed into an online fan community with more than three million "friends" adding their own testimonials about the beloved brand. Close behind Coke on Facebook is another consumer brand, Nutella, whose page was originally built by fans. With almost no advertising budget, the hazelnut and chocolate spread has nevertheless built an intensely loyal following: three million fans are proud to display their love for the brand on their Facebook profile.

Another place where brands are benefiting from customer conversations is mom blogs. These family journals on the Web have become extremely popular: hundreds of thousands of mom blogs generate at least ten thousand page views per month. Mom bloggers love to review products and let readers in on which ones they like. Many companies have started sending them sample products to review, just as they send to magazine editors. When a group of top mom bloggers convened at the South by Southwest (SXSW) digital conference in 2009, record producer Steve Greenberg brought along one of his new artists, singer-songwriter Diane Birch, to meet them over lunch and share some of her music. The mom bloggers immediately connected with Birch's songs and sumptuous voice, reminiscent of Janis Joplin, Rickie Lee Jones, and Carole King. They jumped at the chance to help spread the word about her music, writing about it on their blogs and including a widget linking to Amazon and iTunes that would donate one dollar to a charity picked by the bloggers for every album sold. Venture capitalist and music lover Fred Wilson mused that mom blogs may be "the new radio"—the place where bands (and other consumer products) need to be in order to get heard and be discovered by today's networked customers.[24]

Six Approaches to CONNECT Strategy

The conversations in customer networks are happening every day, and their impact on any business or organization cannot be ignored. This fact poses great challenges for managers seeking to shape the image of their brands, products, and organizations. But it also highlights an opportunity to better connect with customers by participating in these digital conversations.

This participation may be limited, confined to listening in and answering questions when asked. Or it may be extremely active, focused on building new relationships with and among customers and leveraging them to benefit brands and add value to the business.

By looking at businesses that have successfully connected with customer networks in their online conversations, we can see six approaches to a CONNECT strategy:

- *Listen and Learn:* Monitor and learn from the online conversations your customers are already having about your business and your industry.

- *Join the Conversation:* Respond to issues, answer questions, and make friends by joining the give-and-take of online conversations.

- *Provide a Forum:* Create new places for your customers to express their views and connect with each other around shared interests.

- *Ask for Ideas:* Solicit ideas from customers to tap into the wisdom of the crowd and show that you care about what they think.

- *Integrate Their Voice in Yours:* Bring customers' stories into your own content and marketing.

- *Let Conversations Add a Layer of Value:* Make the conversations among your customers an added source of value for your business.

By examining these six approaches and how they have been used successfully by a wide range of organizations, we can gain insights into how becoming a part of customers' conversations can help any business to better connect with its customer network.

Listen and Learn

The first thing any company should do as part of a CONNECT strategy is to begin listening to the conversation in customer networks and learning from it.

Monitoring for Your Brand

Monitoring online conversations that relate to your brand or business can begin quite simply. Free tools such as Google Alerts (for news), Technorati (for blogs), and Seesmic Desktop (for status updates on Twitter and Facebook) allow you to set up automatic searches of social media on key terms. Google Trends allows you to measure the frequency of search terms on Google. This reflects far more of your audience (because more people use Google search than blog or tweet) and can provide a good measure of the zeitgeist (a coffee retailer might learn: Are more customers looking for "espresso" or "cappuccino"?). Whichever tool you use, key words should be chosen to monitor social media conversations about your brands, products, businesses, and senior leadership, as well as conversations about your competitors. Key conversations to listen for include customer compliments, complaints, or problems with your business, as well as comments that provide evidence of the impact of your marketing campaigns. You will also want to monitor topics related to your business category and the key issues that you solve for your customers (for example, discussions of "ERP software," if that is what you provide to clients) in order to hear the conversations going on at the point of need for your potential customers. For organizations with many customers and a great many mentions in social media, paid services from such vendors as Visible Technology and Radian6 provide sophisticated tracking with analytics that quantify measures including volume of comments, share of voice online, sentiment (positive versus negative comments), associated words (what words does your brand name frequently appear next to), and even influence and impact (by measuring which customers have the most visibility and "reach" online). With tools of this kind, social media monitoring can yield detailed maps of your brand's image and show how ideas and opinions are propagating within your customer networks.

Gaining Valuable Insights

Once monitoring is established, it is important to be ready to capture ideas, respond, and act on insights. MasterCard has generated ideas for sweepstakes prizes and creative elements of its ad campaigns from listening to conversations in customer networks and discovering what people were most interested in. General Mills introduced its successful line of gluten-free baking products after listening to the conversations of customers who were avoiding gluten because of Celiac disease or other reasons. When side effects for Pfizer's Champix smoking cessation pills were discussed in the press, the company considered a costly ad campaign as a response until social media monitoring revealed that customer sentiment toward Champix remained positive. On the other hand, when Tropicana launched a major redesign of its orange juice cartons in 2009, the response from their most loyal and influential customers online was deafening. The sleeker new design was judged "generic," "ugly," even "stupid." Tropicana promptly reversed course and announced it would return to the classic packaging that featured the image of a straw piercing a ripe orange.

Customer Networks as Market Research

Networks can supplement, or even take the place of, much traditional market research, typically at much less cost. Pharmaceutical companies and academic research labs have purchased data from the PatientsLikeMe social networks of disease sufferers, after it has been aggregated and stripped of personally identifying information (the data is shared with consent of the site's members). Data from patients' online conversations about symptoms and treatments can provide insights available nowhere else and lead to new hypotheses for drug research. In other cases, pharmaceutical companies have used the networks to quickly recruit subjects for clinical trials. With as many as 5 percent of all U.S. patients for a given chronic disease already enrolled on the site, the population and data sets are larger than anything available anywhere else. Drug maker UCB helped set up a new group within PatientsLikeMe for epileptics in order to gather data about comparative effectiveness of different therapies, understand quality of life for patients, and measure drug safety and side effects. (The site is open to all epileptics, not just those on UCB treatments.) On Sermo, a social network for physicians, pharmaceutical companies pay for anonymized polling comments and data from doctors and for the opportunity to survey doctors directly within the social network. The opportunities for social media as a market research tool are still being uncovered. Today, any company should start by listening to its customer networks before spending money to hire a focus group.

Join the Conversation

Once they are listening, businesses need to be ready to join in on the conversation as well, responding where needed, and taking advantage of the opportunity to make new connections and reach customers. There are several ways to join the conversation.

Respond to Issues and Concerns

I am a frequent user of Google Maps, so I was frustrated one day when I found that it was no longer reloading properly in my Firefox Web browser, even after rebooting. I was not optimistic about getting help from Google, so instead I turned to Twitter, which I had recently begun using. Perhaps my contacts there would have an answer or at least share my outrage. "Why the #$%! does Google Maps not work on Firefox?? Try changing the address and hitting return to refresh—nothing. Can we start a revolt?" I tweeted. Two hours later, I received a reply in Twitter, not from my followers, but from an account named @firefox_answers. The message helpfully suggested that it might be a conflict with the Skype plug-in and told me where to switch that off in Firefox. I was stunned. I immediately tried the solution and reported back that it didn't work. Firefox suggested that I test my other plug-ins and see if turning any of them off fixed the problem. Within minutes, I had identified the conflict: a recording plug-in for RealPlayer that I had added the week before. I eagerly tweeted this news back to Firefox, which thanked me and said it would share the information with others. In thirty minutes I received another tweet, this time from RealPlayer, saying that it was looking into the faulty code. Obviously, Firefox had found my initial comment because they had someone monitoring the universe of Twitter (probably via a free application). With a few brief 140-character messages, the company had found an unhappy customer (before I even reached out to them!), identified a product bug to be fixed, solved my problem, and turned me into a loyal fan who would go on to share this story with many others.

This is what customer service looks like in the age of social media: proactive (be on the lookout), genuinely helpful (no shrugging off the customer with "it's not our problem"), and in a human voice (no bureaucratic rules or officious language). Companies including Microsoft, General Motors, Marriott Hotels, and Wells Fargo bank have all incorporated social media response protocols into their customer service and communications. Even airlines have found that they can win over some of their dissatisfied customers with this approach, rather than inspiring them to compose musical satires on YouTube. With Wi-Fi access now available to passengers on its flights, Virgin America has its Web marketing team monitor Twitter for inflight customer complaints, forwarding issues on to public relations, to guest care, and to onboard crews as appropriate. Providing helpful information and customer care on Twitter is quite visible too, especially if the company has a lot of followers (Southwest and JetBlue each have more than a million). So the good service offered to one customer may be seen by many more.

Be Visible, Make Friends, and Be Viral

How does an airline get a million followers on a social network? Isn't that kind of popularity supposed to be reserved for movie stars? Joining the conversation in social networks is not just about lurking in the background and responding to customer complaints. Businesses large and small can use the most popular networks to create a visible presence online beyond their own Web site and make friends with new and potential customers

Many organizations, from politicians and bands to mass market brands, have developed a major presence on Facebook. Companies often attract fans by offering incentives to get customers to "like" them online. Keeping customers engaged, though, takes attention.

Best practices include: a regular flow of creative content (comments, videos, and images), active discussion (on discussion boards and in wall comments), and a fun and casual tone to match the medium. Starbucks, for example, posts interesting status updates every couple of days that cover a mix of coffee topics, as well as reviews of music and books sold in their stores. Each post receives thousands of comments by their Facebook fans. Adidas attracted many friends on Facebook with a contest to win an MTV house party. After the contest, it featured a stream of content from the party on its page (blog posts, photos, and party video). Red Bull displays the brand's edgy humor for its young target audience by offering funny apps on its Facebook page, such as one that lets fans rate the phone calls of drunk callers to Red Bull's phone line.

All of this content and interaction benefits from the viral element of Facebook: every time a customer "likes" Starbucks for a coffee discount or comments on its music reviews, "likes" a video they see on Adidas's page, or uses a humorous app on Red Bull's page, this interaction appears in the customer's personal Facebook feed and is seen by all of their friends. When you see a friend interacting with a brand, you can click and become a friend of the brand as well. Starbucks has found that for every four customers who interact with one of their content items, three new friends join. A single post announcing a mini-Starbucks card drew thirteen thousand comments and "likes" from friends: thus, one post could yield nine thousand new followers.[25]

Interact Like a Real Human Being

Joining the conversation on social networks is not just about content, prizes, and links, however. It is also about online interaction with customers: a genuine dialogue based on listening, responding, and exchange. First-time author Stephenie Meyer reached out to her fans this way when they started the first fan Web sites for her book

Twilight, a horror-romance between Bella, a teenage girl, and her vampire schoolmate Edward. Meyer answered readers' questions about Bella and Edward on MySpace. She responded to creative writing on fan fiction sites and filled in backstory details on her characters for their Twilight Lexicon Web site. She created a personal Web site with pictures of herself with fans at book readings and with her family at home. She even used customer networks to arrange "I Love Edward" parties and to organize a real-life high school prom for Edward and Bella, attended in full costume by hundreds of her fans. Readers responded enthusiastically, traveling thousands of miles to participate in events, joining online discussion groups in the tens of thousands, introducing Meyer's books to their friends, and championing each new release on Amazon. This network of enthusiastic customers helped buoy *Twilight* and its three sequels to such success that in the first quarter of 2009, they held all four of the top sales spots on *USA Today*'s best-sellers list, accounting for one in seven books sold that quarter.[26]

Larger companies can also show a personal face online by having specific employees represent them in social media. Shashank Nigam, a top airline industry blogger and CEO of Simpliflying, observes that this personal face of the company is often critical to gaining customers' trust. "Why do so many travelers trust what they read in a customer review on Trip Advisor? Because under that review is the customer's name, and they can click and read the profile of a real person who is sharing their opinion. Too many businesses are still speaking online in the faceless voice of some anonymous corporate communications department, and that undermines trust."[27]

Take Customer Service to the Customer

Given the impact of word of mouth in customer networks, customer service is an essential part of any digital communications strategy. This means responding to complaints and issues that you overhear (as Firefox did in my case) and more than that; it means letting customers know they can connect with you online about concerns, questions, or issues.

Many companies use dedicated Twitter accounts for customer service as an ancillary to phone and email. This approach was pioneered by Comcast (which needed some better buzz in social media after its sleeping technician video). Frank Eliason, senior director of Comcast Customer Service, leads their effort, monitoring an onscreen scroll of inquiries directed to his account @comcastcares or to the public Web. If the customer is venting (rather than asking a question), Eliason's first reply may be just "Can I help?" or "We try." Then, if the customer opts to continue, he will get the details to pursue the problem. That may involve checking a customer's modem remotely, clearing up problems with a collection agency, suggesting a change of settings that may solve a customer problem, or sending a technician to the customer's house. This approach has earned Eliason more than twenty thousand followers on Twitter and helped to reshape the image of his company online. Eliason is known to answer tweets on his BlackBerry from the beach. But when he announced he would be on vacation for a family event, several customers spontaneously volunteered to answer other customers' questions during his day off.

Municipal governments are following suit as well. San Francisco has launched an @SF311 channel to allow citizens to file complaints or questions about city services via Twitter. The city of Boston has created an iPhone app called Citizen Connect that allow citizens to snap photos of potholes, graffiti, and illegal trash violations in their neighborhoods and upload them directly to the appropriate city agency. Start-up SeeClickFix has created a simple Web platform that allows municipal governments anywhere in the country to collect information like this from citizens' phones or computers. All these connections increase government's responsiveness while ensuring that requests are submitted in a centralized and effective fashion.

Make Them an Offer

Of course, one of the friendliest ways to get customers to join you in conversation online is to make them an offer—whether it is a discount, a product giveaway, an invitation to an event, or just first dibs on a new menu item. Dell has sold over six million dollars of excess inventory through Twitter, simply by announcing sale items on its @DellOutlet account to more than 1.5 million followers (not bad for a free direct-marketing channel).[28] In Los Angeles, a traveling taco cart called Kogi Korean BBQ sends out a steady stream of updates, via its blog and Twitter, to let customers know where it will be parking each night to serve its unique Mexican-Korean fusion fare (kimchi hot dogs and spicy pork tacos, anyone?). Kogi's followers show up by the hundreds each time it parks, spread the word on their own social media, and help the truck find new locations on the occasions when it is asked to move. With more than forty thousand followers, the customer community has contributed names for the taco trucks and even produced a music video, "Chasing the Dragon," on YouTube. The online buzz has landed Kogi's founder, Mark Manguera, several investment offers and a chef's position at a nonmobile restaurant, L.A.'s Alibi Room.

Provide a Forum

When asked why he robbed banks, Willie Sutton famously said, "Because that's where the *money* is." For many businesses pursuing a CONNECT strategy, it makes sense to go where your *customers* already are. That is: Facebook, Twitter, or whatever the next popular social media platform may be. But in certain cases, organizations may also benefit from creating their own unique forums for customer connection.

Give Room for Comments

Allowing comments on the content of your own Web site is the first step to hosting a conversation on your own turf. For corporate blogs, this turns a channel for broadcasting updates into a forum for genuine discussion with customers. Media companies are also discovering the benefits of allowing users to comment on their sites. In the Toronto *Globe and Mail*'s Cover It Live feature, professional reporting on breaking stories is combined with video and real-time comments from readers. Coverage of the confirmation hearings for Supreme Court Justice Sonia Sotomayor on newspaper sites like NYTimes.com gave us a first peek of what may be the future of online newspapers: displaying live video streams (CSPAN-style) alongside detailed articles by reporters and near-real-time comments from users.

Aggregate Ratings of Others' Stuff

Another valuable type of forum that businesses can provide for customers is aggregated ratings sites. Yelp has become one of the most popular applications for the iPhone by collecting ratings of local businesses from bars and restaurants to optometrists and fabric stores. Users can log in on their phone or computer to add their own ratings and read others' reviews. CitySense allows users to share their votes for the hippest nightlife in cities like San Francisco, so that savvy locals and out-of-towners can log in via their phones to find the place to be. Vitals.com offers users a rating system for medical doctors by combining empirical data with consumer reviews. With the growing trust that customers give to the opinions of other customers, forums like these will continue to add value and attract users.

Give a Forum to Express Views on Your Own Brand

Media brands often have customer networks that are especially eager to share opinions on their brands. Bravo Media has channeled the enthusiasm of its audiences for shows like *Top Chef* and *The Real Housewives of Orange County* in its own online customer forums. Before, during, and after the TV shows, avid viewers log on to vote for and against contestants, answer polls, chat with other viewers, and send in live comments that may run across the bottom of the screen. Lisa Hsia, senior vice president of Bravo Digital Media, turns all this interaction into millions of dollars of extra revenue for the network via sponsorships, advertising, and fees for users who vote or download ringtones and wallpaper. Hsia is building affinity groups among Bravo's customer network, focused on themes of food, fashion, style, and design. She has also recruited customers to take a trivia quiz to join the "Bravo Influentials," a new tastemaker panel offering opinions on programming and advertising and receiving free gifts for participating. Says Hsia, "My job is to try to interact and engage our users before the program, during the program, after the program, and always."[29]

Before the introduction of the Ford Fiesta in the U.S. market, Ford Motor Company invited one hundred social-media-savvy young consumers to test drive the car for six months and gave them a forum to share their uncensored opinions: FordFiestaMovement.com. More than four thousand consumers applied by submitting online videos, and winners were chosen for their passion, story-telling ability, diversity, and sociability—that is, the number of friends in their social networks. "Agents" included California actress Olga Kay, twenty-six, who posted photos of herself inside the hatchback, and Andy Didorosi, twenty-two, an aspiring race car driver and automotive journalist from Michigan. They were given monthly "missions"—drive a friend to the ocean who's never been before, drive your Fiesta until it runs out of gas, and so on. The missions stimulated stories to tell in blog posts, tweets, and videos. The results were positive (most thought the Fiesta was a great car for the price), authentic (with some genuine suggestions to improve the car), and exuded personality. Ford's goal was to spur interest in Generation Y consumers (born 1979 to 1995), who are hard to reach by television but make up 28 percent of U.S. drivers. The campaign resulted in 3.5 million YouTube views, 2.7 million Twitter impressions, and an astonishing 38 percent awareness of the Fiesta among Gen Y consumers. Getting these customers familiar with the Fiesta before its launch also yielded valuable insights into how the target audience would perceive the car.[30]

Give a Forum to Connect around Lifestyle or Interests

Other companies are connecting with customers by providing them a forum to discuss shared interests and lifestyles rather than specific brands and products of that business. Automotive site Edmunds .com hosts the online forum CarSpace, where auto enthusiasts create profiles, join discussions, vote in polls, and upload photos and video, all around car brands, companies, models, and engineering. Nike hosts its Ballers Network, which basketball fans use to organize neighborhood pick-up games. Using a Facebook application or a mobile Web site, Ballers Network members can scout out courts in their cities, connect with other "ballers," and manage their own league. Online stock trading service TradeKing hosts the Trader Network, where participants can see what securities are being traded that day, follow the picks and performance of top traders, share advice, and find out why fellow members made specific trades. In each of these cases, network members are discussing the category (cars, basketball, or stock trading), not the specific company hosting the site. But creating the forum allows the business to become an important part of their customers' networks and lives.

Create a Temporary Forum Tied to a Major Event

When a major public event is particularly important to customers in a business's network, it can leverage the excitement by providing a temporary forum for customer communication. CNN partnered with Facebook to create an online event around the television broadcast of the 2009 U.S. presidential inauguration. More than eighteen million viewers watched live video coverage at CNN.com. They logged in using their Facebook accounts and posted up to three thousand comments per minute in a sidebar that allowed them to chat live with their friends.

Other major live televised events—such as sports games and awards ceremonies—may provide similar opportunities. One in seven TV viewers of the 2010 Super Bowl were online while watching the game. That capped a year in which the Winter Olympics and awards shows like the Grammys and Emmys all saw marked increases in television audiences, many of whom were having simultaneous conversations via Twitter and Facebook.[31]

In other cases, the online forum may be tied to an event that the business organizes itself. In 2008, Nike sponsored the Human Race, a ten-kilometer run held in twenty-five cities worldwide, from Chicago to São Paulo. Nearly eight hundred thousand members of their nikeplus.com network participated in 142 countries, many of them running on their own and logging their times online to compete in the event. For businesses that don't already have a network like nike plus.com, Facebook offers a widget that any company can place on its own site to host customers' Facebook chat alongside the company's own live-streaming content.

Create a Private Forum for Loyal Customers

Creating a private forum or social network can be a way to invite select customers to provide feedback and feel that they have a hand in shaping your business. Mercedes Benz invited members of its Owners Club to join the GenerationBenz social network. Customers can create personal profiles, invite friends, upload photos and video, and interact with one another during special sessions, such as a sneak peak at an upcoming car model. The Intercontinental Hotels Group runs three private communities for members drawn from its loyalty program. Using surveys and threaded discussions, these customers are asked what is most important to them during hotel stays and what they think of new planned promotions. The customer insights that are generated are integrated into Intercontinental's strategic planning, creative briefs for marketing and advertising, and employee training programs. Community members have also shown marked increases in their likelihood to recommend the brand to others.

What to Expect When You Manage Your Own Forum

If you do plan to create your own forum for your customer network, make sure that customers have a compelling reason to come to your site and keep coming back. Bear in mind that they probably have already taken the time to create a profile at one or more large public networks. The motivation to join your smaller forum may stem from a true passion for discussing your products and news (such as Bravo's hit television programs), or it may be an enthusiasm for the specific product category you are in (such as stock trading). If your network is based around a product category, make sure you are not replicating a site that already exists.

It is also critical that you devote enough resources to launching a network and have realistic expectations of its results. Keeping customers coming back to a stand-alone forum requires constant investment in fresh content, discounts, and offers, as well as careful moderation of comments (to establish norms and preclude spamming and nasty behavior). In measuring the participation of your customers, keep in mind Jakob Nielsen's "90–9–1 Rule" (discussed in chapter 2). Roughly 1 percent of the participants in a social media forum will contribute significant content (posting blogs, uploading videos, or initiating discussion topics), another 9 percent or so will post comments on that content, and roughly 90 percent of users will simply read and be influenced by the discussions of the others.

Last, you should recognize that one of the benefits of running your own forum is that it will tend to attract your most loyal, engaged, and high-value customers. TradeKing has found that although only 5 percent of its members participate in the Trader Network, they are responsible for 10 percent of the trades and commissions. Among those participants, the traders who network more actively in the community also have significantly higher balances and funding; they are TradeKing's "high-value clients." Hosting your own forum can be a way to identify your highest-value customers so that you can more effectively market to them and deepen your relationship with them.

Ask for Ideas

Asking customers or employees to share and vote on ideas for new products, services, and business ventures is another valuable approach to a CONNECT strategy. Because customers and employees may have different levels of knowledge about your business, they may be best served by different tools for idea generation.

Ask Customers to Submit, Discuss, and Vote on Ideas

Starting in 2007, Dell's IdeaStorm forum began asking customers to submit, discuss, and vote on new ideas for Dell products and services. In its first three years, IdeaStorm generated more than ten thousand ideas, eighty thousand comments, and half a million votes cast by customers. Dell implemented hundreds of the ideas, ranging from a SupportPro service program for business customers to a DataSafe service that allows customers to remotely access and share data online for a fee. When teachers suggested that Dell offer a cheap, kid-tough laptop for the education market, Dell launched its Latitude 2100 netbooks. Starting at under four hundred dollars, they come in a rubberized case with optional flash memory (sturdier if you drop it), a vent-free bottom to protect the netbook from drink spills, optional carrying strap, touch screens for younger children, and cases in five bright primary colors: School Bus Gold, Chalkboard Black, Ball Field Green, Blue Ribbon, and Schoolhouse Red. The netbooks even sport a network activity light, so that a teacher can tell when students are going online in class.

An IdeaStorm platform was used in a very different product category to run the MyStarbucksIdea.com Web site, announced by Starbucks founder and CEO Howard Schultz in 2008. The site encourages customers of the coffee chain to offer ideas on how to improve the Starbucks experience: from coffee flavors to packaging to the in-store and online music selections. MyStarbucksIdea.com taps into three key ways that customers connect online: sharing ideas, discussing and commenting on ideas, and voting. Within the first hour, three hundred customer ideas were posted; within the first week, a hundred thousand votes had been cast; within the first year, more than seventy thousand ideas were shared.

An algorithm on the site pushes the most popular ideas to the top based on votes received, how recently the votes were cast, and the volume of comments. Forty-eight Starbucks employees ("idea partners") help moderate the discussion, prune out duplicate ideas, and take those with the most votes back to their own departments to advocate for their consideration. Dozens of customer ideas have already been implemented, and many more are under way. These include: free Wi-Fi in stores for customers; a Starbucks music application for the iPhone; reusable "splash sticks" to plug the hole in drink lids and prevent sloshing; the return of the Yukon Blend coffee flavor; a Mini-Starbucks purchasing card; and a more natural food menu with fewer artificial ingredients, no high-fructose corn syrup, and more healthy foods like egg whites, multigrain muffins, and whole fruit.

Starbucks and Dell do not offer their customers any rewards or compensation if their ideas are used, but they don't have to. Customers are usually happy to share ideas and try to improve your business if they feel that you are listening. That feeling of being listened to is one of the best benefits of creating a platform to ask customers for ideas.

Another context for soliciting customers' ideas can be seen in the American Express Members Project. Rather than being asked for business ideas, card members were invited to submit ideas for charities that Amex could support. Members then discussed their ideas with other customers and voted for them online (again: submit, discuss, vote). American Express gave two million dollars to the winning charity in the first year, and five million dollars total to the top five charities in the second year. Customers rallied around their favorite causes and spread word of the contest with photos and videos, as well as widgets and banners that they shared on Facebook and MySpace. Over two years, more than eight thousand charitable projects were submitted and more than half a million members registered to vote and participate.

For the top-winning charities—a water purification program for rural children and an early detection education program for Alzheimer's—the Members Project delivered both money and valuable publicity. For American Express, the benefit to its brand was substantial, with hundreds of blog, print, and TV news articles and more than three million visitors to its Web site. The Members Project was the most recognizable campaign in the company's recent history, with over 50 percent recognition among current and prospective card members. Amex's "net promoter score"—the chance that a current customer would recommend the company to a friend—was lifted an amazing 85 percent.[32]

Ask Employees to "Invest" in an Idea Market

Employees can also be a valuable network to ask for ideas on improving your business. The U.S. government's Transportation Security Administration uses an "IdeaFactory" much like Dell's IdeaStorm to invite ideas from its forty-three thousand employees. Within its first year, more than forty-five hundred ideas were submitted on this non-public site, thirty-nine thousand comments posted, and about twenty ideas implemented as national policy.

When asking employees for ideas, however, organizations may want to use a different tool to tap the intelligence of their networks. Given their greater knowledge of the details of your business, you should probably judge employees' ideas using a more sophisticated technique than simple vote counting. A more robust tool to evaluate such ideas is the "idea market" or "exchange."

In an idea market, network members have the opportunity to propose business ideas; they then choose to invest a fixed amount of their own virtual money by dividing it among the ideas they feel have the most value. Employees have the option to invest more of their money in an idea they strongly support or to spread it across smaller investments in several ideas. The effect is a sort of stock exchange for ideas, with the ideas that attract greater investments bubbling to the top, like assets whose prices rise on an exchange. (Note: Idea markets are frequently confused with "prediction markets" such as the Iowa Electronic Markets, famous for beating many polls in predicting elections. But the mechanism and use of prediction markets is quite different.)[33]

Cisco has used idea markets to generate employee ideas for new start-up ventures. The ideas that attract the highest "stock price" from the employee network are not always those that upper management thought were promising; instead, the market provides access to the wisdom of engineers and employees on the ground level. Cisco has used its idea market to pick several winning ideas to invest in through its Emerging Technologies Group. The employee who proposes a winning idea is given the option to lead the project.[34]

Motorola has used a similar idea market to sort through the thousands of ideas its employees submit to its ThinkTank system. The system generates ideas for new products and process innovations to improve productivity. Each idea starts at ten dollars a share, and each employee gets a virtual hundred thousand dollars to invest. The stock values of ideas rise as employees buy and sell shares. GE has developed a similar process for idea markets called the Imagination Market, which it uses to help answer such questions as "What new technology ideas should we be investing in?" and "What new products should we develop?" GE also licenses its own process to other organizations seeking to run idea markets in their own networks.

Integrate Their Voice in Yours

One of the most powerful ways to strengthen your relationship with customer networks is to incorporate their own voices, stories, and opinions into the public voice and face of your organization.

One way to do this is by tapping the content created by your customer networks for use in your marketing. Sprint created a great deal of excitement with its "Now Network" clock, the first advertisement on YouTube's homepage to be built with user-generated content. Building on Sprint's marketing campaign around its "Now Network," the YouTube clock displayed the current time throughout the day with four digits culled from user video submissions to Sprint. For example, at 12:48, the four squares in the clock would show four different videos in which users had represented the numbers 1, 2, 4, and 8. YouTube visitors who clicked on the "add yourself" button could upload videos of themselves depicting a number and hope to be added in the real-time ad as the minutes ticked by through the day. Thirteen million visitors saw the ad in its first day, and it lived on as a widget on Sprint's Now Network Web site.

Sometimes your customers will be willing to produce the entire ad for you. Doritos has run contests in which customers create Doritos ads to run during the Super Bowl, the most expensive advertising slot of the year. While this might seem risky, the results have been more popular than many of the ads produced by agencies to plug other brands. In 2009, an ad dubbed "Free Doritos" created by two unemployed brothers was rated highest among all Super Bowl ads by *USA Today's* Ad Meter poll. The same ad was the most talked about ad online, according to Zeta Interactive. A year later, the customer-made Doritos ad "Snack Attack Samurai" was the most viewed advertisement of all time.[35] On a smaller scale, the March of Dimes charity has reached out to members of its online community, EveryBabyHasAStory.org, inviting members to create a virtual scrapbook out of videos and blogs. Community members submitted video advertisements telling their own story for a March of Dimes public service announcement to raise awareness of premature births. More than eighty ads were submitted, over three thousand votes were cast, and the winning ad was distributed on TV stations nationally. Networked customers are increasingly interested in each other's stories (and less interested in advertising), so including the authentic voice of your customers in your own communications is a great CONNECT strategy.

If your organization is a media company or publisher, you can integrate the voice of the customer directly into your content and programming itself. This approach has been hugely successful for Nickelodeon's television show *iCarly*, helping to make it the number-one television program in America for kids fourteen and younger (beating out *American Idol* and *Hannah Montana*). The show is a scripted comedy series about a teenage girl who runs her own Web TV show with her best friend and her neighbor. Their show-within-the-show features talent contests, interviews, and wacky comedy. In a television first, it also features homemade videos submitted by the real-life viewing audience. Responding to requests within the program ("We need some dance videos!"), kids log on to the Web site iCarly.com to submit their own videos, hoping for a shot at being featured on television or on the Web site. While visiting the site, they can also read the characters' blogs, post comments, and vote in polls. The concept was so eagerly received by the audience of digital kids that more than two thousand videos were uploaded and nearly forty thousand kids registered before the first episode of the show had even aired. By its third season, *iCarly* was drawing twenty-six million viewers each week and had become the most watched cable television program on Saturday nights.

Let Conversations Add a Layer of Value

Enabling the conversation within your customer networks can do more than just enrich your relationships and communications with customers. It can also add value to the core products and services that your business offers. By sharing their expertise and insight with one another, customers benefit as they strengthen the community around your organization.

One way they can do this is by answering one another's questions about your products and services. That is why Intuit created a user forum for its popular TurboTax tax preparation software. On every page of the program, while users are filling out their tax returns, they can pose questions and look up past answers on the TurboTax Live Community. Within only a few weeks of launching the community, one-third of the customer questions were being answered by other customers rather than by Intuit's internal tax experts. That number soon reached 40 percent. Intuit also watched carefully to see what kinds of answers customers would provide. They were pleased to find that users were providing accurate, relevant information and that the conversation was self-correcting: as users continued to discuss a topic, they refined their answers to improve them.

Having saved 40 percent on its customer support calls for TurboTax, Intuit went on to add a similar community for its popular QuickBooks accounting program for small businesses. In the QuickBooks live community, diehard users answer product-related questions. They also blog and post on general small-business issues, including offering local help to each other in finding a good lawyer, marketing coach, or accountant. Especially active community members choose to answer countless questions for fellow members. Michelle Long, an accountant in Lee's Summit, Missouri, has posted more than 5,600 answers to questions on the forum.[36] As in any user forum, the answers are searchable, so many more users have read and learned from Long than the 5,600 who posed the questions she answered. As a result, Intuit has found that 90 percent of users are able to get their questions answered successfully on the community site rather than calling Intuit's call center. Beyond that huge savings in customer service cost, the conversation in the QuickBooks community makes Intuit's product much more useful for new customers. The strategy helps Intuit to sell over a million copies of the two-hundred-dollar software and boost its market share to 94 percent.

Highly active customers like Michelle Long may have multiple motivations for contributing so much time and expertise in a customer forum. For some, the psychic rewards of helping others, being thanked, and getting to demonstrate their knowledge are the primary motivator. For others, participating may offer a chance to network professionally and raise their profile among a community that is important to their career. Business software company SAP has nearly two million members worldwide in its SAP Community Network. To encourage the customers who connect and share answers there, SAP established a Customer Recognition Program that awards points to customers based on their contributions, such as responding to forum questions, adding to a wiki page, or maintaining a blog. There is no direct compensation from SAP, but these points benefit the network's most active members—who are software developers, vendors, and industry thought leaders—by communicating their reputation and expertise to others who may consider them for a job, a contract, or a sale.

Similarly, Microsoft uses an MVP Award to recognize top contributors on its developer network, which spans ninety countries, thirty languages, and ninety Microsoft technologies. MVP's include people like Yongguang Zhu, who has translated Microsoft articles into Chinese for other readers and helps organize a club for .NET developers; Mr. Tutang MM, a book editor in Indonesia who published an article on how laptop users can stay connected with Windows as they travel between work and home; and Deb Shinder, who wrote a blog post on how to enhance your productivity using the new "jumplists" feature in Windows 7.

Customers sharing ideas online can contribute value to even less technical businesses, however, as long as there is a topic that spurs active discussion and contributions. Cooking Web sites like Epicurious.com feature thousands of professionally developed recipes, but they also allow customers to comment. Those comments include more than just a rating ("4 forks") or an appraisal ("My wife loved this, and it went great with mashed potatoes"). The most active customers log in to share their own advice on how to modify, amplify, or sometimes significantly change the recipe. I'm a fan of homemade enchiladas and found a highly ranked recipe on Epicurious's site. The first of 130 comments begins: "Following a number of reviews, I made a bunch of changes to add flavor and use up a bunch of veggies. For the sauce, I used swiss chard instead of spinach, all milk (no cream), and added a chopped jalepeno, some garlic scapes, chili powder, and lime, and omitted the coriander. Salting the sauce properly seemed important: 1 tsp Kosher." Another reviewer wrote: "I've made this quite a few times and think it's tasty as is, especially as part of a buffet. However, I now make it with the following changes—make 1 ½ times the white sauce and use the entire package of spinach and the whole can of chilies."

Enchiladas are not haute cuisine, nor is this a community of professional chefs, but Epicurious's customers are passionate about food and love finding ways to improve or customize the recipes to suit their tastes. Whenever I make a recipe from the site, I start by reading the comments to find additional ideas.

When customers share this kind of passion and desire to connect and communicate about your product or service, make that conversation part of your offering. By harnessing your customers' knowledge and willingness to share ideas, your business gains a layer of value that you would never be able to add on your own.

The Future of CONNECT

The ways that customer networks connect—sharing ideas, opinions, votes, and links—will continue to evolve with new expressive technologies such as widespread mobile video, and new platforms, like the next Facebook or Twitter.

One important trend will be how mobile and location-based technologies continue to merge the world of our online networks and connections with our offline ones. Social networking tools for mobile devices will allow us not only to share a thought as we hop out of a taxicab but to find out which members of our network happen to be nearby. Mobile social networking games like FourSquare already allow you to check which friends of yours have recently visited the bar you are walking into, and perhaps even check their drink recommendations. As connecting becomes more mobile, our digital networks may start to resemble Meetup, the Web site that helps nearly six million members organize local groups online to meet in real-world locations over shared interests, passions, or professional goals.

Another area of rapid change will likely be in the extension of our "social graph" from networking sites to other digital experiences. The social graph (a term popularized by Facebook's founder Mark Zuckerberg) is the web of relationships that we establish digitally within social networking services like Facebook or LinkedIn and contact lists like our email address book. Viewed as a literal map of all our connections, the social graph will yield many more possible applications beyond just communicating within a social networking site.

Facebook Connect allows customers to transport their social graph from Facebook into partner Web sites or game consoles, adding a social dimension to them as well. I've used it to share articles with my Facebook friends while reading NYTimes.com or to find out what music my friends are listening to on Pandora. Twitter is developing similar capabilities with its @anywhere initiative. Many developers believe that our social graphs should be freely portable, so that if you "friend" me on one service, that tie can be carried across any other Web site, or even another social networking service. MySpace, Ning, Orkut, and most other services have rallied around a shared open system called Open Social. But so far, Facebook, the eight-hundred-pound gorilla in the room, is keeping its data to itself.

The prospect of incorporating our social graph into every other digital experience seems enticing. But the power of the social graph may be limited by the fact that a "link" within a social network can mean something very different to each of its hundreds of millions of users. Sometimes a "friend" is not quite a friend. This was revealed rather humorously by a Facebook advertising campaign started by Burger King in December 2008 called "Whopper Sacrifice." The campaign consisted of a Facebook application that enticed customers to "sacrifice" ten Facebook friends in order to receive a coupon for one flame-broiled Whopper burger. The user would open the application in Facebook, pick their friends to be sacrificed, and then watch their profile images vanish in smoldering flames while Facebook erased them from the user's friends list—and sent the friends a message that they had been sacrificed for a shot at a burger coupon. Would you do that to a friend? Burger King customers did, sacrificing nearly 224,000 "friendships" before Facebook disabled the application, canceling Burger King's campaign only three weeks after it started.

One area you can expect the social graph to be exploited is in advertisement targeting. Marketers have long known that their most effective ad dollars are those spent on existing customers, who are known to have an interest in their product. Beyond that, finding the right targets among the population of noncustomers has always been a challenge, as well as the goal of segmentation, media buying plans, and the zip code and street-level demographic analysis that drives modern political canvassing.

A 2006 study by Shawndra Hill, Foster Provost, and Chris Volinsky found that the network "friends" of a company's current customers may be three to five times more likely to respond to product advertising than the targets identified by traditional segmentation and targeting.[37] It is not clear how much of this effect is attributable to word of mouth (customers actually discussing the product with their friends) versus homophily (customers choosing friends who have similar interests and likes), nor whether the impact would be quite as dramatic across different product categories. (The research was done with a large sample of customers for AT&T.) But you can expect to see advertisers try to put your social graph to work in choosing who to target with advertising in the near future. Media6Degrees licenses user information from social networking sites to help advertisers target the friends of their customers. Companies like Lotame and 33Across are mapping social graphs by tracking the creators of user-generated content and the followers who consume it. MySpace is scraping information from the profiles of users to allow hypertargeting of ads across Web sites owned by its parent, News Corp., and Facebook will likely follow suit.[38] The next wave of Web advertising may likely be based on mining social networks.

Keys to a CONNECT Strategy

The desire to connect—by sharing ideas, opinions, and social links—is at the heart of today's customer networks. Whether your organization is a software maker, a media company, a coffee retailer, or a nonprofit charity, a CONNECT strategy can help you grow closer to your customers by contributing to that digital conversation. This can be done by joining the conversation on large social media platforms or by providing a unique forum of your own for your customers to connect and share.

The conversation in networks is already shaping businesses and defining brands. By joining this conversation effectively, a CONNECT strategy can yield customer insights; improve relationships with key customers; and build your brand image through improved customer service, positive word of mouth, and opportunities for customers to affiliate with your brand.

Successful approaches to a CONNECT strategy include: monitoring and learning from online conversations already happening around your brand and industry; responding to issues, answering questions, and building relationships in existing online forums; creating your own forum for customers to express views and connect with others; asking customers for their ideas on how to improve your business; integrating the voice of your customers into your own content and marketing; and letting the conversation among customers add additional value to your business.

Whatever the approach taken, the first step for many businesses will be to learn to listen. Customer networks and new media have made it easier than ever to find out what your customers are thinking, wanting, and saying. The challenge for many organizations is: Are you ready to listen? Before implementing a CONNECT strategy, you must be ready to take back the lessons you learn from your customer networks and to evaluate, respond, and implement or build on them. Bringing the voice of the customer inside your organization is useless if decision making will continue to be dominated by past practices, bureaucratic inertia, and disdain for anything "not invented here."

Companies should also remember to focus on their passionate customers—both passionate fans and disappointed critics. These will be the customers who are most actively discussing your business, the ones who will share the most ideas, and influence others, and the ones whom you might easily convert from critics to lifelong supporters by giving them a little respect and attention.

Last, before you try to connect with customers in conversation, be sure you know what's in it for them. Whether it's quicker service, answers to technical questions, a community of like-minded friends, special discounts and offers, or a shot at social media fame—there needs to be a clear reason for them to spend their time online connecting with you rather than with their friends, colleagues, and all the other brands and businesses that they know. Replicating the benefits of a popular service that already exists doesn't count. Even though you may be a great camera company, if your customers already use Flickr.com, they don't need you to build them a photo-sharing site with your brand on it. Before you embark on a CONNECT strategy, take a hard look at whatever you are offering and ask yourself: If I were the customer, would I join in?

By helping customers connect with one another around what is most important to them, you can deepen your relationships with existing customers and build ties to valuable new ones.

But sometimes networked customers want to do even more than express themselves, cast their vote, and put their ideas out into the world. On the things that matter most to them, they want to work with others. They want to join together toward shared goals. They want to collaborate in an ongoing fashion and feel that they are a part of something larger than themselves. The deepest connection that a business or organization can have with its customer networks is built on this desire to collaborate. To tap into it requires a full knowledge of how, when, and why customers contribute so much of themselves to the work of their network.

CHAPTER 7

COLLABORATE
Involve Your Customers at Every Stage of Your Enterprise

 Thomas Gensemer was watching his computer monitor carefully when Senator Barack Obama took to the stage in Springfield, Illinois, to announce his long-shot candidacy for the presidency of the United States. It had been only nine days since the Obama campaign had hired Gensemer and his partners at the small, new media company Blue State Digital to prepare for the launch of his candidacy. Those nine days had been spent furiously transforming Obama's Web site into the digital platform for a new kind of voter participation in politics: myBarackObama.com.

Gensemer's partners had tried to use the Internet four years before to energize another insurgent presidential candidacy, Howard Dean's. But despite intense online excitement and donations, that campaign failed to channel its supporters' energy into action that counted: votes and boots on the ground. After months of money and buzz, Dean's campaign sputtered and crashed at the first voting in the Iowa caucuses.

This campaign would be different. From the beginning, the myBarackObama Web site (called MyBO by the campaign) was designed not just to elicit donations, Facebook friends, and exuberant YouTube videos. It focused also on the hard, unsexy work that wins contests—voter registration, phone banking, and door-to-door canvassing. It gave Obama's supporters the tools to organize for real campaign work. Other candidates were visible advertising on as many Web sites as Obama. But when a viewer clicked on an ad for Obama, they were first asked not to donate money (as they were by the other campaigns), but to sign up to volunteer and be invited to events.

In the first twenty-four hours after Obama's announcement speech, Gensemer saw hundreds of thousands of profiles created by new members on the MyBO network. As the numbers climbed to millions, MyBO provided each of them with a broad array of online tools to collaborate with the campaign. Supporters downloaded voter registration forms. They attended and organized house parties and meet-ups in bars to recruit others. They formed online fundraising "hubs" where they set personal goals, solicited donations from friends, and tracked progress with a personal fundraising "thermometer." On the MyBO network, they could download targeted lists of phone numbers to call before a primary vote or lists of names and addresses of undecided voters in their own neighborhood to visit, door to door. The campaign even launched an iPhone app that sorted the phone numbers in a user's address book by the priority of states (with friends in key battleground states like Virginia appearing first) and allowed users to track which friends they had called on behalf of the campaign. Most importantly, the MyBO platform recognized that different supporters would have varying degrees of commitment and available time. It allowed supporters to contribute at their own level—be it a twenty-five-dollar donation at a friend's Obama party, two hours of phone calls on election eve, or a trip out of state to spend a weekend canvassing door to door in a key electoral county.

The results of this unprecedented online platform for collaboration with voters were unmistakable. In the first caucuses in Iowa, the Obama campaign stunned political observers by winning the contest, thanks to countless house parties and an incredibly organized group of local supporters. In the South Carolina primary, the MyBO network was directed toward a massive get-out-the-vote effort. As the Democratic nominating race turned into the first true fifty-state political contest in decades, the ability of Obama's supporters to self-organize provided a critical edge against the better-known candidacy of Hillary Clinton. When the multistate primary day dubbed Super Tuesday arrived, Hillary Clinton held a daunting lead in polls in Texas, but thanks to MyBO, Obama had nearly five times as many volunteers signed up to organize his efforts within the state; he won the delegate count ninety-nine to ninety-four.[1] Every week, as both campaigns' professional staff arrived in a new state in preparation for the next contest, Obama's team found that their supporters had already prepared the infrastructure for their local campaign using tools that they found on MyBO.

By the end of the campaign, thirteen million volunteers had joined Obama's online network. They had organized more than two hundred thousand local events, formed seventy thousand fundraising hubs, and helped raise a record-shattering $750 million dollars, most of it in donations of fewer than a hundred dollars.[2] In the final four days of the general election, Obama's network made three million phone calls to turn out voters, helping to spur the highest voter participation rate in the United States since 1908. With this surge of Net-enabled activism, Obama eked out close victories in traditionally "red" states like Indiana, Virginia, and North Carolina.

The digitally organized network of supporters behind the Obama campaign certainly contributed to the margin of his ultimate victory in the November general election over John McCain. More important, however, his network was probably the deciding force behind his unexpected victory in the Democratic nomination, which allowed him to even compete against McCain. At each stage of the campaign season, Obama's online strategy showed that by giving supporters the tools to collaborate, he could outmaneuver the more experienced political candidates who were still using a traditional run-from-the-top campaign strategy.

The COLLABORATE Strategy

Like Barack Obama's digitally connected supporters, the most energized customer networks want to do more than just share ideas, opinions, and conversations online. They seek to collaborate on collective projects toward shared goals, and they flock to online platforms that allow them to act independently.

The drive to collaborate has always existed. With the growth of digital networks, however, we have gained the ability to collaborate with much broader groups of individuals. Limitations of geography, time, and existing relationships have been largely surmounted by the ability of ad hoc networks to form, communicate, and collaborate via the Internet.

The first landmark case of network collaboration was the Linux operating system, started by Linus Torvalds in 1991 and developed by thousands of software developers around the world, each writing small contributions to the huge quantity of computing code required to build an alternative to Microsoft's Windows. Linux was created out of free labor and is free to anyone to use. Although the operating system is not known to many average computer users, the success and scope of the Linux project proved to the developer community the power of network collaboration.

Wikipedia, the free online encyclopedia that started in 2001, took network collaboration and made it mainstream. Where Linux was an operating system used by a small, tech-savvy minority, Wikipedia quickly became one of the ten most frequently visited sites on the Web. Just as important, Wikipedia is a project that anyone can contribute to by editing or creating their own articles. Don't know anything about technology? No problem. Whatever particular knowledge you have—on fly fishing, Ghanaian cooking, or the jazz music of Charlie Parker—you can use it to add to, or improve, the site. Wikipedia soon grew to encompass over two hundred languages, with its English-language site offering articles on vastly more topics than any printed encyclopedia in human history.

Linux and Wikipedia were both nonprofit efforts where the collaborators worked for free, knowing that no corporation was profiting from their efforts. Their success implicitly raised the question of whether collaboration in customer networks could be used by businesses working with average consumers.

The first proof that it could may have come from the T-shirt company Threadless (as detailed in chapter 1). Launched in 2000, Threadless reinvented the concept of a clothing company by inviting its customers to collaborate in every stage of the enterprise, from product design through to marketing and sales. In a fashion industry that usually expends significant cost on product development, Threadless operates with almost no product development costs and has a 100 percent success rate for all its new products, because it prints only the T-shirts its customers have chosen in advance. By 2008, what started as the hobby Web site of two teenagers had grown into a thirty-million-dollar business with a 30 percent profit margin.[3]

Network collaboration can be used to generate not just a product but also an ongoing service or process. Starting in 2006, CNN proved this in the field of news gathering. With CNN iReport, the channel invited viewers to contribute ground-level journalism by uploading photos, videos, and eyewitness reports from anywhere in the world. In a few short months, iReport grew from its first user submission (a photo of a squirrel) to become a groundbreaking tool for incorporating viewer videos and reporting from the front lines of earthquakes, terrorist attacks, and political revolutions around the world. CNN retains complete editorial control over which submissions it chooses to air and how it frames, edits, and adds detail to them. But by engaging thousands of citizen journalists around the world, CNN has expanded the reach of its news gathering from the level of national and regional bureaus down to street-level eyes and ears. As Vivian Schiller, CEO of NPR, has said about collaborative journalism, "No matter what story you are covering, no matter how brilliant a reporter you are, there is somebody out in your audience that knows more about that than you do."[4]

Apple's iPhone App Store has shown one more model for profitable collaboration. After the initial launch of the iPhone in 2007, independent software developers recognized its potential as a mobile computing device and began coding programs for the iPhone. Apple resisted these efforts at first, and iPhone users had to hack into the phone to install the programs (a process dubbed "jailbreaking"). With the launch of the second iPhone in 2008, however, the famously secretive company reversed course. This time, Apple invited the outside developers to build programs (or "apps") for the iPhone and arranged for the apps to be sold in an official App Store. By opening the iPhone up as a platform to others, Apple unleashed a torrent of innovation far beyond anything it could have matched itself. Within a year, developers had created more than eighty thousand customized applications for the iPhone, ranging from popular games like Tetris to Oracle business software for tracking finance and manufacturing. More than a billion apps were downloaded that same year, with sales on the paid apps estimated in the hundreds of millions of dollars.[5] In addition to keeping 30 percent of that revenue, Apple saw sales of the iPhone jump 245 percent the year the app store launched.[6] By collaborating with others, Apple had turned its iPhone from a promising gadget into a groundbreaking product.

Collaborating is the fifth core behavior of customer networks. It goes beyond the conversational give and take and exchange of ideas that we saw in the previous chapter. When networked customers collaborate, they choose to participate in real work—organizing voter events, writing software code, raising money, reporting breaking news, designing T-shirts, or writing encyclopedia articles. This kind of network collaboration provides a powerful opportunity for businesses and organizations of all types to work with their customers to achieve their goals.

The fifth customer network strategy for business is the COLLABORATE strategy—to invite customers to help, build, and drive your enterprise. This can be done by inviting customers to work together on a project or by inviting them to each take a piece of the project to work on independently. Customers may participate for a range of motivations, from curiosity, personal passion, or deeply held social values to a desire for status, fame, or financial reward.

By inviting customer networks to participate in projects, a COLLABORATE strategy can help an organization achieve key business objectives, including: increasing efficiency despite limited resources, extending the reach of marketing and communications, expanding the capacity for innovation, and building deep audience engagement and support.

But developing an effective COLLABORATE strategy is not always easy. The success of projects like Linux and Threadless has generated a great deal of interest in network collaboration. A variety of terms, including "mass collaboration,"[7] "crowdsourcing,"[8] and "peer production"[9] have each reflected a different part of the phenomenon or a different point of view on how we are collaborating in digital networks. But although there have been notable success stories, attempts to replicate them have often demonstrated the challenges and limitations of network collaboration. Several imitators of Threadless have failed, including one launched by Threadless's own parent company that attempted to enlist customers to design products other than T-shirts.

In order for a COLLABORATE strategy to succeed, it needs to begin with an understanding of several issues. What are the key technologies used for network collaboration? What mix of motivations will inspire outsiders to contribute to your enterprise? How can you divide a project into pieces for collaborators to tackle, and how much expertise will they need to participate? And finally, who will make the final decisions on the project now that you have opened it up to your network as partners?

Technologies for Collaboration

A variety of digital tools have emerged recently that can assist in group collaborations. Each brings its own capabilities and may be suited to solving different problems.

Let's start with the wiki. A wiki is a Web site that allows contributors to easily create and edit the wiki's *own pages*, using a simplified editor that anyone can operate within a Web browser. Altering a wiki page involves no more difficulty than filling out a form on a standard Web site. The self-editing software that makes wikis possible was invented in 1994 by Ward Cunningham. Jimmy Wales was leading a foundering effort to create an online encyclopedia written by experts (dubbed "Nupedia") when he tried out Cunningham's software for a side project, open to the public, and inadvertently launched the world's most famous wiki, Wikipedia. Other organizations have used wikis for a variety of projects where they want to enable a geographically dispersed group of people to contribute to a shared collection of knowledge. While many wikis are open to the public, others are for internal use only. In 2005, the U.S. government's intelligence agencies launched Intellipedia, a set of three wikis running on the same software as Wikipedia but used to gather unclassified, secret, and top-secret information about regions, people, and issues of interest. By using a more collaborative and real-time approach to sharing knowledge among agencies, Intellipedia aims to change an internal culture that has previously failed to "connect the dots" between knowledge in different agencies.

Collaborative office software, such as Google Docs, Microsoft Office Web Apps, and Zoho's software suite, allow users to perform the tasks of typical office software (word processing, spreadsheets, databases, and presentation design) in a collaborative environment. Based on the Web, this type of software can allow a team to work together on a single shared document, even editing it at the same time while working at computers in remote locations. For small teams, such software allows a simple, dynamic platform for quick collaborative work.

Other digital tools are effective in organizing in-person, face-to-face gatherings for collaboration. The largest platform of this type is the site Meetup.com, started in 2001 with the aim of using the Internet to help people connect not just in virtual chat rooms but locally and in person. More than six million members use Meetup to create or join groups and events organized around professional networking, personal interests, or politics. Popular social networks like Facebook have incorporated event organizing features as well.

Custom-designed social networks have now begun to incorporate all of these types of collaboration tools in a powerful fashion. The myBarackObama site developed by Blue State Digital was one example. Enterprise 2.0 software from companies such as Cisco and Microsoft allow businesses to create internal sites for their employees that combine wikis, collaborative office software, event organization, project planning, social networking, and more collaborative features.

Three other tools are geared specifically toward collaboration in the development of software and web applications: software development kits (SDKs), Application Programming Interfaces (APIs), and open-source software. SDKs, such as the one for the iPhone App Store, give outside developers the information they need to write programs that will work on a given device or in a given operating system. APIs allow outside development by defining kinds of information that can be exchanged with a data library or operating system on a device or over the Internet. Open source is an approach to software in which the software's code is made publicly available so that anyone can modify and create their own version of it or create add-on or "plug-in" programs that will work with the commonly used version. Later in this chapter we will see examples of how SDKs, open APIs, and open-source code can each be used to foster open collaboration.

Motivations: For Love, Glory, or Money?

Besides providing the right tools or platform for collaboration to take place, any organization must ask what will motivate its customer network to participate. Why would anyone contribute an article to Wikipedia? News footage to CNN iReport? A T-shirt design to Threadless? In some cases, customers may be motivated by curiosity, personal interests, or deeply held social values. In other cases, they have more commercial goals or a desire for personal benefit. The biggest cause of failure in network collaborations is likely a misunderstanding of the customer's motivation. Thomas W. Malone, Robert Laubacher, and Chrysanthos Dellarocas of MIT's Center for Collective Intelligence describe the motivations for network collaboration as love, glory, or money.[10] These three categories can provide a good starting point for understanding why customers choose to collaborate.

Love

In many cases, participants choose to collaborate with others out of purely social motivations. These motivations may include: altruism (the desire to contribute to the common good); a passionate interest in the topic; work that is entertaining, fun, or creative; participation and connection in a community; the chance to contribute to social values they believe in (such as a cause or candidate); or a sense of duty or obligation (perhaps because they are already enjoying the benefits of the project).

These social motivations are the kind that spurred supporters of Barack Obama to participate in the MyBO network for his candidacy. They also explain why users contribute to Wikipedia without financial reward or byline. New Wikipedia articles are typically written by users with a particular knowledge of their subject and often a passionate interest in it. Other users who frequent Wikipedia may take the time to fix an occasional misspelling or error that they spot out of gratitude for the value they gain from the site. The power of the networking tools behind MyBO and Wikipedia is that they allow all these small acts of generosity to add up to very large impact, far beyond what was feasible in our prenetworked past, when it was virtually impossible to amass and assess contributions of people scattered around the world.

As Clay Shirky has observed, "We have always loved one another. We're human. It's something we're good at. But up until recently, the radius and half-life of that affection has been quite limited. With love alone, you can get a birthday party together. Add coordinating tools, and you can write an operating system. . . . In the past, we could do little things for love, but big things, big things required money. Now, we can do big things for love."[11]

But what if your cause is not an inspiring political candidate or a charity or a free public service? It is very unlikely that you will get people to contribute for "love" alone, even if they do have a passion for the project. Your customers may love taking photos of local events, but they may not want to share them anonymously on your news platform if you will be earning a profit from and retaining the rights to the images they produced. Fortunately, humans harbor other motivations.

Glory

The key to CNN attracting unpaid collaborators to its iReport news project is that their submissions are *not* anonymous. If a customer's photo, video, or story appears on CNN's Web site or broadcast, his or her name is credited for all to see. The opportunity to be seen as a "citizen journalist" contributing to such a famous and popular network provides a powerful motivation to the iReport customer network.

Even without such a mass-media spotlight as CNN, mechanisms that highlight and confer social status can be an effective motivator for active collaborators. As we saw in the last chapter, the top participants in technical forums will answer thousands of questions posed by fellow customers when they are recognized in the forum as a major contributor. Forums can use public markers of status—awards, name recognition—to draw attention to users' high level of contribution, their expertise and knowledge, or their creativity, taste, or style.

Money

Of course, sometimes the best way for a for-profit business to motivate network collaboration is to offer money or other commercial benefits.

When Cisco announced its Innovation Prize, or I-Prize, in 2008, the company placed an open call for teams anywhere in the world to identify billion-dollar business opportunities for Cisco's Emerging Technologies Group. After several rounds of winnowing down twelve hundred business proposals received from 104 countries, Cisco announced the winners: Anna Gossen, Niels Gossen, and Sergey Bessonnitsyn, a wife, husband, and brother team of two computer science students and an engineer. The three not only received $250,000; they were also given the opportunity to work for Cisco on their proposed new venture, a "smart grid" framework to reduce the passive consumption of power by electronic devices. The prize award was a small price to pay for Cisco, which estimated that the project could generate a billion dollars in revenue within five to seven years.[12]

It is important to note that while the prize was a good deal for Cisco, it also represented an extraordinary reward for the recipients, who were doing work (business plan development) that was not part of their normal careers or business. Some short-sighted companies have seized on the notion of "crowdsourcing" as a means to exploit the same vendors they would normally hire to carry out a professional task. Rather than hiring one firm to complete work, they simply ask many to submit a solution and offer to pay "the winner" at a rate similar to what would normally be professional work for hire. This kind of spec-work masquerading as "collaboration" can yield resentment and a bruised reputation, as ad agency Crispin Porter + Bogusky found when it tried to solicit logo designs for an advertising client with a thousand-dollar prize.[13] Businesses should not confuse collaboration with exploitation. But money can be an effective reward when the sum received or the type of work is out-of-the-ordinary for participants.

Hybrids

In many cases the motivations for members of a network to collaborate with a business are a hybrid mix of social, status, and financial rewards. Threadless contestants may be motivated as much by the chance to see their design advertised and worn by others (they are not, generally, professional clothing designers) as by the cash reward. In the Netflix Prize (discussed in chapter 5), the team that produced the winning solution to improve the company's recommendation engine received not only a million dollars but extensive coverage in mainstream media such as *BusinessWeek*, *Wired* magazine, and the *New York Times*. And although a quarter million dollars may have attracted participants to the Cisco I-Prize, the winners were probably motivated just as much by passion for their business idea as for their long-shot chance at winning the money.

Slicing the Problem and Slicing the Crowd

Another key issue in developing a COLLABORATE strategy is to understand whether and how to divide up the task at hand.

The key to a collaborative project like Wikipedia or the Linux operating system is that the core task can be divided into many very small tasks that can each be tackled independently by others. No single person could have written the millions of articles in Wikipedia. But to contribute, all a participant needed to do was to write one article—or, even less, to make a minor change or improvement to an article begun by another. Similarly, the entire Linux effort was possible only because its founder, Linus Torvalds, organized the project so that individual programmers around the world could work on the code of one small piece of the operating system and submit that piece for inclusion in the whole.

The ability to divide a collaborative project into smaller parts, which Jeff Howe calls "modularity," is not essential, but it is an important and defining aspect of many COLLABORATE strategies.[14]

Some tasks, however, cannot be effectively broken into discrete pieces. The attempt to create an experimental wiki novel entitled A Million Penguins generated nothing but disjointed rubbish. A much publicized effort to incorporate online suggestions into the horror movie Snakes on a Plane did little to rescue it from mediocrity. No doubt, the singular vision behind a narrative work of fiction cannot be easily doled out in pieces to a crowd, no matter how eager.

A related issue for collaborations is whether contributing to the project requires any special expertise that will limit the pool of potential volunteers. In the case of CNN's iReport, anyone with a digital camera can perform one of the key tasks—capturing an image of a breaking news event he or she happens to be near. As a result, CNN can solicit collaborators from an extremely broad pool. Creating a Wikipedia article requires, by comparison, a specialized knowledge of the subject of the article (say, the history of genetics). But because you can contribute an article on any subject of expertise, no matter how obscure, the pool of potential collaborators is also quite large. To contribute source code to Linux or a mathematical algorithm for the Netflix Prize, by contrast, requires a specific set of skills not held by the general population. The power of digital networks is that even in these cases, a collaboration with very narrow requirements may still attract numerous participants from around the world, thanks to their ability to connect and organize easily over the Internet.

The Bottom Is Not Enough

Much of the excitement around network collaboration stems from a belief in the power of bottom-up thinking and the infallible wisdom of networks. However, numerous instances show the shortcomings of these beliefs. When the Finnish soccer club Pallokerho-35 adopted a text-message polling system that let its fans vote on the club's recruiting, training, and game tactics, the season ended poorly, the coach was fired, and the crowd polling was scrapped.[15]

Network collaboration still requires top-down leadership and vision to be successful. Obama supporters were given independence and initiative to carry out a great many tasks on the MyBO network. But it was the Obama campaign that set the goals of the project and carefully steered the group's range of actions. Unlike the online political group MoveOn.org, the campaign made no attempt to subject its policy positions or strategy decisions to a vote.

Similarly, the editing and maintenance of Wikipedia has relied from the beginning on a mix of both open contributions by everyone and editorial control by an elite group of mostly unpaid, but heavily involved volunteers. If I were to make an edit to the page on "Portuguese Water Dogs," an alert would likely appear soon in the in-box of a volunteer expert on dog breeds who had signed up to observe such content. They could quickly determine if my error was mischievous vandalism and then immediately revert it, spoiling my fun. Otherwise, the editor could quickly judge if my addition violated

Wikipedia's guidelines (such as adding a personal story about my neighbor's dog), merited further review for accuracy, or was good enough to leave as it was. Jimmy Wales has said that Wikipedia works "by a confusing but workable mix of: consensus (minority views count); democracy (but not usually simple voting); aristocracy (those who have built respect in the community have greater sway); and monarchy ('benevolent dictator'—someone to make a decision when it needs to be made)."[16]

Kevin Kelly, whose book *Out of Control* in 1995 predicted the growth of "bottom-up" collaborative systems, has consistently tempered his enthusiasm for networks' ingenuity with a sober belief in the need for some centralized design and planning. In his seminal article "The Bottom Is Not Enough," Kelly points to Wikipedia's need for top-down control and argues that any collaborative network needs a role akin to an editor to "select, prune, guide, solicit, shape, and guide the results from the crowd" to achieve excellence.[17]

In designing a strategy to collaborate, an organization needs to decide which functions it will control from the top and which it will let go "bottom up." (Designing campaign ads requires central control; phoning undecided voters is perhaps best led from the bottom.) Sometimes there are different stages where work may be generated by participants and then evaluated or edited by the organizers.

Five Approaches to COLLABORATE Strategy

No single model for network collaboration will fit all objectives, organizations, or customers. In order for a COLLABORATE strategy to work, the organization leading it needs to find an approach that suits its goals, as well as those of the participants. Success will hinge more on these human and problem-definition issues than on specifics of technology.

By looking at businesses that have successfully harnessed the ideas, energy, and expertise of customer networks for major projects, we can see five distinct approaches to a COLLABORATE strategy:

- *Passive Contribution:* Participants agree to contribute to a project via actions that they are already taking.

- *Active Contribution:* Each participant actively contributes work to part of a large project.

- *Open Competition:* Many participants create their own solutions to a single project, competing to be chosen as best.

- *Defined Platform:* Each participant builds his or her own project on the platform, but the project type is narrowly defined.

- *Open Platform:* Each participant builds his or her own project on the platform, with wide latitude for what the project will be.

The first three of these are "project-based" approaches to collaboration, in which the organizer defines the scope of what will be done. (Wikipedia saying, "We are building an encyclopedia; please help us.")

The last two listed are "platform-based" approaches to collaboration, in which the organizer creates a foundation on which others can initiate their own projects and contributions. (In announcing the iPhone App Store, Apple was saying, "We have a touch-screen pocket computer; create any program you can imagine for it.")

Each of these approaches is marked by different characteristic elements, including: the type of motivations for participants, the modularity of the project, the breadth versus expertise required of participants, and the mix of top-down versus bottom-up decision making. In addition, the different approaches tend to have varied levels of interaction among participants and different ownership of the final results of the collaboration (table 7.1).

By examining these five approaches and how they have been used successfully by a wide range of organizations, we can gain insights into how inviting customer networks to collaborate can help any business achieve its goals.

Passive Contribution

In a passive contribution system, participants opt in to contribute to the work of a collective task or process, but their contribution is merely a byproduct of effort or activity they are already engaging in. It does not demand additional work. Passive contribution is easy on the contributor but can still lead to quite powerful collaborations.

Capturing accurate real-time information about traffic flows has long been a daunting problem for transportation planners. The traditional approach—placing roadside monitors alongside major traffic routes throughout a metropolitan area—is a huge undertaking with high costs to implement with any geographic detail. Several companies have discovered that a much more effective solution can be created by getting drivers to voluntarily transmit automated information about their location as they drive. This data shows their current speed on the road they are driving, and collectively it provides an up-to-the-minute record of traffic flow in a metropolitan region. The Dash Express navigation system built this voluntary system into a GPS device, as does the Inter-Navi system for Honda vehicles in Japan. John Geraci, founder of DIYcity.org, has pointed out that after twenty years of New York City trying to develop a real-time tracking system for city buses, the transit authority would do better to allow cell phone users to voluntarily run phone applications that transmit their location, direction, and speed while riding the bus.[18]

Other examples of passive contribution systems include SETI @home, which since 1999 has allowed users to download a program that runs in the background during their computers' idle moments, processing radio telescope readings from outer space in search of signs of extraterrestrial life. With nearly two hundred thousand participants

Table 7.1 Elements of the Five Approaches to COLLABORATE Strategy

COLLABORATE Approach	Examples	Definition	Motivation for participants	Modularity of the project	Breadth versus expertise of participants	Decision making (top versus bottom)	Interaction between participants	Ownership of results
PROJECT-BASED								
1. Passive Contribution	*Dash Express, SETI@home, GWAP*	Participants agree to contribute to a project via work that they are already doing.	Love (fun or benefit).	The project must be divisible into discrete pieces.	Maximum breadth, with no expertise usually required.	All decisions made by the organizer.	No interaction between participants.	Owned by the organizer, or made freely public.
2. Active Contribution	*Wikipedia, TaxAlmanac. org, MyBO, CNN iReport*	Each participant works actively on a small part of a larger project.	Love (Wikipedia, MyBO) or glory (CNN iReport); participants are too numerous for money.	The project must be divisible into discrete pieces.	Preferable to require least expertise, in order to attract maximum breadth.	Decisions are divided between participants and the organizer.	Interactions among participants may vary from none to quite a lot.	Owned by the organizer or made freely public.
3. Open Competition	*Netflix Prize, Cisco iPrize, X Prize, InnoCentive, Threadless*	Many participants create their own solutions to a single project; the solutions compete to be chosen as the best.	Money, love (excitement for project), and usually glory (unless anonymous).	Single project is given to all participants to work on in parallel.	Expertise needed will depend on the project, and determine the breadth of participants.	Winner is usually picked by organizer, but sometimes with input from participants.	Participants work individually or in teams, usually with no interaction with others (unless participants will vote on the winner).	Owned by the organizer.

PLATFORM-BASED

4. Defined Platform	*eBay, craigslist, CD Baby, YouTube*	Each participant builds his or her own project on the platform, but the project type is narrowly defined (e.g., ten-minute videos).	Just money (craigslist, eBay); just glory (YouTube); or a mix of love, glory, and money for entrepreneurs (CD Baby).	Single project, designed by each participant.	Little technical expertise is needed, allowing for wide breadth of participants.	Decisions made by participants; organizer may play a limited "gatekeeper" role.	Participants work individually; however, discussion forums may arise.	Owned by participants but with revenue share or fee to the organizer.
5. Open Platform	*Linux, Twitter apps, iPhone and Android apps*	Each participant builds his or her own project on the platform, with wide latitude for what the project will be (e.g., any software application).	Mix of love, glory, and money for entrepreneurs.	Single project, designed by each participant.	Technical skills (e.g., programming) required, leading to narrow range of participants.	Decisions made by participants; the organizer may play a limited "gatekeeper" role.	Participants work individually; however, discussion forums may arise.	Owned by participants; they may pay revenue share or fee to the organizer or simply add value to the organizer's platform.

volunteering small amounts of power on their computers, the SETI@ home project has enough computational power to make it the fourth fastest computer in the world.[19] More recently, "games with a purpose" (GWAP), like Luis von Ahn's ESP Game, have provided entertaining online games for users that contribute to some data-processing task (such as image labeling, to assist with cataloging a large dataset) as part of the game play.

In passive contribution systems, the motivation for participants is usually either that they enjoy contributing or they feel obliged to opt in because they benefit from the shared information—as in the Dash navigation system. (Note that I am excluding involuntary user input systems from the definition of COLLABORATE.)[20]

The shared project for passive contribution must be divisible into discrete pieces. Because large numbers of participants are needed, these collaborations should require little or no expertise to join.

Because of their passive nature, all decisions (such as how to manage the data or results) are made by the organizer, and there is little or no interaction among participants. The results of the collaboration are owned by the organizer, although they may make it freely public (perhaps under a Creative Commons license).

Active Contribution

In the second approach to network collaboration, participants actively contribute a piece of work to a single, large collective project, such as building an encyclopedia, running a presidential campaign, or providing images and reporting breaking news. Wikipedia, MyBO, and CNN iReport are all examples of an active contribution approach to COLLABORATE.

Financial software company Intuit has used an active contribution system to build a closer relationship with one of its core customer segments: professional tax preparers. To better serve them,

Intuit launched TaxAlmanac.org, a wiki where users can contribute and access detailed information on every topic or question related to U.S. tax filings, no matter how obscure. Intuit launched the site with 150 articles written by its own tax professionals, as well as searchable copies of the Internal Revenue Code, Treasury Regulations, and court cases that would be helpful to accountants in doing research. Then Intuit opened the site up à la Wikipedia, so that tax professionals could add questions, answers, articles, and news of their field. Thanks to their collective efforts, the site has grown to more than 170,000 pages, and is used by four hundred thousand unique visitors—nearly the same number as professional tax preparers in the United States.[21] TaxAlmanac keeps a revision history for each page and a list of "recent changes," which allow for easy fact checking and cleaning up of entries by the community and by the small group of administrators Intuit assigns to deleting, protecting, and maintaining site content. Intuit's customers benefit from being able to quickly research and find answers to obscure questions (such as how to file Oklahoma's "Bonus Depreciation Addback") and the latest IRS rules and temporary deductions to incentivize home or car buyers. Tax professionals can easily post questions, answer others' queries, search the site, or sign up for watch lists on topics of interest. Intuit benefits by visibly sponsoring a unique and unmatched resource for its core customers and by advertising its products on a site that has minimal costs and an ideal and engaged target audience.

The *Guardian* newspaper in London has used an active contribution system to catch up with a competitor and greatly expand its ability to sort through a huge amount of data. In 2009, a national scandal erupted when the *Guardian*'s rival, the *Daily Telegraph*, broke the news that members of Parliament had been claiming expenses for unjust reimbursement for many years (such as thousands of pounds on gardening, dry cleaning, and second homes). The *Daily Telegraph* already had taken the lead in breaking the story when a

Freedom of Information Act request made public the records of seven hundred thousand expense claims. There was no way the *Guardian's* reporters could sift through that much data in time to begin their own reporting. Instead, the paper hired a Web developer and launched a Web site in under a week that invited outraged readers to chip in a few minutes of time sorting through some of the expense claims and flagging any that looked erroneous for the *Guardian* to investigate.

Thanks to the immense public outcry, the site attracted more than twenty thousand volunteers who sifted through 170,000 documents in the first eighty hours alone.[22] Part of this success was due to the site design by Simon Willison. A four-button interface let users quickly flag each expense they viewed; a progress bar on the front page showed how much of the work the community had completed so far; mug-shot-style photos of each parliamentarian were added to their expenses; and a leaderboard showed a running tally of which readers had reviewed the most expenses. The site made the hunt for government miscreants feel less like a civic duty and more like a computer game.

Others are successfully using an active contribution system to raise donations from supporters, a phenomenon sometimes called "crowdfunding." When musician Brad Skistimas was planning to record the next album by his band, Five Times August, he realized he couldn't afford to pay for it all himself. As an independent musician, he was keenly aware that once he recorded and released an album, many listeners would find a pirated copy for free rather than pay to download. So he asked his fans for the money *before* making the album. Using the Web site Kickstarter.com, he posted a challenge, asking his fans to pledge $20,000 within thirty-one days to finance the recording, mastering, and promotion of the album. Donors received a variety of benefits at different pledge levels, starting with a digital download of the album for a five-dollar pledge; adding a CD, T-shirt, and thanks in the album's liner notes for pledges of up to fifty dollars; and offering more personalized awards such as a video message, dinner with Brad, or a private concert and signed acoustic guitar for those donating up to $2,500. Total pledges had to reach the full $20,000 by the fundraising deadline, or no money would be collected at all, as per Kickstarter's rules. In the end, the project raised $20,546 from 398 backers. Skistimas, who was the first unsigned artist to get national distribution through Wal-Mart stores, proved that the generosity of fans could provide a new business model for independent music.

Other organizations are using collaborative funding to support projects in film, visual art, and even journalism. On the Spot.us Web site, journalists pitch stories they would like to investigate, and donors sign up to fund them. The final articles are either published publicly under a Creative Commons license or sold to a news organization, with donations returned to the funders.

In active contribution systems, participants may be motivated primarily by the opportunity for recognition and fame (such as being seen on air in CNN iReport) or they may participate more from a belief in the value of the project (Wikipedia or Spot.us). As a rule, financial reward will not be an effective motivation because participants are too numerous to be sufficiently incentivized.

As in passive contribution, a shared project must be divisible into discrete pieces for active contribution to work. It is usually preferable to demand less expertise from participants in order to attract as many as possible.

Because of the large number of participants, decision making must be carefully divided between the collaborators and the organizer. For example, participants in MyBO had the latitude to choose who to call on their phone lists and to adapt their call scripts to the talking points they felt most comfortable with, but the campaign set the overall strategy, such as where volunteer resources would be devoted in different states. As Wikipedia has shown, quality control in such collaboration requires a mix of community supervision and top-down oversight to ensure quality on a large scale.

Interactions between participants may vary from none (such as for contributors to iReport and for many who make small edits to Wikipedia) to quite a lot (such as MyBO participants who hosted fundraising events and participated in online forums). The results of the collaboration are owned by the organizer, although they may be made freely public (for example, Wikipedia licenses its content under Creative Commons and GNU Free Documentation).

Open Competitions

The third approach to COLLABORATE strategy is the open competition. In this approach, the project to be tackled is not easily broken down into smaller pieces that can be given to different contributors; it must be tackled in its entirety by one person or team. The improved algorithm sought by the Netflix Prize, an innovative business plan for Cisco's I-Prize, the design of a new T-shirt for Threadless—each of these projects required focused attention and an understanding of the whole. Each project also benefited from attracting a wide variety of solutions from the diverse minds of their customer network. This approach—throwing out a single problem to the network in hopes of generating many competing solutions—is the heart of an open competition. Such competitions have existed for centuries (notably, the solution to measuring a ship's longitude at sea was found by clock-maker John Harrison in the eighteenth century after a decades-long open competition).[23] But the rise of customer networks today allows open competitions to draw contributors from around the world and allows the participants to collaborate in teams at great distance. The result can yield a much broader range and diversity of participation.

In open competitions it can be useful to pose a problem to

an established network of innovators. These kinds of networks are managed by companies like InnoCentive, NineSigma, and yet2.com. InnoCentive has a global network of 175,000 of these "solvers"—independent academics, graduate students, and experts in a variety of fields who are based in 175 countries and linked by the Internet. More than a hundred organizations, among them Procter & Gamble, Eli Lilly, and the Rockefeller Foundation (called "seekers"), turn to InnoCentive's network to tackle the toughest problems that have stymied their own research and development departments.

Sun Microsystems cofounder Bill Joy famously said, "No matter who you are, most of the smartest people work for someone else." InnoCentive's network brings the advantage of a much larger and more diverse set of minds. Typically, the toughest challenges are solved by someone from outside the standard area of expertise. When the Ocean Spill Recovery Institute posed a challenge to separate frozen oil from water in an Arctic sea cleanup, the solution was proposed by John Davis, a nanotechnology expert from the cement industry who applied a technique normally used to vibrate cement and keep it in liquid form. When another "seeker" company was looking for a chemical to use in art restoration projects, the answer came from a twenty-year-old chemistry student in Indiana based on a solution he had found to help his mother dye cloth. The winners of a challenge for a new polymer design included the owner of a small agriculture business and a veterinarian.

InnoCentive's global reach is also evident in its competitions. Texas-based nonprofit SunNight awarded an engineer in New Zealand for the design of a solar-powered flashlight that is now bringing light to communities without electricity in Africa and the Gaza Strip, providing safety outdoors and allowing children to study at night.

More than a thousand previously unsolved problems have been posted to InnoCentive, in these and other fields such as remote sensing, public transportation, and plant genetics. An independent analysis for a Swedish packaged goods company found that it received a 74 percent return on its investment and a faster research cycle by using the InnoCentive network.[24]

InnoCentive's process begins with the "seeker" developing a clear technical problem that can be posted publicly without giving away vital trade secrets (for example, a company developing a new shampoo might post a challenge seeking one chemical compound that will bind effectively with another under specific circumstances). The challenge is posted along with a prize amount, ranging from five thousand to a million dollars. Solvers then review an initial description of the challenge; if they are interested in pursuing it, they sign a nondisclosure agreement to receive more detailed information. After solvers submit their solutions, the seeker can choose to buy one or more solutions at the agreed prize amount, with InnoCentive ensuring the transfer of intellectual property and the rights of all parties.

During the open competition for the Netflix Prize, the company found that many of the participants were sharing information on their online forum and eventually forming teams to pool their ideas. Similarly, InnoCentive has found that many of its most productive "solvers" have assembled their own teams of collaborators, whether in an academic lab or on an ad hoc basis. To better leverage the formation of teams within its network, the company is developing tools based on discussion forums, shared workspaces, and social networking sites. The goals are to help solvers find others with complementary skills anywhere in the world, to encourage team formation, and to easily manage teams' shared intellectual property.

Where innovator networks like InnoCentive are focused on narrowly defined technical problems, the X Prize Foundation has taken the opposite approach to open competitions. Starting with its first Ansari X Prize, which awarded ten million dollars to the first person to develop a vehicle that could be used for commercial space travel, the foundation has sought to inspire game-changing innovations that will reshape industries or launch new ones. The Ansari X Prize was awarded in 2004 to SpaceShipOne designer Burt Rutan. He provided the technology for Space Adventures, Virgin Galactic, and other companies to enter what is so far a field of tourism for the ultrarich (thirty-five million dollars for a ride into space, anyone?). Since then, new X Prizes have included the Archon Genomix X Prize, aimed at developing high speed, low-cost sequencing of human genomes; and the Progressive Automotive X Prize to build a commercially-viable 100 mile-per-gallon car. The X Prize approach is similar to the Netflix Prize in that the award is high, the challenge is extremely difficult, and solutions are pursued by global teams over multiple years.

There are many other variations on the open-competition approach to collaboration, including Threadless's contest for amateur designers to create the most popular new designs for its T-shirts and Cisco's I-Prize in which teams around the world competed to develop plans for new business ventures. Another example is uTest, whose quarterly Bug Battle competition brings together more than a thousand software testers around the world to compete for prize money in finding bugs in popular software platforms. Thousands of software bugs have been uncovered in uTest Bug Battles of Web browsers (Chrome, Internet Explorer, and Firefox), social networks (Facebook, MySpace, and LinkedIn), and Twitter applications—for only a few thousand dollars in prize money at each contest.

The motivation for participants in an open competition is mainly the chance to win, which may bring with it significant money (such as the Netflix Prize, Cisco I-Prize, and X Prizes), usually combined with public recognition (although not for InnoCentive's anonymous "solvers"). Excitement about the project, however, is also often a powerful motivator. No doubt the three winners of the I-Prize were particularly excited by the opportunity to work at Cisco to bring to life the smart-grid energy framework that they had conceived.

In open competition, the project does not need to be divisible into parts, because the same project is given to all participants to work on in parallel. However, that project may be a discrete part of a larger business issue—like many of the technical challenges submitted to InnoCentive. Open competitions may require widely differing levels of expertise (such as the ability to design a T-shirt versus a space craft), which will result in much broader or narrower groups of participants.

Typically, the organizer decides who wins in an open competition. However, the decision may be made by participants in cases where they have enough information to decide and the feasibility of the winning solution is not an issue (for example, customers voting on the winning T-shirt design for Threadless, where the cost of producing one T-shirt versus another is not an issue).

Participants in open competitions usually work individually or in teams, with no interaction with others. But in projects where participants vote on the final decision, there tends to be much more interaction. In some cases, teams will spontaneously share information with competitors (as during the early rounds of the Netflix Prize). The results of open competitions are owned by the organizer, except in nonprofit cases, such as the X Prize, where the goal is purely to spur innovation by others.

Defined Platforms

The last two kinds of approaches to COLLABORATE strategies are based on platforms. In these cases, the collaboration's organizer creates a foundation upon which others can create their own projects, conceived and driven by their own initiative. Microsoft Windows, for example, is a platform: the operating system provides the environment in which countless other companies, independent of Microsoft, have built software businesses (including companies such as Adobe Systems, Electronic Arts, and Intuit, each worth billions of dollars). In

Microsoft's case, it has profited indirectly from businesses using its platform. The ecosystem of companies writing software for Windows has allowed the Windows product itself to achieve a dominant market share and extremely high profit margins. Other platforms, such as the auction site eBay, yield profit directly, by taking a share of revenue from all businesses that use the platform. The power of a platform approach to collaboration is its scalability, speed, and openness to innovation. A lightweight platform can grow rapidly if it attracts collaborators. The core code for the entire eBay Web platform was written by its founder, Pierre Omidyar, over a long Labor Day weekend. Omidyar's simple but flexible auction service has attracted millions around the world who use it as the platform for their own small businesses, growing eBay to more than sixty billion dollars in total payments per year.

Ebay is an example of a defined platform, our fourth approach to network collaboration. Defined platforms are those that provide clear specifications of what others can build on top of them. On eBay, anyone can set up an item for auction or sale to be delivered by mail. On YouTube, another defined platform, anyone can upload videos to share. On neither site can you sell MP3 music downloads, however. Craigslist is another defined platform: anyone can create a classified advertisement in a wide range of categories, but you cannot post videos or run an auction on craigslist. You cannot even create another Web page that pulls data from craigslist and adds another layer of functionality to it (some have tried, and craigslist promptly shuts down their access to its site).[25]

The power of defined platforms lies in their simplicity, which limits make possible. As discussed in chapter 3, simplicity is a key value in spreading new products, services, and behaviors through customer networks. It is much easier for others to build their own small business on top of craigslist or eBay than it is to build one on top of Microsoft Windows (which requires fairly advanced programming skills). That is because the narrow scope of what can be built on defined platforms allows them to have extremely intuitive user interfaces that are as easy to use as sending an email or uploading a video. That ease of use allows them to attract numerous collaborators who will build their own businesses on the platform.

CD Baby is the world's leading online store for independent musicians selling CDs and music downloads directly to consumers, with more than two million tracks for sale. But CD Baby wasn't started by a large retailer or by an e-tailer like Amazon. It was started by one musician, Derek Sivers, as a Web site to sell his own CDs, and then the CDs of his friends, and then the CDs of any other artist not signed to a major record label.

CD Baby is a clearly defined platform: it allows any artist with a music CD of their own to set up their own storefront by paying only thirty-five dollars, filling in a few paragraphs of marketing text, and mailing in the first four copies of his or her CD. Its phenomenal growth is due, no doubt, to the fact that it was built by an indie musician, Derek Sivers, and built to match his exact image of the perfect store for indie musicians. All musicians get paid weekly. Musicians set their own prices, with CD Baby taking a flat four-dollar cut per disc (much less than such retailers as Amazon). Musicians receive the full name, email, and address of every customer they sell to (unless the customer opts out), allowing bands to build and network with fan lists. CD Baby even offers actual credit-card swiping machines to musicians, equipping them to sell CDs and merchandise at live shows (often the largest venue for sales for indie bands). CD Baby's site accepts no advertising and no payments for preferential placement of CDs on the home page or anywhere else. And as a matter of fundamental trust, no musician will ever have his or her album dropped from CD Baby's catalog for lack of sales. By understanding what independent musicians want and need, Sivers created an unmatched online platform, which quickly grew to more than thirty million dollars in annual sales. Most remarkably, even as CD sales were contracting industrywide, CD Baby's platform bucked the trend and grew 28 percent in 2008.[26]

In defined platforms, the motivation for participation may be primarily money (for example, selling an item on craigslist or eBay) or fame and glory (many videos posted to YouTube). For platforms like CD Baby that allow entrepreneurs to showcase their work, the motivation will be a mix of both money and glory, along with the participants' love and excitement for their projects.

Modularity is not an issue for collaboration in platforms, as participants each design their own projects and complete them in entirety. A wide range of participants is possible, since a well-defined platform allows for easy participation with no technical expertise.

Decision making in defined platforms rests mostly with the participants, although the organizer may play a limited "gatekeeper" role (setting standards for what can be added or listed). Participants tend to work individually; however, they may interact in discussion forums (such as the numerous eBay and craigslist user forums). Participants almost always retain ownership of their projects that they build for defined platforms, but they agree to a revenue share or a service fee paid to the organizer.

Open Platforms: SDKs, APIs, and Open Source

The fifth and final approach to COLLABORATE strategy is the open platform. In open platforms, the range of possible projects by collaborators is not narrowly defined. Microsoft Windows is an example of an open platform because, unlike CD Baby or YouTube, the organizer does not know what kinds of projects others will build on its platform. Microsoft did not just allow others to write music editing software for Windows; it allowed them to write *any* software for any task. This is what has led to the vast ecosystem of software for Windows computers. The iPhone has created a similar platform for developing software in the mobile computing space. Rather than tell developers something like "You can sell your music on our platform," Apple said, "You can design any kind of application you can imagine for the iPhone."

Participant motivations and interaction are similar on open platforms to what we saw in defined platforms, as is the lack of modularity (participants work on their own whole projects). However, open platforms usually attract a narrow set of participants, because an open platform requires more technical skills to participate (such as programming skills).

Typically, the organizer still plays a gatekeeper role and requires a revenue share or service fee from participants. However, in some cases, such as Microsoft Windows, the platform's organizer takes no financial cut and allows participants to join in without an approval process. In this case, the primary objective is for participants to build projects that add value to the underlying platform, which the organizer owns.

The critical difference in open platforms, however, is the freedom and flexibility that they allow collaborators. In order to allow this, open platforms need a much more open architecture than the kind of Web interface used for posting an ad on craigslist or selling an album on CD Baby.

Three powerful tools for software and web development have provided the building blocks for open platforms to date: software development kits (SDKs), Application Programming Interfaces (APIs), and open-source code. Each can be a powerful tool for open platform collaboration.

SDKs

Lim Ding Wen was only nine years old when he wrote his first application for the iPhone. Called Doodle Kids, it allows users to sketch colorful pictures and patterns with their fingers on the screen, take a snapshot of their creations, and clear the screen by shaking it (a sort of digital, multicolor Etch-a-Sketch). Lim, a fourth grader in Singapore's Lianhua Primary School, spent just three days writing the application, which he developed for his little sisters Xin Quan, age five, and Xin Mei, three. But as a free application on the iTunes App Store, Doodle Kids went on to be downloaded 480,000 times in its first three months.[27]

Lim Ding Wen is not an employee of Apple Inc., but he is one of more than fifty thousand independent developers who have been the driving force for innovation on Apple's iPhone (and later, iPad). Each one has downloaded an SDK, which allows them to write programs coded to work in Apple's unique operating system. While Lim's app is free in the App Store, many others have written successful paid apps. Ethan Nicholas coded the iShoot game in his free time and eventually quit his day job when the game earned him more than thirty thousand dollars in a single day.[28] Others have started small businesses writing programs for the iOS platform. Ian Schenkel, cofounder of EuroSmartz, says that its app, which allows users to print from the iPhone, took only three weeks of work to develop but grossed three hundred thousand dollars in three months.[29]

The phenomenal success of the iPhone and iPad has been in large part because they are open platforms for innovation by developers like these. Apple's SDK (only ninety-nine dollars to download), its huge built-in audience of customers, and the relatively small share of revenues that it takes (only 30 percent) have all attracted developers to write programs. The devices' unique hardware has given developers a creative set of tools to play with: large touch-screen interfaces, accelerometers that detect movement (allowing them to respond to users' shaking or turning), location awareness, camera, compass, and more. For Apple, making the iPhone and iPad open platforms has unleashed an army of collaborators who have created more software than Apple could have ever imagined, let alone designed in such a brief period. Apps turn the iPad into a magazine, chessboard, or work-space; the iPhone into a language translator, gaming device, musical instrument, restaurant finder, mass transit guide, and more. As the iPhone redefined the smartphone category, competitors like Black-Berry had no choice but to begin developing app stores of their own. Their platforms will need to be at least as open as Apple's if they hope to foster as much innovation for their devices.

Open APIs

One of the most powerful recent tools for open platforms is the use of open Application Programming Interfaces. Where an SDK gives collaborators the keys to programming for a particular device, an open API gives them access to the organizer's data and ways to "talk" to the organizer's applications.

The rapid growth of Twitter in 2008 and 2009 was an example of the ability of open APIs to grow a platform. Twitter's core is quite simple: a service for transmitting 140-character messages via the Web and SMS. Twitter started as a small company and allowed itself to be radically open to others. It was so open that independent companies were soon developing add-on services (such as specialized iPhone apps to use Twitter) that were making them money, while Twitter itself still had zero revenue. As a result, however, Twitter's platform was able to grow at a phenomenal rate (buoyed by an ecosystem of great apps) while the company's owners invested very little in product development and focused on maintaining the core messaging service in the midst of rapid growth in the number of users. Even Twitter's tool for searching real-time conversations around the world (arguably, the one central feature of Twitter besides sending and receiving messages) was developed by another company using Twitter's open API. (Twitter used some of its early venture capital to buy that company, Summize.) Twitter's open platform approach reflected not just a technical choice but a philosophical one as well. Its founders intentionally left Twitter open to others to help define it as it grew. Many of the most popular uses of Twitter—retweeting, hashtags, and even the word *tweet*—were invented by Twitter's customers, not the company. Twitter's founders were not even sure what the service would be used for when it launched. What they expected to be a social networking tool was turned by users into more of a microblogging platform and real-time search tool. Twitter did not even define a business model before launching. Instead, it waited for others to find profitable uses for its platform (from direct selling to customer service, broadcasting, and advertising) before deciding what the best model for its own revenue might be.

Open APIs are not only used by Web companies, however. Any organization with a database can use open APIs to create a Web-based platform for open collaboration. Under the direction of Vivek Kundra, the federal government's first chief information officer, the United States began a series of initiatives in 2009 aimed at opening up government data to the public online, using tools such as open APIs to encourage collaboration and innovation. On the Web site Data.gov, data sets such as the Federal Register and the U.S. Geological Survey are providing massive amounts of data to the public in a machine-readable format that can be analyzed by anyone. In response, citizen groups like Sunlight Labs are organizing volunteers to sort through government data to track congressional earmarks, spending on stimulus projects, and how contracts are being awarded. Media companies such as the BBC, the *New York Times*, and NPR have opened up their APIs to encourage others to develop innovative new applications that combine their articles with other sources of information, thereby reaching new readers and linking some of them back to the news services' own sites. By opening up its API, Google Maps has become the platform on which a wide range of companies and non-profits build their own customized maps. When customers of Netflix first started using iPhones, they clamored for an iPhone app to manage their accounts on the go. Rather than commit the resources to developing an app, Netflix simply opened up its API to let others quickly build one for them. Developer Brent Jensen soon launched a $2.99 iPhone app called iPhlix, which, thanks to Netflix's API, can search the database of available movies on Netflix, add a new order for one that you want, or tell you which movies are already in your order queue. Netflix's iPhone customers can now reserve a movie at any time (such as when hearing about it from a friend in a coffee shop), thus increasing their loyalty to the service at no innovation cost to the company.

Open Source

The third tool for building open platforms for innovation is open source, an approach to software design in which the source code is made public with few or no copyright restrictions. This approach allows for extremely open collaboration among independent developers, who may each develop software contributions and share them freely with the community. Benefits to business can include lower IT and innovation costs, quicker development of new solutions, and broad participation in a new platform.

The seminal success of the open-source model for software was the development of the Linux operating system. Finnish university student Linus Torvalds began the project in 1991 and soon had attracted thousands of other developers around the world to contribute code to this mammoth project. Today, much of the Internet runs on servers using a combination of software known as the "LAMP stack"—Linux operating system, Apache server software, MySQL databases, and PHP programming code—all open source. Nearly 90 percent of the world's supercomputers (used for running incredibly data intensive processes such as modeling of weather, climate change, and aircraft aerodynamics) run on Linux. Linux is installed on countless devices, including cell phones, video game consoles, and MP3 music players. Since 1999, IBM has made Linux-based products a core part of its technology consulting. With the rise of netbook computers (an inexpensive, ultraportable style of laptop), the Ubuntu version of Linux has even entered the mainstream consumer marketplace.

As the worldwide market for smartphones continues to grow, the biggest challenger to Apple's iPhone as a platform for mobile phone applications is the Android open-source operating system. Based on Linux and introduced to the market by Google, Android is becoming the operating system for a wide range of mobile devices. Although the iPhone established a large head start in its consumer base, Android competes with a platform that is even more open in a number of ways. First, it offers a greater diversity of devices and phone networks (versus the iPhone's single product model, offered only on AT&T in the United States as of 2010). Android was offered on dozens of phones from every major phone carrier by the end of 2010, as well as on other mobile devices such as the Nook e-reader. Second, Android's diversity allows for greater customization. Where the iPhone's design must balance the different needs of many business and consumer segments, handset makers are using Android to offer different phones with interfaces tailored to different needs. An early example is the Motorola Cliq, a phone optimized for fans of social networking services, with a home screen that combines email, Facebook, MySpace, and Twitter into a single feed. In the race to develop many phone apps to compete with the iPhone, Android hopes to attract more developers with an easier programming language (Java), and the do-it-yourself Google App Maker for nonprogrammers. Just as important, anyone who creates an app for Android phones can sell it to consumers without seeking permission from a centralized app store like the iPhone's. Given that Apple has rejected some high-profile apps that seemed to compete with Apple's own business (like Google Voice and Google Latitude), Android's lack of a gatekeeper could attract many developers to innovate for Android phones.

Perhaps the biggest example of the innovation possible with an open-source platform is the World Wide Web itself. Its open standards and protocols have allowed anyone, from Fortune 500 companies to individual students and hobbyists, to develop Web sites, services, and applications. As Howard Rheingold has pointed out, the Web has provided a "platform for cooperation" that unleashes the creative energies of entrepreneurs, the market, and society at large, to the great mutual benefit of all.[30]

The Future of COLLABORATE

The rise of collaboration within digital networks poses opportunities and challenges to existing organizations of all kinds. As Yochai Benkler has pointed out, the greatest disruption wrought by Wikipedia was not upon the business model of encyclopedia publishers but upon our collective definition of "authority."[31] Instead of turning to a select group of professional experts for answers to our questions, Wikipedia has trained us to look to ourselves and to the collective knowledge of the network.

Network collaboration will continue to play an especially large role in the future of nonprofit organizations, due to their ability to inspire passion and commitment to dearly held causes. New innovators like TheExtraordinaries.org are exploring the possibility of what is called "microvolunteering"—where citizens can use idle moments on their phones and computers to contribute five-minute bursts of effort (translating a text into another language, tagging an image for a museum, or reviewing congressional bills for pork) that may add up, Wikipedia-like, to a large social impact. The challenges of dividing socially beneficial work into such small tasks, however, may mean that the greater impact of network collaboration is in projects where a smaller number of participants are committed to work in a more sustained fashion. Blue State Digital's Thomas Gensemer has remarked that it is easier to garner a large email list of people concerned about a political issue than it is to lead them into effective action. The critical difference in networks like myBarackObama.com may be that they combine online coordinating with face-to-face meetings and interaction by their network members in the real world.[32]

For-profit businesses will need to find careful ways to balance value creation for their enterprise with appropriate rewards and motivation for their network collaborators. The success of Twitter and the iPhone in attracting a network of innovators may point to an increasing role of open platforms for new businesses. The new business model of the digital age may be smaller, leaner companies that do less work developing their business. Instead, they create a great business idea, keep their work simple and focused, and leverage an open platform like an API to attract a network of ancillary businesses to feed their growth.

Keys to a COLLABORATE Strategy

The desire to collaborate with others on collective projects is one of the greatest potential opportunities of customer networks. Whether your organization is a political campaign, a news organization, an online business, or an offline enterprise, a COLLABORATE strategy can help you to tap into the knowledge, skills, expertise, and enthusiasm of your networked customers.

With widely varying levels of expertise required, and more or less interaction between participants, a COLLABORATE strategy can be used to help design products, to solve intractable technical questions, to analyze large sets of data, to organize key stakeholders, or to identify new business opportunities.

Successful approaches to a COLLABORATE strategy include: offering a chance to passively contribute to a project via work customers are already doing; inviting customers to actively contribute to a small piece of a large shared project; sponsoring an open competition for customers to vie in creating the best solution; building a defined platform that allows customers to easily create their own project of a specific kind; or using an open platform, such as an SDK, an API, or open source, that allows participants wide latitude for inventing contributions to your enterprise.

Whatever the approach, it is important to be sure that you are creating value for all parties. A successful collaboration cannot be just about your organization and its needs. Make sure you understand the values, wants, and motivations of your network. For some collaborations, love of the cause alone is enough: just make sure that you are rewarding participants with a clear sense of how they are contributing and the importance of their work. For other collaborations, an opportunity for social recognition—whether fame or the esteem of select peers—or financial reward may be the right motivation.

Be sure to leave the door open for collaborators to surprise you, too. You may begin a network collaboration with a clear set of goals in mind. Once your network participants become involved, however, they may very well uncover new opportunities for your organization that you had not imagined. Be flexible in leading any network collaboration and be ready to follow or lead it in new directions.

By inviting customers to collaborate with your organization on vital and important projects, you can harness their talents and energies while building a closer relationship. This COLLABORATE strategy is the last of five strategies that any organization or business can use to thrive with customer networks.

But although these five strategies are distinct, they are certainly not separate. In many of the businesses and nonprofits we have seen, these strategies work in tandem. This raises several questions. When should the core customer network strategies be combined? How should a manager begin assessing his or her organization, customers, and needs in order to determine which strategies to apply? And how will customer networks change the shape and culture of the organization as a whole? In the final part of this book we will examine these and other issues for the management and leadership of customer network strategy within an organization.

PART III

Leadership and the Customer Network–Focused Organization

CHAPTER 8

Planning and Executing a Complete Customer Network Strategy

As we have seen, the five core strategies for customer networks—
ACCESS, ENGAGE, CUSTOMIZE, CONNECT, and COLLABORATE—can be
used by companies and organizations of all kinds and sizes to build
more fruitful relationships with customers and to drive such key business objectives as product differentiation, customer loyalty, sales efficiency, reduced costs, brand building, and innovation capacity.

No two organizations will apply these strategies in precisely
the same way. A midsize retail chain, a Fortune 100 financial services
company, and a small technology start-up each have very different
customers, they possess different organizational skills and strengths,
and they have to contend with very different sets of competitors. Not
surprisingly, then, each company should execute an effective customer network strategy in its own way.

A key challenge for any organization, therefore, is how to plan
and implement a complete customer network strategy in a way that
best matches its specific business. This chapter provides a management process for strategy planning and implementation that can be
applied to any organization.

The Five-Step Customer Network
Strategy Planning Process

Any organization that is serious about customer networks will want to develop an overall customer network strategy—that is, a broad plan that includes one or more of the five core strategies of ACCESS, EN-GAGE, CUSTOMIZE, CONNECT, and COLLABORATE and is matched to the specific needs of the organization or business.

Such an overall strategy may be a companywide initiative led by the CEO or founder of a business or the president of a nonprofit. In other cases, developing a customer network strategy may be an initiative assigned to a specific division, brand, or business within a larger company. In each case, the manager in charge of creating an overall strategy faces several key questions:

- Where do you begin, and what goals should you set for your project?
- How should you match your strategy to your customers' needs and to your business and brand?
- How do you decide which of the five core strategies to deploy and how to connect them to one another?
- Which divisions of your business do you need to involve in executing the strategy successfully?
- How do you sell your project to upper management, and if you move ahead, how do you know if your project is working?

The Five-Step Customer Network Strategy Planning Process presented below answers these questions and can be used by any organization to guide the development and successful execution of an overall customer network strategy designed to meet the needs of its business (fig. 8.1). This process includes:

Step 1. *Setting Objectives:* Defining key outcomes for your organization that your strategy will aim to achieve.

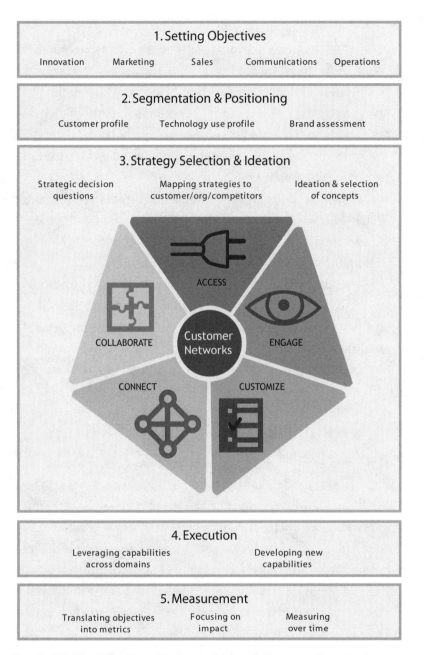

Figure 8.1 The Five-Step Customer Network Strategy Planning Process (complete). *Illustration by Anna Fokina.*

Step 2. *Segmentation and Positioning:* Understanding your customers and their network behavior, as well as your brand positioning, to provide the foundation for any new strategy.

Step 3. *Strategy Selection and Ideation:* Selecting which of the five core strategies to include and understanding how to fit them to your business, your customers, your competitors, and your objectives; concept ideation and testing must then be used to select specific innovations to implement.

Step 4. *Execution:* Enlisting the right team to carry out your strategy across functional disciplines—from research and development to operations, customer-facing services, outbound communications, and top-level leadership.

Step 5. *Measurement:* Putting metrics in place that can measure the results of your project against the objectives you defined in the first step. Metrics should measure the strategy's impact and return on investment (ROI), as well as what is working and why, in order to improve and build on the customer network strategy.

Step 1: Setting Objectives

The first step to developing and executing an overall customer network strategy is to identify your primary objectives. Are you undertaking this initiative to build your brand and increase loyalty among repeat customers? To generate more leads and improve online sales? To lower your customer service costs? By defining the objectives up front, you can ensure that the development of your customer network strategy will focus on achieving real impact for your organization.

As we have seen in numerous cases, customer network strategies can help organizations of all kinds achieve real business impact. Recall the toymaker Ganz, which created a hundred-million-dollar product by linking online and offline play in its Webkinz toys. Or Ford, which drove a 38 percent prelaunch awareness of its Ford Fiesta among Generation Y consumers with its online customer "movement." Computer maker Dell generated more than ten thousand new ideas for products and services simply by inviting customers to share ideas at Dell IdeaStorm. By mixing utility and mobility, Kraft Foods created an iPhone app that promoted recipes for its products and sold over a million copies to paying customers. And the iPhone itself built a library of more than a hundred thousand such apps and helped drive a surge in sales in its second year by launching its App Store, which tapped the open innovation of a network of developers.

Objectives that have been achieved by these and other customer network strategies range across the domains of innovation, marketing, sales, communications, and internal operations. Specific objectives that an organization may consider as it begins strategy development include:

Innovation Objectives
- Gaining customer insights
- Capturing and evaluating customer input and ideation
- Differentiating products
- Differentiating service
- Expanding the capacity for innovation

Marketing Objectives
- Building brand image
- Building audience engagement, loyalty, and support
- Amplifying positive customer word of mouth
- Marketing to hard-to-reach customers
- Marketing to high-value niche audiences

Sales Objectives
- Generating new customer leads
- Driving direct marketing sales

- Achieving greater efficiency in online sales channels
- Earning permission to market to customers directly
- Educating your market to grow it

Communications Objectives

- Managing reputation and crisis response
- Breaking through media clutter
- Improving product support and documentation
- Mobilizing employees through better communications
- Improving data transparency within the organization

Operations Objectives

- Extending the global reach of your business
- Lowering customer service costs
- Increasing productivity despite limited resources
- Increasing speed of business decision making

Of course, all of these objectives may appear worthwhile. Who doesn't want to generate leads on new customers or build their brand image? But just like any other project, starting a customer network strategy requires prioritizing and choosing objectives to focus on. When IBM began developing the Innov8 online game, its objectives were to "reach niche customers" and to "educate its market" on business process management, and thus grow its customer base. By contrast, Intuit was focused more on "lowering customer service costs" when it launched its TurboTax Live Community to help customers ask and answer one another's questions on tax preparation. In neither case was their primary aim to "capture customer ideation," so neither one muddled their project by trying to add something like Dell's IdeaStorm into the mix. Different organizational objectives lead to a different focus for customer network strategies.

The objectives of your strategy will likely evolve, or become more defined, as it is developed in Steps 2 and 3. However, it is important to begin with an initial list at the start, even if it is somewhat exploratory and will be refined later. By identifying clear objectives, you can be sure you are focusing on a strategy with real business impact in the subsequent steps, and not just one that creates buzz and excitement over the newest shiny gadget of the new media world.

Step 2: Segmentation and Positioning

The second step in planning and executing an overall customer network strategy is to understand who your customers are, how they are participating in networks, and what your brand positioning or value proposition is for them. This background research—which fits under the traditional marketing practice of segmentation and positioning—will provide an essential foundation for creating effective new strategies.

Customer Profile

Traditional segmentation focuses on understanding your customer demographics (age, sex, income, geography, and so on) and pertinent psychographics (interests, social values, popular activities, self-identity). The point of segmentation is that any organization serves more than one kind of customer. An automaker may need to understand and serve the needs of young adults making their first purchase in the category, parents whose family size dictates their purchasing needs, and a smaller group of affluent consumers who are seeking a different kind of automotive experience. An auto company does not seek to produce one car model—or ad campaign—to reach all of these customer segments. Similarly, one customer network strategy may not effectively reach all these segments, either.

Technology Use Profile

In addition to traditional market research on each segment, it is critical that businesses examine their values, their behaviors, and their technology adoption in customer networks. Is your customer segment more focused on using networks to connect socially with friends, to solve problems for their family, or to meet goals in their professional life? Which new media have they adopted, and how actively do they use them?

In answering these questions, it is important to rely on relevant and recent data and not simply the standard assumptions of your industry. New technologies are not only adopted by the young (the growth of Twitter was driven largely by adult professionals, and Facebook and YouTube have a lot more grandparents on them than you might expect). After years of resisting the online world, major luxury fashion brands like Prada, Bulgari, Fabergé, and Burberry discovered that younger consumers and working women were replacing baby boomers as their dominant consumer group and that these new consumer segments are extremely active online. In the recessionary year of 2009, Burberry doubled its share value as it shifted to more direct-to-consumer sales and pushed its classic British brand into the digital age using Facebook, Twitter, YouTube, and Burberry's own social network.[1]

When engaging customer networks, go where your customers already are. Barack Obama's campaign raised millions of dollars through its own myBarackObama.com network, but it also made a point of engaging millions of supporters on other networks that they were already using, including Facebook and MySpace, but also Black-Planet, MiGente, and AsianAve. If your organization operates globally, it is important to realize that the ways customers connect to networks vary greatly by country and region. Different social networks dominate in different countries. Japan and South Korea have average broadband speeds ten times that in the United States, but usage is much more likely to be on the mobile Web.[2]

Brand Assessment

In addition to understanding your customers, it is critical to start with a clear understanding of your brand and what it means to them before developing a customer network strategy. Strong brands communicate and deliver a clear promise to customers, whether it is an experience (for end consumers) or a more functional value proposition (for business customers). Strong brands have a powerful message at their core. Here are a few:

- *Nike*: Athletic aspiration ("Just do it")
- *Apple*: Your digital life made easy
- *Kiva*: Make a difference for a real person ("Loans that change lives")
- *Starbucks*: A"third space" to relax between work and home
- *SAP*: Making your business a best-run business

Taken together, an understanding of the customer and of the brand promise will provide clear guidance for the kind of experience that any new customer network strategy should create. For Burberry, any customer network strategy should focus on rich media (to convey the vivid aesthetics of luxury fashion), social sharing (luxury is inherently conspicuous), and the ability to connect to others. For Apple, no matter what it does, it has to be incredibly easy to use (Apple's core value proposition) and appeal to people who like technology but often do not know a great deal about it (the brand is not just for geeks). For Nike, a network strategy has to help customers push themselves as athletes, whatever their current level.

Step 3: Strategy Selection and Ideation

The third step in customer network strategy planning is where managers must decide which of the five core strategies to pursue, develop specific ideas for new innovations and initiatives, and then select which of these to include in their final plan.

Strategic Decision Questions

In selecting from the five core strategies—ACCESS, ENGAGE, CUSTOMIZE, CONNECT, and COLLABORATE—you will want to explore and answer a set of key decision questions.

The first question is: *Which of the five core strategies will you prioritize for your own organization?* The five strategies do not have any fixed priority of their own. We therefore cannot generalize and say that "COLLABORATE is more important than CONNECT," or even that "If you are successfully helping your customer network to EN-GAGE, then you should focus your attention on helping them CUS-TOMIZE." Rather, in answering the question of prioritization, each organization should look at its own objectives, at its customer seg-mentation, and at its positioning and brand—that is, the insights from Steps 1 and 2 of the planning process. Likely, there will be evident opportunities to achieve your objectives through more than one, or even all five, of the core customer network strategies.

The second decision question, then, is: *Should you focus on only one strategy, on a few, or on a holistic approach that encompasses all five?* Each approach has trade-offs. If a business can effectively employ multiple strategies for customer networks, the benefits to the customers and the business will be greater: more opportunities for differentiation, more business objectives achieved, and a deeper, more holistic relationship with the customer network. However, that does not mean that a single stand-alone initiative focused on one or two customer network strategies should not be implemented if there is a clear opportunity. We have seen several cases of such fo-cused initiatives that have been quite successful. The Ford Fiesta Movement—which focused solely on a CONNECT strategy—was used to effectively drive prelaunch awareness of the Fiesta car model among a target of Generation Y consumers by creating a forum for one hundred of them to share their experiences as test drivers of the car. By contrast, Apple Inc. has eschewed any sort of CONNECT strategy, virtually ignoring social media and maintaining a culture of intense secrecy. Yet the company's successful products like the iPhone have delivered game-changing value in customer network ACCESS (to the Web, to media, to email) and have harnessed a COLLABORATE strategy to build its breakthrough iPhone App Store. The decision to pursue either a narrowly focused customer network strategy or a more holistic one using several strategies will depend on how broad your mandate is, how much of your resources you can commit, and how quickly you need to launch the project and show results.

If you have chosen more than one network strategy, then your third decision question is: *Should the strategies be connected or separate?* Different customer network strategies may be developed in stand-alone fashion if they are targeting distinct customer groups. However, if two or more of the five strategies are being developed for the same audience segment, they will benefit from coordination. In the case of Nike+ (seen in chapter 3), both the digital shoe sensor and the online running community benefited greatly from each other and their sharing of data (rather than being two separate and unconnected offers for Nike runners). Similarly, the Kraft iFood Assistant phone app creates a powerful branded experience for customers by integrating an ENGAGE strategy (providing relevant content on cooking simple meals for the target audience of busy working parents) with an ACCESS strategy (offering a seamless mobile app design that lets you find a grocery store, buy your ingredients, and follow your recipe, all with the phone in your pocket).

Your last decision question, if you are including multiple network strategies, is: *In what sequence should the strategies be developed or launched?* Once again, this will need to be decided on a case by case basis, as there is no generalizable rule that any of the five strategies should be developed before any others. For example, the Nike+ running platform could have easily started development as an idea for a CONNECT strategy (to build an online community where Nike's most passionate runners can share their stats and routes and set challenges with one another) and then been extended to incorporate the ACCESS strategy (to strengthen the community experience by letting runners connect to it via their shoes while they are running and not just via their PCs when they are at home). But in fact, the strategy for Nike+ actually arose in the reverse order: ACCESS and then CONNECT. Nike started experimenting with how runners could capture and track data on their running as early as the 1980s, with an experimental Nike Monitor that was strapped around your waist and used radar and headphones to calculate and communicate your running speed. Years later, Nike brought back this idea of embedded data measurement (ACCESS) and added the idea of an online community (CONNECT), and Nike+ was born.[3]

Mapping Your Strategies to Your Customers, Your Organization, and Your Competitors

Once you have selected one or more of the five core strategies to focus on, you will need to understand how you will implement them. To do so, you should map the selected strategies against your own customer needs, organizational capabilities, and competitive environment.

Any customer network strategy must be developed to match the needs of your identified customer segments. If you are considering an ACCESS strategy, you need to understand what drives access for your own customers: Are they young consumers who make heavy use of the mobile web? Are they business customers for whom data portability is critical? Or are simplicity and speed of online transactions critical motivators?

If you are considering an ENGAGE strategy, you need to develop a clear sense of the kind of content that will be most valuable and relevant to your customer segments: Is it gaming and interactive entertainment? Specialized information in a technical field or general news and perspectives on a particular industry? Do your customers seek out long-form or short-form content?

If you are considering a CUSTOMIZE strategy, you will need to identify the specific elements of your value offering that customers would most like to have more control over: Product design elements? Choice of service plans? A more personal touch? A greater reflection of their style and identity? Or just a variety of options for how and when to hear from your business?

For a CONNECT strategy, you will need to understand why, where, how frequently, and with whom customers are already connecting online: Are they better reached in a broad social networking platform that they already participate in, or are they open to joining a more specialized one? How much can you learn by simply listening in to the connections they are already sharing online?

For a COLLABORATE strategy, it is critical to understand what kind of relationships you might have with key customer networks and how they might be motivated to collaborate with you: Do you have passionate followers who believe in your mission and may contribute to it out of shared values? Or will they be more motivated by commercial incentives or a chance at fame and glory? Do you have any customer segments with specialized skills that could collaborate with you, or will your collaboration do better to rely on a broad pool of contributors without deep expertise?

Next you must consider the unique capabilities and culture of your organization and assess how your chosen strategies might be a good match. Is yours a technology focused company that is likely to innovate a new piece of hardware, software, or Web service that creates a breakthrough experience for customer networks? (Think of Research in Motion's development of the BlackBerry or Amazon's continuing innovations in online interfaces.) Or are you a nontechnological company with a strong marketing and innovation orientation—one that can harness existing technologies to create a new and compelling experience for customers? (Think of Nike's development of Nike+ or Affinia Hotel's use of basic Web technology and an extraordinary service culture to offer a radically customized hotel experience.) Are you a media-focused company with proven ability to generate compelling content that your customers seek out and value? If so, could that content be combined in new ways with networking technology to create new platforms for your customers? (Think of Nickelodeon's development of the *iCarly* TV show.) Are you an organization with a powerful operations focus that might use customer networks to improve speed of business, knowledge sharing, or innovation within your organization? (Think of GE's imagination market and Cisco's I-Prize.)

Finally, you need to examine the competitive landscape that you face for each strategy you have chosen. Whether you are considering the launch of a branded online forum, the design of a new online commerce experience, a newly customized service offering for your customers, or a sponsored content channel for high-value customers, you first need to understand the current state of your business category (be it charitable giving, discount airlines, athletic clothing, or online movie rentals). What are the current expectations for your category, in terms of your chosen strategy? For example, if you are planning a new kind of mobile customer experience, how high is the current bar for your category? Are you already falling behind, are you leading the pack, or are you somewhere in the undifferentiated middle along with your competitors? When assessing your category, be careful not to assume that the status quo is justified and that there "must be a reason" no one is meeting a customer need that you may have identified. Often, by benchmarking outside of your category—learning lessons from some of the businesses we've seen in prior chapters—you can easily apply a customer network strategy that is new to your category and leapfrog ahead of your competition. Imagine what might happen if a car rental company followed the example of Affinia Hotels in offering its customers an easily customized set of low-priced extra amenities.

Ideation and Selection of Concepts

Through the questions above—assessing customer needs, organizational strengths, and competition within your category—you may have already identified several ideas for innovative applications of your chosen strategies by your organization.

Your ideation—the generating of new ideas—should continue in a formal process led by designers, engineers, and marketers from various divisions in your organization. Ideation should draw on your greatest insights into your customer's values and needs, as well as careful benchmarking of other companies. Benchmarking is too frequently conducted by examining only what has been done by competitors in your category. It is often far more productive when you look at organizations outside your industry. For example, if you are looking to create an open competition to benefit your consumer packaged goods brand as part of a COLLABORATE strategy, look at successful network competitions run by other businesses, whether they are clothing makers (Threadless's design competition), online retailers (the Netflix Prize), or automotive designers (the Progressive Automotive X Prize).

Your ideation process should be wide open and yield a wide variety of concepts, many more than you are likely to implement. After ideation is complete, you will need to select which to keep through a process of concept testing. The key areas to test for are:

- *Feasibility:* Can you pull it off? Do you have the required skills and capabilities for the innovation you are considering?

- *Relevance:* How appealing is your idea to your target customer? Don't take your colleagues' word for it. Use simple prototypes to get feedback from real customers on whether your idea will matter enough to shift their behavior.

- *Differentiation:* How different is your idea, really? Has your competition already done something similar? Will your new initiative actually stand out and be noticed by your customers?

- *Sustainable Advantage:* If your idea is a great success, how easy will it be for others to mimic? How long will it take your competitors to knock it off?

- *Return on Investment:* How much resources will your idea require? If it does succeed, will the objectives met more than justify the expense? If one of your objectives is to generate revenue, do you have a clear business model for your idea?

To see how these tests might work, consider IBM's initial concept of building an online game to teach prospects about business process management and to demonstrate IBM's expertise. Sandy Carter, the project leader, needed to ask several questions before committing to the concept. *Feasibility:* Could her team build a game with the right features, or would they need to hire an outside party with game design skills? *Relevance:* How could the game appeal to its two different audiences, business managers and information technology professionals? *Differentiation:* Did a competitor already have a similar game in the marketplace? *Sustainable Advantage:* How hard would it be for a competitor to copy IBM's game? Could IBM maintain an edge by continuing to update the game or by using it to build tighter relationships with the businesses and universities it was targeting? *Return on Investment:* What budget would the project require, and would the potential revenue from new customers justify this expense?

In applying these tests to your project concepts, keep in mind that not every initiative aimed at customer networks needs to be your next front-page, game-changing, blockbuster new product. That type of project can have high rewards but typically carries high risks as well. Other projects may have a more focused scope and audience, but they can easily justify their investment. In general, a broad customer network strategy should incorporate two tiers of initiatives: "Quick Wins" and "Big Plays." Quick Wins are elements of your strategy that are relatively easy, cheap, and certain to be popular. They are likely to rely on smart deployment of existing platforms (such as YouTube and Facebook). Their impact is likely to be either limited (to a specific audience) or of temporary advantage (a great, simple idea that your competitors will start offering within three months, too). But they can be effective in terms of winning customer support, as well as internal support, for more ambitious endeavors. Those ambitious Big Plays are your strategic initiatives that require more investment and more risk but that you expect to have a great impact. Big Plays will be much harder for your competitors to easily knock off because they draw on your unique strengths as an organization. These are the initiatives that typically lead to tangible product or service differentiation or powerful, self-energizing communities and network collaborations.

Step 4: Execution

Once the core strategies have been selected (for example, COLLABORATE) and specific ideas have been ideated and chosen (such as an open competition to develop new variations on your most popular product line), your organization must begin the execution of your customer network strategy. To do so will require an interdisciplinary mindset and a broad range of capabilities. Some of those capabilities may already exist in different domains within your organization. Others may need to be developed.

Leveraging Capabilities across Domains

Customer networks do not fit neatly into one organizational bucket, such as "advertising" or "product engineering." Therefore execution of customer network strategies will require leveraging capabilities from different domains within your organization. These typically include:

- *Customer-facing Domains:* Customer service and call centers; sales, retail, and other front-line positions; e-tail, mobile commerce, and other sales channels

- *Research and Development Domains:* Market research, customer insight, innovation, and product development

- *Outbound Communications Domains:* Advertising, public relations, corporate communications, and internal communications

- *Operational Domains:* Finance, business model planning, human resources, and knowledge management

- *Strategic Leadership Domains:* Market entry, business strategy, and business process management

Developing New Capabilities within the Organization

Customer network strategy may also require the development of new capabilities. This may require the formation of new units or teams within the organization, focused on areas including:

- *Social Media:* A team focused on interacting with customers using new platforms like Facebook, Twitter, or discussion forums (versus traditional call centers or help desks)

- *Idea Capture:* A team capable of capturing, assessing, and directing ideas from customers in order to feed them into product innovation and business process improvement

- *New Media Production:* A team capable of generating regular content for customer networks that is neither traditional advertising (because it focuses on content and utility, not selling messages) nor traditional public relations (because it is aimed at customers instead of the press)

Leadership of this kind of interdisciplinary effort must, of course, operate under someone's sponsorship. Depending on the size of the organization and the scope of the strategy, it may be sponsored by the CEO or president, by the head of a business unit, by a divisional head such as the chief marketing officer (but with clear mandate to tap resources outside the division), or by the head of a new division charged with leading customer network strategy across the organization (we will see examples of this new structure in the next chapter).

Step 5: Measurement

As you begin to execute your customer network strategy, it is essential to have in place a set of metrics to measure the customer response and ultimate impact of your initiatives, as best you can. No measurement system will fully capture the precise monetary benefit of every initiative you undertake, but with careful planning, a good approximation can be made for whatever strategy you implement.

Translating Objectives into Metrics

Measurement should begin with the key objectives which you set for your strategy back in Step 1. At this point, with a full-fledged strategy planned out, you may need to revisit and recalibrate those objectives, as some of them may have proven unfeasible and others may have emerged as additional benefits that you hope to gain from the strategy you have developed.

Whereas your objectives may be very broad ("product differentiation" or "brand engagement"), your metrics need to be specific enough to be measured quantitatively. Typically, one objective may be measured with the use of multiple metrics.

For example, one of Apple's likely objectives for its App Store strategy was to increase the product differentiation of the iPhone during its second year on the market (compared with other smartphones like the BlackBerry). That objective could be measured in terms of perceived differentiation in the minds of consumers (via surveys before and after asking, "How different is the iPhone from other phones?"), as well as in terms of changes in both market share and sales volume of the newly differentiated product.

One of the stated objectives for the Nike+ community was to increase customer engagement with the brand. That objective could be measured by several metrics, including: the amount of time spent on the site per user, the likelihood of users to return and continue to upload their running information on the site, the number of friends users connect to and share running information with on the site, and users' likelihood of clicking on links to learn more about Nike products, sponsorships, and promotions.

Focusing on Impact

Overall, it is important to make sure that metrics focus on results and impact (sales, brand perception, leads generated, reduced customer service costs), and not merely on measuring activity. If you are running an online forum for your brand, and the only thing you are measuring is site visitors, you need to ask, "To what end do you want visitors to come to your site?"

If Intuit's goal with its TurboTax community is to reduce customer service costs, then it should be measuring not just how many customers are visiting the forum but how many questions they are answering for one another, how many times other customers are finding and reading those answers, how favorably they are rating these peer answers ("very helpful" or "not helpful"), and how many fewer customer questions paid employees are having to respond to each week.

If the goal of MyStarbucksIdea.com is to generate valuable product ideas from customers, then Starbucks should be sure to measure not just the number of ideas generated but also the number of ideas that it evaluates and deems worthwhile, the number of ideas that the company implements, and any measure of ROI or new business generated by these ideas.

By shifting metrics from focusing on activity (how many people are joining your forum) to focusing on impact (what that is doing for your business), you can avoid the temptation of judging a customer network strategy on "buzz" and "cool factor," which, in the end, may do little to help your organization.

Measuring over Time

Metrics that are carefully designed and measured both before and after your strategy gets off the ground will help you achieve several important goals.

First, they may help you the sell your strategy internally—as upper management gets a more specific idea of how it will see a return on its investment of resources. Demonstrating how IBM's Innov8 would be measured for its lead generation and market education helps make the case for designing an online game for customers.

Second, knowing the metrics you will be judged by will help you focus the implementation of your strategy on your key objectives and not just on the technology or on interesting but ultimately diverting initiatives. IBM's goals kept the focus of its game design on what mattered most: educating and holding the attention of prospective customers.

As your strategy is implemented over time, good metrics will help you measure its success and ROI in order to determine whether to continue it, wind it down, or increase your investment in the strategy. By seeing the results of the first generation of Innov8, IBM knew that it was worth continuing the game and building another generation aimed at additional customer segments.

Finally, metrics should include some qualitative measures (such as open-ended questions and feedback from participants), which, along with your quantitative metrics, may help you to improve, learn from, and build upon the initial success of your strategy.

We have now seen a five-step process for planning and implementing an overall customer network strategy: from setting objectives to customer segmentation and positioning, strategy selection and ideation, execution, and finally measurement. You should now be ready to begin implementing a customer network strategy in your organization.

As we have seen, customer network strategy does not sit comfortably in one division of a company. In fact, a true customer network orientation requires a broad shift in the culture of the organization, a way of doing business that differs greatly from the processes and organizations that arose to meet the age of mass markets.

In the future, the rising influence of customer networks and the spread of new and emerging technologies may lead to a very different type of organizational structure than we have seen in the businesses, governments, and nonprofits of the past fifty years. To get a sense of what that may look like, we will want to first look at the nature of a few large companies that have already begun focusing on customer networks broadly throughout their organization. By looking at these and other cases, we may get a sense of what is coming in the customer networked organization of the future.

CHAPTER 9

Creating the Customer Network– Focused Organization

The rise of customer networks is very recent. Yet we can already see how networks have begun to transform many aspects of organizations, from communications to innovation to strategic planning. The scope and impact of customer networks are not confined to any single department, though, as they reshape marketing, public affairs, engineering, sales, senior leadership, and more. What then are the implications of customer networks for the shape of organizations as a whole? And how will the organizations of the future change to adapt to them?

From a Customer Focus to a Customer Network Focus

At the end of the twentieth century, most thinking on how organizations should relate to their key constituencies was embodied in the notion of the "customer focused organization." Within academic literature, this concept (also known as customer orientation or market orientation) was studied to identify the factors most important for organizational success. In an influential article synthesizing research on the subject, Ajay Kohli and Bernard Jaworski identified three key elements of customer focused organizations:

- *Intelligence Generation:* The ability to gather information about customers and use it to identify current needs and anticipate future needs. Intelligence generation may employ traditional market research tools such as surveys and focus groups, secondary research such as industry reports and databases, and informal contacts with customers and business partners.

- *Intelligence Dissemination:* The ability to communicate the findings of intelligence generation among a company's divisions. Intelligence dissemination may include newsletters and internal training programs, as well as casual mechanisms such as interdepartmental lunches and water cooler conversations.

- *Responsiveness to Intelligence:* The ability to respond quickly and efficiently to the customer needs uncovered by intelligence generation. Responses can include a choice of which customers to focus on, the development of new goods and services to meet the needs of those customers, and effective marketing and promotion of those goods and services to them.[1]

These three elements remain important to any organization today. And for their own era, they offered a fairly comprehensive summary of how organizations might focus on customers' needs. But they also reveal how the model of a customer focused organization arose to suit the reality of customers in an earlier age. In this model, intelligence is only gathered *from* customers, who remain passive actors. Within the organization, interaction and knowledge-sharing are based on periodic broadcasts (*dissemination*) between company "silos" that otherwise go about their business separately (sales, marketing, engineering, and so on). Responses to customer needs are carried out by the organization, with no further input from the customers themselves. All three elements, then, reflect a model that was created in the age of one-to-one communications, when customers were isolated from each other, unable to coordinate, and easily reached by mass media.

Now, of course, we live in a different age, one transformed by the use of many-to-many communications tools by customers. No longer are customers passive bystanders in the research, planning, and development of new products and services, waiting patiently for companies to roll them out to a mass market and trumpet them with blasts of one-way communications. The Internet's many-to-many tools have given rise to customer networks that are dynamic, interconnected, and able to act independently of the strategies and plans of businesses. This age demands a different model for companies: a model of a customer network–focused organization.

What would a customer network–focused organization look like? We do not yet have a clear picture. Few organizations have arisen under the pervasive influence of customer networks, and fewer still have grown to a large size in industries outside of digital media. But we can glimpse the future by looking carefully at established businesses that have been particularly forward-leaning. These companies have embraced customer network strategies broadly—not just in a single experiment but in multiple initiatives, and across the divisions of their company. In these organizations a vision of customer networks is pervasive and emanates from the most senior leadership. These organizations, for different reasons, started thinking about networks earlier than others and have made networks central to their strategy. By looking at three such vanguard organizations, we can gain insights into what the customer network–focused organizations of the future will look like.

Dell: Trial by Fire

Computer manufacturer Dell started thinking seriously about customer networks early on because it had to. Starting in 2005, Dell faced two trials by fire (one figurative, one literal). First, there was the storm of complaints by bloggers, set off by Jeff Jarvis's blog post about customer service in "Dell Hell," and spread rapidly by a host of other bloggers as the company failed to react because of a hands-off policy toward blogs. Within a year, the company was facing another public relations nightmare in the form of a laptop that was photographed bursting into flames owing to a faulty battery. By then, the company had already made a dramatic shift in policy, having formed a "SWAT team" of the best and brightest members of its tech support division to contribute to the customer forums on Dell.com (which had been running since 1996) and to reach out to external blogs and forums. This allowed for a rapid response to the flaming laptop incident (a quick "autopsy" led Dell to pull its laptops much faster than competitors' laptops facing the same problem), which garnered respect from the network of bloggers and customers.

Under direction from the top, Dell began building on its blogger outreach program to find new strategies for connecting with customer networks. Urging the company toward a wider embrace of customer networks, founder and CEO Michael Dell spurred his employees: "These [customer] conversations are going to occur whether you like it or not. Do you want to be part of that or not?"[2]

As the company followed Michael Dell's directive to join the conversation in customer networks, it continued to launch new initiatives: Direct2Dell became the company's own blog, run out of corporate communications, with topics that quickly branched out beyond technical support to such matters as discussing the company's shifting retail strategy. By 2007, teams working in tech support and in community support were fused into a new "communities and conversations" division with a mandate to generate new ideas. "We created it as a greenhouse for a whole bunch of quick experiments," says Richard Binhammer, a manager who was instrumental in the effort. "We wanted to fertilize new ideas, let things die if they didn't work, consolidate others, and keep learning."[3]

Among the ideas that came out of the greenhouse was Dell IdeaStorm, the online platform for customers to propose new product and service innovations for the company (discussed in chapter 6). Another initiative was digitalnomads.com (described in chapter 3), the content and community site for members of the laptop-toting mobile workforce. When Twitter became popular among its customers, Dell launched Twitter accounts focusing on such topics as enterprise servers (@dellservergeek) and the education market (@edu4u), as well as personal accounts, such as Binhammer's own @richardatdell. The @delloutlet Twitter account was launched as a sales channel to announce discounted inventory, and by 2009 it had made $6.5 million in sales.[4] Numerous other initiatives have included Dell's community forums (where customers answer most of each other's questions, so Dell doesn't have to), and the environmentally focused site regeneration.org.

Dell had always been a very customer-focused organization because of its direct-selling model of building computers to order for consumers. In 2009, Michael Dell reorganized the company into four units based on their key customer markets: consumers, small and midsized business, large enterprises, and public sector and government. By then, Dell's customer networks focus was ingrained throughout the company and no longer resided in any single place. Established initiatives were therefore taken out of the greenhouse and "planted" into each of the four business units with appropriate teams and tech skills to support them. A smaller team was left behind in a streamlined version of the greenhouse under the new name of Social Media & Community. "We wanted to make social media not a special expertise, but part of the whole direct business model and how Dell connects with customers," Binhammer told me. "It needs to be throughout the organization. That's why the greenhouse team has shrunk, as it has expanded and pushed out into the business units."[5] The focus of the streamlined greenhouse was on nurturing new innovations, identifying best practices, driving adoption and coordination across business units, and developing governance and metrics.

Those metrics vary widely, depending on the business objectives of a given project.

Dell has seen many returns on investment for its focus on customer networks, including: cost savings in customer service, improved brand reputation and sentiment, and the ability to serve as an early warning system for any business, product, or customer issues that the company may face. Most important, perhaps, are the benefits of a general orientation toward listening to customer networks. Combining forums, communities, Twitter, and more, Dell has over 3.5 million follower and subscriber connections—all with customers who have opted in to connect with the company. No wonder it is the second most mentioned brand on the Web, with over four thousand mentions a day.

SAP: An Ecosystems Strategy

Another company that has embraced a far-reaching focus on customer networks is SAP, the global leader in database and resource-management software for businesses. Like Dell, SAP's focus on customer networks has begun to reshape the very structure of its organization.

SAP's focus on customer networks may not be surprising, given the extremely Web- and tech-savvy population that it deals with every day, from IT departments of its corporate customers to independent developers writing software to work on top of SAP's systems, service companies that specialize in installing and customizing SAP's software for businesses in every industry, and companies developing complementary software (such as Adobe) or hardware (such as Dell) that must run effectively with SAP's enterprise databases.

SAP's focus on customer networks reflects something else, too. Much more than its direct competitors, SAP has chosen to pursue a business strategy focused on collaborating with this ecosystem of developers, service providers, and software and hardware companies.

Rather than narrowly defining and focusing on its own piece of the market, SAP has focused on collaborating with partners, sharing knowledge, and thereby increasing the value of its products and their utility for customers. In essence, SAP's very business strategy has been modeled on a network, in which its own company is linked to a web of nodes representing all the other businesses that are critical to the information technology success of SAP's customers.

As a result, customer network strategy has a special place at SAP. Rather than being a subject that is managed by a division like marketing or sales, SAP has created its own stand-alone division called SAP Global Ecosystems. Although smaller in staff (with approximately five hundred employees, including those in the field, or 1 percent of the company's employees), Global Ecosystems sits parallel to the four other divisions of the company: Marketing, Sales, Product Development, and Support. The head of SAP Global Ecosystems reports to the CEO along with the heads of the other major divisions.

This offers many advantages, not the least of which is direct access to top leadership. It also means that SAP's customer network strategy is not filtered through the lens of marketing, product support, or any other division. "If communities are viewed just as a marketing activity within an organization, then other channels are disadvantaged," says Mark Yolton, senior vice president within Global Ecosystems. "Other opportunities for communities—for product insight, for innovation, for product support, or direct customer feedback—are disadvantaged."[6] Part of this is a matter of measurement. If customer networks are the responsibility of marketing, then they will be measured only in terms of marketing objectives. By placing Global Ecosystems outside any single division and tasking it to support the goals of all of them, SAP has made it the new division's responsibility to connect with every stakeholder in the outside world and to feed back the results of those connections to every part of the organization without bias.

This approach can be seen in the many initiatives emerging from Global Ecosystems. The largest initiative, which Yolton heads, is the SAP Community Network, home to nearly two million customers, employees, partners, analysts, and thought leaders in the market who influence the purchases of others. Many of these members have been hired, invited to pitch for business, or promoted within their own company based on the recognition they earned in the SAP Community Network. Other initiatives by SAP Global Ecosystems have included official corporate Twitter accounts, such as @SAPnews, @SAP network, and @SAPcrm, along with over two hundred personal accounts by employees like Yolton who identify themselves as SAP employees and use their accounts to track what is being said about SAP online and join in where appropriate. Docupedia is SAP's new documentation wiki, which hundreds of customers are contributing to, thereby providing product documentation that is most suited to their own uses and needs. SAP is also an investor in InnoCentive (described in chapter 7), with which it has launched an online Innovation and Technology Pavilion that invites outsiders to propose solutions to such questions as how best to demonstrate the power of SAP's software to manipulate billions of records of information.

SAP Global Ecosystems has yielded important benefits in the efficiency of customer service. Consulting-type questions not focused on core support issues (such as "What's a best practice for using this in my own industry?" or "What did I do wrong in this planning?") are more quickly, effectively, and cheaply answered by peers within the SAP network. Another major benefit has been in market insight—allowing the company to better understand what customers are looking for in products, what their contracts will allow, and what tools can support their partners. A third major benefit has been in expanding the global reach and speed of SAP's enterprise with a global network of touch points to listen to, respond to, and engage with customers. When a new product is not adopted as quickly as expected, SAP

Global Ecosystems will reach out to the right customers and influencers and make sure they have enough information and answers to questions, dramatically accelerating product adoption in the marketplace.

Perhaps the biggest impact of SAP Global Ecosystems, though, is in breaking down barriers between the company and its many types of external customers and constituencies. "We have become a much more porous organization," says Yolton. "There is much less of a wall between our company and the enterprises we engage with."[7]

Obama '08: Community Organizer in Chief

The remarkable role of customer networks in Barack Obama's 2008 campaign for the presidency stemmed in large measure from the candidate's roots in community organizing in the housing projects of Chicago. Even before his candidacy was launched, it was decided that the Obama campaign would rely to an exceptional degree on using the power of new many-to-many communications technologies to extend the principles of local community organizing to a national scale.

To do so, the campaign hired Blue State Digital, whose partners had begun developing such tools four years previously while working for the presidential campaigns of Howard Dean and Wesley Clark. After the 2004 election, they joined forces to form Blue State Digital and were hired by the Democratic National Committee (by then headed by Dean) to build Web-based tools to deliver on the DNC's new fifty-state organizing strategy. In 2004, Dean had used Meetup.com to organize supporters on a local level, but all the data on this grassroots network stayed in the hands of Meetup. To tap into the real power of its network, Obama's campaign would need a custom platform, my.BarackObama.com. The campaign had more fans on Facebook, but it was able to raise far more money per capita on its own platform than on any other network. More data about members allowed the campaign to shape each fundraising "ask" around the personal activities of different members.

More effective fundraising was the first visible impact of the campaign's new approach to networks. Another major impact was in organizing, particularly as the contest for the Democratic nomination stretched on into a full fifty-state contest, going where no Democratic presidential campaign had gone in recent times. "When Idaho became relevant," says Thomas Gensemer, managing partner of Blue State Digital, "no one had planned for that in their budgeting scenarios."[8] Hillary Clinton was forced to pull a campaign team member from a tough contest in vote-rich Pennsylvania to fly out to Idaho for a traditional campaign outreach, talking to local labor unions. Clinton herself had to take time to fly in to drum up support. By contrast, the Obama campaign was able to use its digital network to quickly identify those grassroots supporters who were already most active in Idaho and use them to coordinate meetings across the state. It was a much more efficient organizing model.

The success of the campaign's network strategy may have had much do with its role within the organization as well. Joe Rospars, who was in charge of the digital component of the campaign, reported directly to David Plouffe, the campaign manager (the CEO or COO equivalent). As a result, Rospars sat in on all top campaign meetings alongside the finance director, fields director, and communications director. Hillary Clinton's campaign, by contrast, had very talented technology people, but not one was represented in the senior staff or garnered the influence or budget that comes with that position.

"Traditionally, the digital group is brought into a campaign by finance or by the fields operations," says Gensemer. "The problem is, if you don't have a seat at the table with top leadership, you have to deal with competing interests."[9] This affects what the customer network strategy is measured and judged by. If it is run out of finance, the goal may be to focus on numbers of new donors brought in each week; an effort run out of the fields operation will be asked to deliver on the number of volunteers signed up. For Obama's digital campaign, all of these goals were placed on an equal level of importance. Most important, the customers themselves were not put in silos—judged to be either "donors" or "volunteers" or "activists" when, in fact, a single supporter might be all three at the same time.

The Three Elements of the Customer Network–Focused Organization

In each of these cases—Dell, SAP, and the Obama campaign—the focus on customer networks is central to the overarching strategy and vision of the organization and is supported with leadership from the top. We probably have yet to see a full picture of the customer network–focused organization of the future. But many of the differences from the *customer* focused organization are already clear. New organizations will need to do more than simply *generate, disseminate,* and *respond* to market intelligence. Three new critical elements will define the customer network–focused organization. The organization will be: *borderless, collaborative,* and *pervasively networked.*

Borderless

For the customer network–focused organization, there will be fewer barriers both between the company and its customers and between the company and the other organizations it interacts with.

In the traditional organization, customers were clearly and distinctly outside the organization. The organization captured intelligence about customers and then set to work using that information internally. Customers acted as an information input and, later, as the object of product and marketing outputs.

Boundaries are much more porous in a customer network–focused organization. Technologies are used to bridge between the company's employees and a diverse range of constituencies, including business partners of all kinds and end consumers. A constant level of interaction and exchange connects these nodes in the business's "ecosystem" and blurs the lines between who is inside and outside the company. This can be seen in Dell's constant interaction with its 3.5 million connected customers or the thousands of bloggers on the SAP Community Network or the dynamic participation of millions of supporters in the Obama campaign. The net result is to blur the lines between inside and outside of the customer network–focused organization.

Collaborative

In the customer network–focused organization, interaction with customers is highly collaborative. Rather than simply listening to the company's marketing messages and choosing whether to respond or purchase a product, customers are expected to interact and (to varying degrees) participate.

In the Obama campaign, supporters were not just sending checks and planting lawn signs; they were organizing campaign events, recruiting other volunteers, and bringing the campaign to new primary states before the professional staff even arrived on the ground. In SAP's innovation pavilion and Dell's IdeaStorm site, customers contribute to the development of new products, business ideas, and marketing messages.

The customer network–focused organization does not just observe customers and then plan and develop products and ideas on its own; it actually listens to the customers' perspectives and finds ways to involve them directly in the planning. This does not mean that the organization relinquishes control; management must still make the decisions, and the company's every strategy will not be put to a vote by customers visiting its Web site. But planning, innovation, and communications will be much more iterative. Rather than getting something "perfect" and then rolling it out to the market, organizations will rely on customer input, begin developing ideas, test those ideas for customer feedback, evolve them further, launch a new project or product in beta, and quickly incorporate feedback and new ideas to evolve it rapidly.

Pervasively Networked

The focus on customer networks will be pervasive throughout the entire organization. It will be incorporated in the culture and practice of every division—as in the teams embedded in each of Dell's four divisions and the independent SAP Global Ecosystems division that works will all the other business divisions. Digital networking tools will not be confined to the information technology department. Nor will they sit tucked away in a single department such as marketing or customer service within a company, or fundraising or volunteer organizing within a nonprofit.

The focus on networks will also pervade the internal work and communications of the organization. The traditional customer focused organization relied on a model of "dissemination," whereby information was shared in occasional broadcasts among the separate units of a company. By contrast, the customer network–focused organization will use many-to-many communications tools to continuously connect these units and share knowledge among them in an internal network of employees. Sometimes known as "enterprise 2.0," this internal use of networks harnesses collaborative tools for everything from threaded conversations (via tools such as Google Wave) to collaborative project management (such as Zoho Projects), recruiting employees via social networks (such as LinkedIn), large-scale brainstorming and idea-generation (such as mind-mapping and idea jams), and advanced systems for enterprisewide sharing of market intelligence. The net result is an organization that looks as much like a network on the inside as its customers do on the outside.

The Near Future of Seven Industries

What would an organization built around these three elements look like? How would a large organization that arises in the age of customer networks evolve to be borderless, collaborative, and pervasively connected? The details will vary depending on the industry, of course, yet they are easy enough to imagine based on trends that are already becoming apparent.

Fashion

In the past, businesses in the fashion industry were built on the strength of design skills (for example, Prada), the ability to manufacture and project an alluring brand image (for example, Victoria's Secret), or supply chain prowess that could bring down costs and bring products to market quickly with good inventory management (for example, Zara). The next big fashion house, though, may look more like the user-generated T-shirt company Threadless, but on a much larger scale.

A customer network–focused fashion company would thrive by connecting customers directly with designers, marketers, and retailers. Customers will have opportunities to preview and vote on new product designs, to see what clothing the friends in their social networks are buying or looking at, and to contribute design ideas in open contests (although most products will continue to be designed by employees of the company). Selected products will be available for custom alteration in fit, fabric, and color for those who want a unique statement without paying haute-couture prices.

New fashions, and the image of their brands, will not be based just on visual design but will be connected to pop culture and lifestyle trends in sports, health, technology, and environmental concerns. Fashion innovations could range from wearable technology to biometric sensors. Fashion brands may also bleed over into media, with sponsored content showcased online and personal images, stories, and videos contributed by loyal fans. These same active core users will have the chance to weigh in on early design ideas from the company, connect with one another in exclusive forums, and receive discounts, event invitations, and other perks. Like the street teams who thrive on and support up-and-coming rock bands, the customers will feel a sense of ownership in the fashion brand that brings them into its network.

Retail

Traditionally, retail chains attract customers through a combination of product selection, staff training, ambience, and perhaps a sense of community among those who gather there (think of Starbucks or your favorite independent bookstore). With competition from increasingly facile e-commerce, a customer network–focused retailer will need to attract customers to shop in person by building a sense of community that bridges both physical and virtual space.

Arriving at your favorite wine store or coffee shop will begin with a digital "check in" (as on the FourSquare mobile social network) to see which of your friends have visited recently, to earn loyalty points, and to gain access to complimentary Wi-Fi in the store. Loyal users may gain more points (toward discounts or rewards) by synching their social networking profiles to anonymously share what they are listening to on Pandora, reading on their Kindles, or watching on Netflix.

With local staff in the store joining the online space, a real online + offline community can begin to emerge. Rather than relying on a corporate marketing department to pick recommended books to promote at the counter, visitors may browse a virtual bookshelf that includes different "shelves" showcasing picks by their friends, by the local staff behind the counter, or by the community of customers frequenting the local store (much like the movie suggestions offered by

Netflix that show what others in your zip code are renting). In-store events—classes, tastings, reading groups—may be organized by the store or by the customers based on topics of interest, much like a Meetup gathering. In addition to finding out about the real people on both sides of the serving counter, customers can submit product or recipe ideas for voting and inclusion in the store ("This month only: Karen's cranberry pumpkin bread, $6.99").

Automotive

Traditionally, automotive companies included customers in research and then relied on engineering prowess and outsourced production to compete with products that could be marketed on a mass scale. In a customer network–focused car company, the customer (be it a single driver or the purchaser of a corporate fleet) will have more insight and input into the entire business process. Blogs and other digital content from the company will yield greater transparency and insight into design plans, while virtual test driving experiences will let customers know more about their prospective purchases before they get behind the wheel.

Driving itself will be a much more networked experience, with voice interfaces allowing drivers to access information ("Find me Mexican restaurants ahead with an easy off-ramp from the highway and good reviews") while keeping their hands on the wheel and their eyes on a dashboard that measures carbon emissions as well as fuel consumption. Because cars are such a high-involvement purchase, customers will have the opportunities to customize detailing before they purchase and share their favorite driving experiences in social networks after taking the car home. Loyal customers will have the chance to preview new models, vote on the colors to be offered for next year's lineup, and request the features they most want to be included in the standard packages. Open-source design competitions will allow hundreds of design enthusiasts to submit their favorite concepts for a unique chassis design, with the top winner each year produced for a limited run.

Pharmaceutical

Pharmaceutical companies have traditionally focused solely on their proprietary research to develop unique medicines and therapies that can differentiate themselves in clinical trials. These innovations will continue to be critical. But as the health care industry shifts from pay-for-treatment toward paying for patient outcomes, it will be increasingly important for pharma companies to focus not just on the chemistry of a drug but on how it is or is not successfully integrated into a patient's life.

The customer network–focused pharmaceutical company will develop effective content, training, guidance, and mobile connections between patients, doctors, and researchers in order to ensure that every new therapy has the best chance of success in real patients' lives. Online communities of patients with the same disease, as well as online doctor communities, will provide points of contact for the company to listen, learn, and find out how better to assist in patient health care. They will also help companies understand better the lifestyle issues that shape disease treatment.

Researchers within the company will reach out to scientists around the world to collaborate on key science problems via platforms for sharing or open competitions to find the best solution to a problem. Big decisions about which areas to invest in for new research (with drug development pipelines that span a decade of more) will be made not just with the knowledge of a few corporate strategists but by tapping thousands of points of market intelligence and harnessing the collective opinions of researchers and doctors throughout the company and at laboratories and universities around the world.

Media

The traditional media company was based on holding a near monopoly in the mass distribution of content and relied on teams of creators and editors to produce as much content as possible for as broad an audience as possible. The customer network–focused media business will focus much less on distribution, since that will be much less differentiating in an environment that is open to anyone with a blog. Instead, the business will attract an audience both by finding areas of unique content to produce and by developing a curatorial relationship with independent content producers (of blogs, podcasts, videos, games, and so on) whom it may select, feature, sponsor, or recommend.

The audience will be the biggest source of this independent content, whether it is sending in eyewitness footage of breaking news, contributing to blogs and customer forums, or voting to pick selections for the media company's "best of the year" compilation. A key source of value for a media company will be in artfully moderating the forums and online discussions of its customers, so that genuinely interesting dialogue and exchanges of ideas float to the top, aided by voting by the customers themselves. As customers share their network profiles, media companies can show them what others in their social network are reading, watching, or listening to and can offer content that is selected to match the customers' tastes (as well as a few surprises). Media brands will no longer define themselves by format (magazine, radio, TV), as every publisher will rely on a mix of media and will make its content available anywhere and on any device (although greater access may require a premium price).

Philanthropy

Traditionally, philanthropies focused on telling their customers just enough to get alarmed about the problems of the world and funneling them into a role as small donor, volunteer, or large donor. The customer network–focused philanthropy will seek to build much more active and informed relationships with supporters and will offer them more ways to contribute.

Supporters will have the opportunity to organize fundraising events at their schools, community groups, or places of worship. With content produced and curated by the philanthropy, they may choose to delve deeper into the issues (what microfinance is, what medical needs are in a war zone, and so on) than the bullet points in a public service announcement. Those who volunteer on aid projects will be able to easily share their experiences and success stories with others online and contribute to the stories that the organization uses to market itself to new supporters. Other supporters may use digital tools to volunteer small increments of time working online or choose which projects they want to fund with their money. Open calls for collaboration will be used to develop cheap, effective solutions to pressing social needs (whether a solar-powered flashlight to reduce kerosene consumption or more effective mosquito netting to prevent malaria). And digital mapping and data visualization tools will allow different philanthropies and nongovernmental organizations to share data and identify emerging trends and pressing needs.

Education

Traditional educational institutions have focused on the unique value of face-to-face learning and collaboration among students and teachers at the same physical campus. Learning materials (especially in primary and secondary schooling) were largely limited to mass-produced textbooks, and teachers developed curriculum in relative isolation, sharing ideas only with those in their department.

In the customer network–focused educational institution, students will be able to take advantage of the benefits of virtual collaboration and instruction, as well as face-to-face learning. Online video libraries like the Khan Academy (described in chapter 3) will replace rote lectures in many subjects, freeing teachers to focus more on interactive learning. Classes in core subjects such as math and reading will benefit from the face-to-face interaction of a physical classroom. But at other periods of each day, students may use digital tools (e-readers, video conferencing, and online collaborations) to participate in virtual classes that can focus on much more specific topics and student interests. A student in rural Nebraska may be the only child in that school taking a course on frog ecosystem preservation or the theology of Hinduism in Southeast Asia, but he or she can easily participate in a class with twenty other students in other cities and states, all taught by a teacher with the specialized knowledge to develop an age-appropriate curriculum. Students will learn to use video, audio, mapping, photos, and text in school, but as tools for critical thinking and analysis. Class participation grades will reflect both in-person and online discussions, and students will learn the media literacy skills to find their own content sources and evaluate them for their perspectives and merits.

Students will not be the only ones working collaboratively with digital tools, however. Teachers will use blogs, wikis, and online forums to create, find and share curriculum and lesson plans with one another (using Creative Commons licensing) and to bookmark and vote on the sources that are most appropriate for teaching current issues to students at various grade levels. Instead of scouring government Web sites for a single good article on climate change that is up to date and appropriate for a sixth-grade audience, teachers will be able to easily see what others in their network have already found and shared and to comment and vote on what did or didn't work when they brought it into the classroom. As students and teachers collaborate and learn with peers both in their home community and across the world, translation-powered learning tools will allow them to gain a sense of the global environment the students will need to live in and contribute to as adults.

Why Organizations Are Holding Back

You may call me a dreamer, but the scenarios above are hardly radical or beyond the ken of innovative leaders today. Why then have we not yet seen more customer network–focused organizations? Most of the platforms described in the scenarios above (social networks, collaboration tools, mobile social networking, and so on) already exist. All of the underlying technology is already here, and much of it requires only modest financial investment. What is required of established organizations, though, is organizational change. And that is usually the most difficult investment to make in a large, legacy institution.

While newcomers and start-ups see opportunities for new businesses and new relationships with customers, many older organizations see that their familiar ways of doing business are threatened. For established organizations, the rise of customer networks—and the uncertainty, disruption, and change they pose—brings a great deal of fear. For leaders hoping to thrive in the new era of customer networks, this may pose serious obstacles to organizational change.

The first obstacle is a desire for control. Managers see the open nature of social media and hear the voices of customer networks, and they are afraid to enter into an environment in which they cannot maintain complete control over their organization, their brand, and what their own employees might say. A 2009 report on the use of social media by major brands revealed that Toyota, the world's largest automaker, had strongly resisted the idea of having a blog. Instead, the company had tasked its three-person (!) social media team with using YouTube and Twitter to broadcast the content already being developed by its marketing and corporate communications department.[10] At the same time that movie and television celebrities were using Twitter to stoke the eager attention of millions of fans, the National Football League passed rules forbidding its players to post to Twitter, or even have an assistant post to their accounts for them, for ninety minutes before or after a game. The *Washington Post* passed rules prohibiting staff and reporters from expressing personal opinions in social networks, lest they jeopardize the perceived impartiality of the *Post*. Of course, any organization should apply their rules for confidentiality and disclosure to employees in new media, just as they do in any other communications medium. But for an organization to simply reject online conversation is not an option. The fact is that organizations have already lost absolute control of their message in a world of customer networks. Employees, customers, business partners, and anonymous voices will have their voices in the mix of social media, and silencing a company's own voice will only make matters worse.

Another fear holding back many organizations from embracing customer networks is a reaction against anything "not invented here." In a traditional organization with a clear boundary between company and customers, the expectation is that all innovation, ideas, and value will be created inside the organization. Ideas generated by customers or outside parties are either ignored or seen as a threat to their intellectual property. In 2008, toymaker Hasbro discovered that two fans of their Scrabble board game, brothers Rajat and Jayant Agarwalla of Calcutta, had developed a Facebook application, Scrabulous, based on the game. The application allowed users to play Scrabble with friends online via the social network. Hasbro had failed to capitalize on the potential for social network versions of its game properties, and it watched as Scrabulous quickly attracted hundreds of thousands of users, becoming the most popular application on Facebook. Rather than embrace the Agarwalla brothers or hire them to head up a new social gaming unit for the company, Hasbro slapped them with a lawsuit. The Agarwallas withdrew their game from Facebook to howls of protest from online fans. Hasbro later launched its own version of Scrabble for Facebook but attracted far fewer users.[11]

To innovate in the future, companies like Hasbro will need to be more open to ideas that emerge outside their organization.

A third fear preventing many established organizations from embracing customer networks is the fear of letting go of old business models or experimenting with new sources of revenue. A hundred-year-old newspaper company (with significant assets and personnel invested in physical printing and distribution) will find it much harder to consider moving to a digital-only distribution model than will a start-up publisher like the Huffington Post. A wide range of industries that have been disrupted by digital technologies and open information flows have resisted investing in new, uncertain business models as they watch the profits of their old business models dwindle inexorably. The question for any such organization today is, "What business are you really in?" Is the *New York Times* really in the newspaper business or the journalism business? Is CBS really in the business of broadcasting content via affiliate television stations or the business of creating premium content to distribute in any media that will attract viewers, advertisers, and potentially other sorts of revenue? One reason that Hasbro was out-innovated by its customers with the Scrabulous game may have been that Hasbro still thought it was in the business of making board games rather than the business of making social entertainment experiences.

Cultural Traits That Organizations Will Need

The world is changing fast. Long-standing institutions and organizations of all kinds will need to reorient themselves quickly if they wish to avoid profound disruption and even irrelevance. For any organization today, networks are the future face of their customers, be they business customers, end consumers, voters, or donors.

To succeed in building the customer network–focused organization may require, first of all, new cultural attitudes within the organization. More than new technologies, or new tech-savvy employees, these cultural qualities will be the key to building an organization focused on customer networks.

Interdisciplinary Thinking

Any organization seeking to thrive in a world of customer networks will require a capacity for interdisciplinary thinking. This will mean no longer viewing their own organization as a set of vertical, highly separate silos, like marketing, sales, and product development. For decades, this kind of division has brought structure and efficiency to large organizations, but it has imposed costs as well. In the era of customer networks, the costs of lack of communication between silos are too high to sustain. Specialties and focused disciplines will remain, but they need to be crisscrossed by network ties and interdisciplinary collaboration within the enterprise.

Some of this will be as simple as bringing people together in the same room—so that if a public relations crisis is erupting in a large company, someone thinks to invite the human resources department, which manages internal communications to the thousands of employees inside the organization (who are no doubt sharing their own point of view on the crisis in social media). Some of it will involve using collaborative digital tools inside the organization, so that a formal meeting or interdivisional task force does not need to be called before insights can be shared between the company scientist attending an academic conference, the sales person hearing customer product requests, and the design team working on the next product prototype. Some of it will require insisting that outside partners take an interdisciplinary approach as well—that everything digital is not left to the advertising agency, while the company's public relations agency continues to focus on an old mass-media model for communications.

Companies may choose to restructure their formal divisions

around their customers, as Michael Dell did in reorganizing his company into divisions focused on large enterprise, small business, end consumers, and government customers. Others may keep organizing themselves around traditional divisions such as marketing and sales. In either case, they must use internal networks to foster pervasive connections among these divisions. That will require that the company's focus on customer networks be interdisciplinary as well. This may be achieved with a special unit like SAP Global Ecosystems that has a seat at the top of the organization. Or it may be that the customer network focus is diffused throughout every division, as at Dell, but with an incubator or greenhouse dedicated to innovating new best practices. Whatever the approach, the role of customer networks must become a reason for organizations to become more interdisciplinary, not less.

Trust-Based Leadership

In the chaotic and messy world of combat, every military officer knows the truism "No plan survives contact with the enemy." The same can be extended to organizations in our digital age: "No detailed plan survives contact with the customer network." If an organization is to be truly borderless and powered by collaboration between customers, partners, and diverse employee groups, then a new kind of leadership will be required.

In their book *Made to Stick*, Dan and Chip Heath describe the military leadership concept known as "commander's intent." This approach to leadership does not rely on a detailed plan laying out exactly how an operation is to proceed. Instead, the commander's intent focuses on a spare statement of the most crucial goal of the mission and the means chosen to achieve that goal. The point is to identify the idea at the core of the commander's strategy and communicate it in such a way that when the unexpected happens, personnel at every level can make independent decisions that are aligned by a shared understanding of that strategy.[12]

Leadership in networks, indeed in any collaborative situation, hinges on trust: trusting those you work with and ensuring that they are able to act independently and maintain that trust. Leaders must realize that they will not be able to plan for everything that will happen or sign off on every decision that will have to be made in a dynamic and fluid environment. Leadership therefore requires trust in the independent action of others.

In a network focused organization, there is no option for a command-and-control approach to leadership. Managers can't order their business partners around, and neither can they order around their customers. They can't succeed by trying to control everything their employees do either. It is simply not possible for a large organization to monitor and manage every employee utterance and interaction in networks by running it through a traditional corporate communications vetting process. Businesses that try to take this approach to social media wind up in the hypocritical position of proclaiming their great openness to customers in new media while being unable to respond to some of the simplest queries from people outside the organization (a failure I witnessed several times in researching this book). Employee guidance on communications should focus not on prohibitions, control, and vetting for the utmost consistency. It should rely on employee responsibility (posting online is tantamount to speaking to the press), disclosure (always let people know what company you work for), and knowledge at all times of the commander's intent: what are we doing, why are we doing it, and how can you help support this as part of our network.

Moderation Skills

As many organizations have by now realized, simply opening your virtual door to customer networks is not enough to ensure a thriving and valuable conversation or collaboration. Without the right skills for moderating the give-and-take of an open network, an admirable attempt at openness can run into a lot of unintended consequences.

When NASA announced a call for Americans to vote on a new name for the Space Station module formerly known as Node 3, it may have seemed like a simple way to invite citizen participation. Once comedian Stephen Colbert heard of the contest, however, he quickly enlisted his online fan community to swamp NASA with votes for naming the space module after himself. When the contest ended, the write-ins for "Colbert" came in first among over a million votes cast. Fortunately, NASA had reserved the right to make a final choice from among the top vote getters. They chose "Tranquility"—a name that was also suggested by voters and received many votes—but they made a point to name the Space Station's exercise machine the "Combined Operational Load Bearing External Resistance Treadmill," or C.O.L.B.E.R.T.

Less careful leaps into customer-led branding have yielded more embarrassing consequences. When Skittles sought to embrace its customers on social media, it temporarily turned its home page into a real-time search of everything being said about the brand on Twitter. It wasn't long before pranksters began filling the home page with a stream of vulgarities and criticism of the brand, forcing the company to cancel the experiment.

As organizations reach out to customer networks, they will need more than a willing and open mind; they will also need the skills to moderate the often unruly give-and-take of online communities. This begins with knowing and being clear about your rules of engagement, as NASA was. Another key part of playing the moderator in a network is knowing how to keep things civil. Requiring participants to identify themselves with a verified name is often effective, particularly for internal networks such as employees. At the same time, to keep interactions honest and valuable, participants should not have to fear undue policing and punishment for simply expressing an opinion. Skillful moderation requires keeping all participants invested in participating; companies like SAP and Microsoft use nonmonetary reward points and recognition to encourage and validate the contributions of their network members. And moderation requires the ability to tap appropriate resources, feeding questions and new ideas from customers to the right subject-matter experts within the organization.

In many cases, the biggest challenge of moderation is simply to separate the network's wheat from its chaff, drawing out the most valuable ideas and voices from a crowded conversation. When a blog post receives ten comments from readers, it has sparked a conversation. When it receives a thousand comments, it has sparked a problem. The author will never be able to read through and consider each of them. Sites such as the *New York Times* attempt to tackle this situation by having readers vote (thumbs up or down) on the comments of others, thus elevating highly favored comments to the top of the list. Other less democratic mechanisms may also be used to curate a discussion and draw out voices that are more thoughtful, less sarcastic, or provide a diversity of views. With a brand such as Dell, which receives four thousand mentions a day by users online, moderation begins with separating background noise from what merits close attention. The ability to filter, redirect, judge, and encourage valuable participation in networks—to moderate effectively—will be critical for every networked organization.

Transparency

In 2006, Virginia's George Allen was in a seemingly safe campaign for reelection to the U.S. Senate when he was caught on video taunting a volunteer in his opponent's campaign with a racial slur, "macaca." As questions circulated regarding the comment and allegations of prior racial slurs surfaced, Allen watched his double-digit lead in polls collapse into a narrow loss of his Senate seat. The *Washington Post* speculated that if not for the recording and ceaseless replaying of his "macaca" comment online, Allen not only would have won reelection but would have been a serious contender for the 2008 Republican presidential nomination.[13]

In the age of online social networks, blogging, and video camera phones, we are all George Allen now. No one, least of all a public figure or leader of a major organization, can assume that actions that affect customers and the public can safely escape scrutiny. What is said in private or behind closed doors will not necessarily stay there. The old adage "What happens in Vegas stays in Vegas" has been updated: "What happens in Vegas goes on Facebook."

Michael Wesch describes the moment of confusion that many video bloggers face when they first turn on their Web camera as "context collapse": the realization that whatever they are about to say could be seen by anyone in the digital world, now or into the future, in an infinite range of possible contexts.[14] Organizations today face this same context collapse in all their actions and communications.

What does this mean for them? There is no longer a profit in deceiving customers. Now that customers, and not just large institutions, hold access to the means of mass communication, it is simply not a long-term profitable strategy to try to systematically fabricate or misrepresent the actions of your organization. After the early years of planting fake comments in online forums or secretly sponsoring customers to blog nice things about you, companies have realized it is better public relations to argue for what you are than to try to pretend you are something else.

In a networked world, companies will succeed by embracing transparency with customers and business partners and sharing as much information as possible in order to foster greater collaboration and mutual benefit. In the future, competitive advantage will not lie in keeping an organization's strategy secret from competitors but in sharing it with networks of customers and partners inside and outside the organization.

Responsiveness

No matter how scrupulous, skillful, or well managed, any business or organization will face problems that challenge its relationships with networked customers. Products will fail and need to be recalled (like Toyota's massive auto recall in 2010). Crises will be mishandled by the organization (like Jet Blue leaving passengers stranded on airport runways during the Valentine's Day blizzard of 2007). Customers will be offended by a marketing campaign (like the 2008 Motrin Moms advertisement that enraged many of its target customers). Or employees may just be caught behaving badly (like the Domino's Pizza staff who, in 2009, posted a video of themselves adding disgusting ingredients to their store's food).

In a networked world, bad news will spread fast, and one customer's unhappiness will not stay isolated. Customers have a voice and a platform now, and they will use it to express their displeasure. And when one customer complains of a problem that many others are also experiencing, their voice will resonate and be amplified through networks. This is why Jeff Jarvis's Dell complaint and Dave Carroll's "United Breaks Guitars" song each took on a life of their own and spread virally through networks.

Organizations therefore need to respond to customer concerns much more quickly than in the past. Not only can a bad story about a business spread more quickly today, but customer's expectations for a speedy response are much higher. Where once a company responding within a week might have seemed appropriate, it will now be expected to respond within a day. In many cases, that means the organization will be responding before it knows the answer to what caused the problem or even how serious it is. Companies that are used to waiting behind closed doors until they have a full explanation will now have to speak out before the situation is resolved. Dell took this approach with the flaming laptop, flying a team to Japan to retrieve and investigate the faulty product before Dell knew whether it bore any responsibility for the problem. In the end, the fire hazard was discovered to be caused by a battery problem faced by Dell's competitors as well—but Dell was much faster in recalling the batteries than Apple or HP. Dell's Binhammer says, "Companies today need to get used to the idea of not waiting until they know what the problem is. They need to be comfortable saying, 'Yes, we hear you, we are working on it,' before they have found a solution."[15] Often the solution to customer unease is quite simple: just knowing that you hear their concern may be the most important thing.

Organizations need to do more than respond effectively in a moment of crisis, however. They also need to learn to respond solicitously to the everyday questions and concerns of customers. Responsive and effective customer service has always been one of the best tools for businesses to build positive word of mouth among customers. In an age of customer networks, it is simply more important than ever. As commentators from Brian Solis to Steve Rubel to Thor Muhler have observed, "Customer service is the new P.R." Where public relations traditionally focused on maintaining relations with the press (which used to hold a monopoly on one-to-many communications), today it is equally important to maintain the trust, respect, and support of your customers. When your customers speak about your organization to others, it is their voices that will be heard with the most credibility.

Shared Values

For the borderless organization, there will be no firm and impermeable boundary between customers and company. The organization must share not just products, conversations, and collaborations with its customers; it needs to share their values, too. This may come naturally to many nonprofits and social enterprises. But as more businesses reach out to customer networks to contribute to and collaborate in their mission, these businesses need to make sure that the values they espouse to customers match their internal policies, that walk matches talk, and that practiced strategy matches professed mission.

In the early industrial era, works of social good were left to the philanthropic deeds of business tycoons; the businesses they owned were not expected to reflect an ethical orientation. Later, many large businesses took to setting up corporate foundations to contribute to society, often with little attempt to draw attention to themselves. As mass communications and brand management evolved to become more emotionally driven, companies began practicing "cause-related marketing" wherein partnerships with nonprofits were chosen for maximum public relations appeal and carefully marketed to bolster the company's image. More recently, we have seen the idea of "corporate social responsibility" (CSR), which argues that businesses should evaluate their decisions in terms of a range of social impacts (environment, sustainability, employment, and so on) as well as profits. In practice, CSR sometimes consists of isolated, but well-publicized, good deeds.

Some businesses, though, have distinguished themselves by committing quite broadly to a set of values that they share with customers. This can be seen in Tesla Motors (with its commitment to developing high-performance cars run entirely on electricity), in Whole Foods (which always stressed organic and natural foods but added an emphasis on local growers as this became important to customers), and in Google (with its commitment to open Web standards and its motto, "Don't be evil," which sets tough expectations for the company but has led many customers to view it differently from its competitors).

For the networked organization, values that are shared with customers are critical to maintaining the trust and support necessary to partner fully with customer networks. These shared values need to be represented in more than just one-off initiatives, however. They must be part of the overall strategy of the company, and every aspect of the company should reflect them—from products to communications, vendor relationships, environmental impacts, and human resources policies. Only then can a borderless enterprise succeed with the full support of internal and external networks.

As the Internet continues to grow more mobile, more distributed, and more embedded in our physical lives, the impact of our human networks will be seen not just in individual organizations but in our societies as a whole.

With their growing importance in our lives, networks may come to be more than a means to communicate and share our deepest values. They may become a source and a repository of new values themselves. Openness, connectedness, self-expression—these values hold a special role in many cultures, and for centuries they have been enshrined in our philosophies, religions, and legal frameworks. In a world of networks, these values may have greater weight, nuance, and meaning. But they also are vulnerable to technological censorship and surveillance. The fragility of political freedom worldwide shows us that open networks are not always assured, nor are they immune to threat.

In January 2010, after an international cyber attack on the networks of Google and the Gmail accounts of Chinese political dissidents, U.S. Secretary of State Hillary Rodham Clinton delivered a landmark speech that laid out a new vision of digital networks and their meaning to society. In it she described network access as a human right, linked to the freedom of assembly enshrined in the U.S. Bill of Rights. "Governments should not prevent people from connecting to the Internet, to websites, or to each other. The freedom to connect is like the freedom of assembly, only in cyberspace," Clinton said. She spoke of the universal right to freedom of worship and about how worship takes place today not just in churches, synagogues, mosques, and temples but also online.

"The Internet is a network that magnifies the power and potential of all others," she proclaimed. "Freedom of expression . . . is no longer defined solely by whether citizens can go into the town square and criticize their government without fear of retribution. Blogs, emails, social networks, and text messages have opened up new forums for exchanging ideas, and created new targets for censorship. . . . We stand for a single Internet where all of humanity has equal access to knowledge and ideas."[16]

In the future, we may all be called upon to defend and strengthen that digital access, those digital expressions, and our digital freedoms. If we do, then our future networks will continue to make us not only more connected but, let us hope, more human.

Self-Assessment:
How Networked Is Your Business?

Understanding Your Customer Network

1. *Who is in your customer network?* What types of "customers" determine the success of your organization? (These may include consumers, business customers, investors, analysts, business partners, regulators, donors, volunteers, music fans, voters, and parishioners, among others.)

2. *Who matters most?* Which of these types of customers are most important to the success of your organization? Who are the most important potential customers that you want to bring into your network?

3. *What are your goals for your customer network?* What are your most important objectives for each type of customer in your network? Do you want to gain customer insights and increase product differentiation? Amplify word of mouth and connect with hard-to-reach customers? Drive direct sales and generate new customer leads? Build your brand image and break through the media clutter? Lower customer service costs and increase your productivity? Any customer network strategy needs to start with identifying your most important objectives.

4. *What network technologies are your customers already using?* What hardware are they using to get online (phones, tablets, laptops, desktop computers)? What media are they interacting with (YouTube, Flickr, phone apps, blogs, Web sites)? How do your

customers prefer to communicate (email, phone, text, Twitter)?
What social networks are your customers already using (Facebook,
LinkedIn, MySpace, specialized networks)?

Your ACCESS Strategy

1. *Are you findable?* Are you making it easy for customers to find you
   and incorporate you into their digital lives? Are you optimized for
   search, with appropriate paid keyword advertising? Can customers
   find you on the social networks they are using?

2. *Are you flexible?* Do you offer your services and content to customers
   on their schedule, not yours? Can customers reach you by email,
   text message, Twitter, or phone? Do your Web services run well on
   any browser, smartphone, or digital interface?

3. *Are you mobile?* Does your business work on the small screen in your
   customers' pocket? Can they use their phones and mobile devices
   to find you, learn about you, and pay you? Are you delivering products and services that take advantage of mobility and location
   awareness?

4. *Are you fast?* Do you realize that "I can get that for you in two days" is
   a reason for your customer to look somewhere else? Are you offering on-demand services rather than making customers adapt to
   your schedule? Are you turning out new content while it is fresh
   and current? Are you responding to customers online in a timely
   fashion?

5. *Are you simple?* As technology grows increasingly powerful and
   complex, are you keeping yours simple? Are your products and
   services as easy as emailing on a BlackBerry, searching on Google,
   or uploading to YouTube? Are you eliminating the hoops that customers must jump through to find you, connect with you, or pay you?

Your ENGAGE Strategy

1. *Are you creating valuable content for your customers?* Are you thinking
   like a media company? Are you creating content that earns your
   customers' scarce attention in a busy world? Have you moved
   beyond just running ads online and started creating content and
   stories that actually engage your customers?

2. *Are you sensory and interactive?* Does your content include text, images, and video? Are you incorporating interactive elements like maps or gaming? Is your content easily shared by your customers—through email, on Facebook, or by embedding it in their blogs?

3. *Are you useful for your customers?* Who is your content aimed at? What needs does it answer for them? What problems does it solve? Do your customers have a good reason to return to your content more than once? Is it genuinely useful?

4. *Are you authentic?* Does your content speak in the voice of real people inside your organization? Does it express a genuine point of view? Will customers who have interacted with you in person recognize your voice in your content?

Your CUSTOMIZE Strategy

1. *Do you let customers choose what they hear from you?* Have you stopped broadcasting one-size-fits-all communications? Can customers customize your content? Can they pick the topics they are most interested in? Can they adjust the frequency? Can they pick the format (email versus podcast versus RSS versus Twitter)?

2. *Do you act as a filter for your customers?* Do you help them to pick out what's relevant to them from the cacophony of voices, products, and options in their digital world? Do you curate? Do you make recommendations?

3. *Are your products or services adaptable?* Can customers adapt your services or products to suit their interests and needs? Can each customer find a unique experience of his or her own?

4. *Do you offer a personal choice?* Do you learn from your interactions with customers? Do you know what elements of your offering they would most like to customize? Do you offer choices that reflect their passions and express their individuality?

Your CONNECT Strategy

1. *Are you listening to what your customers are saying?* Do you use tools to track your buzz online? Do you know what is being said about your brand, your competitors, and your business category? Are you

following and learning from the conversations of your current and potential customers?

2. *Are you making connections in popular online forums?* Do you have a presence in such forums as Facebook, LinkedIn, Twitter, or Google Buzz? Can customers find you there to ask a question or report a problem? Can they "like" you or express support for your brand? Can they introduce you to their online friends?

3. *Are you proactive and helpful?* Are you responding quickly to concerns about your business that are voiced online? Do valued customers know they can ask you for help? Are you generating goodwill and positive buzz by showing that you are helpful?

4. *Are you connecting to your most passionate customers?* Are you building relationships online with your biggest supporters? Are you giving them opportunities to connect with you and champion you online? Are you showing your critics that you are at least listening to them?

5. *Are you giving your customers a place to meet and share ideas?* Are you creating your own space for customers to connect and converse online? Are you asking your customers for their ideas on how to improve your business? Are you testing out new ideas, products, messages, or strategies to get their input? Do you have the skills to collect, evaluate, and act on ideas from your customers?

6. *Are you incorporating your customers' voices into your own?* Are the testimonies of your customers reflected in your communications? Are you giving customers a chance to answer one another's questions? Has the conversation among your customers become a vital part of your business?

Your COLLABORATE Strategy

1. *Are you identifying your most motivated customers?* Are you tapping into their knowledge, skills, expertise, and enthusiasm? Are you lowering the barriers of entry for customers to get involved? Are you offering different levels of participation for those who can contribute just a little and those who want to contribute a lot?

2. *Are you giving customers ways to work together?* Are you helping them to collaborate in an ongoing fashion? Are you giving them the tools

to work together on shared goals and projects? Do they feel that they are a part of something larger than themselves?

3. *Are you splitting up large projects into small tasks that customers can contribute to?* Are you using tools like wikis that allow each participant to contribute to a collective project? Are you giving customers a choice of tasks that can be accomplished in a short time? Are you tapping into the full breadth and expertise of customers who might want to collaborate with you?

4. *Are you asking for help on challenges you can't solve yourself?* Are you posing your most bold and vexing business questions to your customers for answers? Are you open to ideas that come from outside your organization and willing to reward them? Do you understand the values and motivations that might inspire your customers to contribute?

5. *Are you leaving parts of your business open for others to build upon?* Are you providing datasets for your customers to freely use? Are you using Web-based platforms to make it easy for others to run a business that contributes to yours? Are you using tools such as SDKs, APIs, and open-source licenses to create an open platform where the innovations of others can add to your own?

Your Internal Customer Network

1. *Is your business transparent on the inside?* How accessible is your own data for yourself and your employees? Can you find up-to-minute information on your critical business metrics wherever you are and at any time? Can you see and update your data through the Web from any secure device?

2. *Are you using collaborative tools for work?* Are you harnessing tools such as wikis, threaded discussions, collaboratively edited documents, and internal social networks? Are you using them to share knowledge, assemble flexible teams, and collaborate on projects?

3. *Is your organization pervasively networked?* Are you training all your employees in new digital skills and tools? Have you liberated your network strategy from the "social media interns" in your public relations department? Are you embracing customer networks in every division of your business: market research, product development,

marketing, sales, customer support, human resources, and more? Are you using networks to collaborate across divisions?

4. *Are you constantly learning, listening, and sharing with networks?* Are you using networks to be more responsive to customers? Are you constantly learning from constituents of all kinds (business partners, end consumers, press, volunteers)? Are you lowering the boundaries that stand between those who are inside and outside your organization? Are you becoming more open to new ideas?

How to Continue the
Conversation Online

This book is complete and will go out into the world without updates, additions, or links; such is the technology of books. But of course, the topic of customer networks will not stand still, and neither will my research and writing.

I hope you will join me at my Web site: www.davidrogers.biz. There, on my blog and media pages, I will continue to share new ideas and put into practice the strategies outlined in this book.

You can, of course, ACCESS the site from any browser on any computer or mobile device. The site will aim to ENGAGE you with frequently updated content, including video, audio, slide decks, blog posts, tweets, links to further reading, and more. The site will offer options to CUSTOMIZE that content by sorting cases by the industries and topics most relevant to you. I hope you will CONNECT with me and others by sharing your ideas, feedback, and questions in the comments sections and on my linked presences in Twitter, LinkedIn, and Facebook. And I invite you to COLLABORATE by contributing examples of effective strategies from your own organizations or from others that you witness. There are far too many important trends and innovative approaches to customer networks unfolding every day for one lone author to properly follow, record, and share.

As I finish this manuscript, I have already started to collect and post more cases from my daily research and the advice of others in my network. So please stop by and join the network. I look forward to seeing you there!

Cases and Examples by Industry

Consumer packaged goods
Coca-Cola
Frito-Lay (Doritos)
General Mills
Kraft Foods
Mars (Skittles)
Red Bull
Tropicana

Consumer durables
Blendtec
Masi
Weber

Fashion
Abercrombie & Fitch
Adidas
Burberry
Nike
Styleshake
Threadless

Etail
Amazon
CD Baby

craigslist
eBay
My Virtual Model
Ponoko
Wine Library
Zazzle

Retail
Burger King
Home Depot
Kogi Korean BBQ
Naked Pizza
Sears
Starbucks

Health Care
Lifescan
Methodist University Hospital in
    Memphis
PatientsLikeMe
Pfizer
Proteus Biomedical
Sermo

Toys and Games
Ganz (Webkinz)
Hasbro
LEGO
Xbox

Telecom
Comcast
Motorola
Sprint

Web
Boxee
CitySense
Evernote
Facebook
Foursquare
Google (Android)
Innovid
Kickstarter
Layar
Meetup
Twitter
Urbanspoon
Yelp

Consumer Electronics
Apple (iPhone)
Dash Navigation
Dell
MakerBot
Flip Video
RIM (Blackberry)

Automotive
Ford Motor Company
Mercedes-Benz
Mini Cooper
Nissan
Toyota

Travel and Hospitality
Affinia Hotels
Intercontinental Hotels
United Airlines
Virgin America
Zipcar

Financial Services
American Express
Bank of America
Fidelity
HSBC
TradeKing
USAA

IT and Software
Amazon Web Services
Dell
HP
Linux
Microsoft
Mozilla (Firefox)
salesforce.com
SAP

B2B / Business Services
Cisco
GE
IBM
InnoCentive
Intuit

Media and Entertainment
Bravo Media
Edmunds
Epicurious.com
Netflix
Nickelodeon (*iCarly*)
OnDemandBooks (Espresso)
Pandora
Wikipedia

Notes

Chapter 1. The Customer Network Revolution

1. The analysis of online comments, conducted by Visible Measures, was reported in Jennifer Van Grove, "United Breaks Guitars Surpasses 3 Million Views in 10 Days," Mashable, July 15, 2009, http://mashable.com/2009/07/15/united-breaks-guitars/.

2. Visitors to Coca-Cola fan page on Facebook, "Wall," Facebook, http://www.facebook.com/cocacola (accessed June 2009).

3. Profitability figures are from Max Chafkin, "The Customer Is the Company," *Inc. Magazine*, June 2008, http://www.inc.com/magazine/20080601/the-customer-is-the-company.html.

4. Deloitte Development LLC, "2009 Tribalization of Business Study: Transforming Companies and Communities with Social Media," October 5, 2009, http://www.deloitte.com/assets/Dcom-UnitedStates/Local percent20Assets/Documents/TMT_us_tmt/us_tmt_TribofBusFlipBook_100609.pdf. The study surveyed "400+ companies that have created and maintain online communities."

5. A. H. Maslow, "A Theory of Human Motivation," *Psychological Review* 50 (1943): 370–96.

Chapter 2. Network Science and Lessons for Business

1. Todd's own telling of his Abercombie & Fitch mission can be found, along with YouTube video of the exploit, on his blog at Charlie Todd, "No Shirts," The Improv Everywhere Blog, October 17, 2007, http://improveverywhere.com/2007/10/17/no-shirts/.

2. Howard Rheingold, *Smart Mobs: The Next Social Revolution* (New York: Basic Books, 2002).

3. Information on Euler's original paper can be found at the Euler Archive, "E53—Solutio problematis ad geometriam situs pertinentis," The Euler Archive at Dartmouth College, http://www.math.dartmouth.edu/~euler/pages/E053.html.

4. Albert-László Barabási, *Linked: How Everything Is Connected to Everything Else and What It Means* (New York: Plume, 2003), provides an excellent introduction and overview of the science of networks. Barabási tells the story of Euler and the Königsberg Bridge problem at 10–12.

5. Barabási, *Linked*, 3–4.

6. Duncan Watts, "Measuring Diffusion and Influence on Twitter" (BRITE '10 Conference, New York, March 31, 2010).

7. Barabási, *Linked*, 27–34.

8. Jakob Nielsen, "Participation Inequality: Encouraging More Users to Contribute," Jakob Nielsen's Alertbox, posted October 9, 2006, http://www.useit .com/alertbox/participation_inequality.html.

9. Barabási, *Linked*, 44–57.

10. Clay Shirky, *Here Comes Everybody: The Power of Organizing without Organizations* (London: Penguin, 2008), 179–81.

11. There are many different measures for what percentage of Internet users are content creators rather than simply consumers, depending on what is measured to represent "created content." This figure is from eMarketer, based on the percent of U.S. Internet users ages fourteen to seventy-five maintaining a social networking profile (in 2008: 48 percent; in 2009: 57 percent). This measure is excerpted from an eMarketer report and reported in Jennifer van Grove, "Baby Boomers and Seniors Are Flocking to Facebook [STATS]," Mashable, http://mashable .com/2010/01/28/baby-boomers-social-media.

12. Clay Shirky, "Tools and Transformations," Penguin Group USA's Blog, March 11, 2008, http://us.penguingroup.com/static/html/blogs/tools-and-transformations-clay-shirky.

13. Elizabeth L. Eisenstein, *The Printing Revolution in Early Modern Europe* (Cambridge: Cambridge University Press, 1983).

14. For a summary of research into the hierarchy of effects, see Thomas Barry, "The Development of the Hierarchy of Effects: An Historical Perspective," *Current Issues and Research in Advertising* (1987): 251–95.

15. These first four stages of the purchase funnel are sometimes labeled Awareness, Interest, Desire, Action—abbreviated as the AIDA model—as per one of the first models of a hierarchy of effects; Edward K. Strong, Jr., "Theories of Selling," *Journal of Applied Psychology* 9 (1925): 75–86.

Chapter 3. ACCESS

1. Jeff Zeleny, "Obama Keeps His BlackBerry in a Hard-Fought E-Victory," *New York Times,* January 22, 2009, http://www.nytimes.com/2009/01/23/us/politics/ 23berry.html?_r=3&scp=15&sq=obama percent20blackberry&st=cse.

2. Al Jazeera, "Focus: One Month In Kabul,"*Al Jazeera*, February 7, 2009, http://english.aljazeera.net/focus/2009/02/20092238554740328.html.

3. Associated Press, "Ex-Taliban Diplomat Hooked on His iPhone," March 4, 2009, http://www.smh.com.au/news/technology/extaliban-diplomat-hooked-on-his-iphone/2009/03/04/1235842465754.html?page=fullpage#contentSwap1.

4. Associated Press, "Ex-Taliban Diplomat."

5. BusinessWire, "Best Buy® Mobile Survey Reveals America's Appetite for Smartphones and the Killer Apps They Can't Live Without," June 30, 2009, http://www.businesswire.com/portal/site/home/permalink/?ndmViewId=news_view&newsId=20090630006051&newsLang=en. This public press release contains key highlights from Best Buy's survey, including the numbers I have cited here.

6. Ben Parr, "In-Flight Wi-Fi: 76 Percent of People Will Change Airlines to Have It," Mashable, http://mashable.com/2009/08/31/w-fi-alliance-poll.

7. Salman Khan, "Khan Academy" (Gel 2010 Conference, New York, April 30, 2010).

8. Coca-Cola Enterprises' use of cloud computing by its merchandisers is detailed in Steve Hamm, "How Cloud Computing Will Change Business," *BusinessWeek*, June 4, 2009..

9. Nicholas Carr, *The Big Switch* (New York: W. W. Norton, 2008).

10. Dan Hope, "IPhone Can Be Addicting, Says New Survey," MSNBC.com, March 8, 2010, http://www.msnbc.msn.com/id/35768107. The survey was of two hundred Stanford University students, 70 percent of whom had owned their iPhones for less than a year.

11. Steve Rubel, "Bye Bye Boredom, We Hardly Knew Ya," Micro Persuasion, June 5, 2009, http://www.micropersuasion.com/2009/06/bye-bye-boredom-we-hardly-knew-ya.html.

12. Roger Entner, "Smartphones to Overtake Feature Phones in U.S. by 2011," Nielsen Wire, March 26, 2010, http://blog.nielsen.com/nielsenwire/consumer/smartphones-to-overtake-feature-phones-in-u-s-by-2011.

13. Hamm, "How Cloud Computing Will Change Business."

14. Six hundred million daily searches included queries to Twitter's API by outside services, as announced by Twitter's founders at the Chirp conference and reported by Nick Bilton, "Chirp, Twitter's First Developer Conference, Opens Its Doors," New York Times's Bits Blog, April 14, 2010, http://bits.blogs.nytimes.com/2010/04/14/twitterers-gather-at-chirp-twitters-first-developer-conference.

15. Hamm, "How Cloud Computing Will Change Business."

16. Jay Greene, "How Nike's Social Network Sells to Runners," *BusinessWeek*, November 6, 2008, http://www.businessweek.com/magazine/content/08_46/b4108074443945.htm. U.S. market share for Nike running shoes is reported byMatt Powell, an analyst at the market research firm SportsOneSource of Princeton, NJ. Powell is quoted as saying that "a significant amount of the growth comes from Nike+."

17. Estimate of 15 billion chips is by Intel, and reported by Stacey Hig-

ginbotham, "Intel Inside Becomes Intel Everywhere," Gigaom, March 2, 2009, http://gigaom.com/2009/03/02/intel-inside-becomes-intel-everywhere.

18. Danah Boyd, "I Want My Cyborg Life," apophenia blog, July 13, 2009 http://www.zephoria.org/thoughts/archives/2009/07/13/i_want_my_cybor.html. This is a great story of culture clashes and the blending of online and offline worlds in public space, both the original blog post and the comments that followed it.

19. Boyd, "I Want My Cyborg Life."

Chapter 4. ENGAGE

1. Dana Goodyear, "I ❤ Novels," *New Yorker*, December 22, 2008, http://www.newyorker.com/reporting/2008/12/22/081222fa_fact_goodyear. I am indebted to Goodyear's excellent article for the story of Mone, Maho-I-land, and Goma Publishing and for her introduction to *keitai shosetsu*.

2. Michael Learmonth, "Time for Networks to Figure Out the Internet: Average Network TV Viewer Now 50 Years Old," Silicon Alley Insider, June 27, 2008, http://www.businessinsider.com/2008/6/average-network-tv-watcher-now-50-years-old. Learmonth's source is a report by media buying firm Magna Global. Fifty is the median age of broadcast viewers (hence, half are fifty or older).

3. Quantcast, *YouTube.com*, measure for U.S. monthly traffic in January 2010, http://www.quantcast.com/youtube.com (accessed March 16, 2010).

4. "Internet Activity Index," Online Publishers Association, http://www.online-publishers.org/internet-activity-index.

5. Bret Swanson, "Eric on the Exaflood," May 5, 2008, Progress & Freedom Foundation Blog, http://blog.pff.org/archives/2008/05/print/005143.html. Quoting Eric Schmidt speech at the Milken Institute Global Conference, April 29, 2008.

6. Kevin Kelly, "Better Than Free," *The Technium*, January 31, 2008, http://www.kk.org/thetechnium/archives/2008/01/better_than_fre.php.

7. Lewis Wallace, "Blink-182 Rocks 'Augmented Reality' Show in Doritos Bag," *Wired*, July 6, 2009, http://www.wired.com/underwire/2009/07/blink-182-rocks-augmented-reality-show-in-doritos-bag.

8. Stephen Voltz, "TV 2.0, Online Video, and the Future of User-Generated Content" (BRITE '08 Conference, New York, February 8, 2008).

9. Voltz, "TV 2.0."

10. Mike Perlman, "American Express Open Forum Leverages Social Media," Compete blog, February 12, 2009, http://blog.compete.com/2009/02/12/american-express-open-forum-twitter/. Compete is a Web analytics firm.

11. Karl Greenberg, "American Express CMO: 'Go from Disrupting to Empowering,'" *MediaPost*, April 18, 2008, http://www.mediapost.com/publications/index.cfm?fa=Articles.showArticle&art_aid=80877.

12. YouTube Channel stats as of July 25, 2009: Youtube.com/whitehouse:

79,000 subscribers, two million channel views. Youtube.com/barackobamadotcom: 175,000 subscribers, twenty-one million channel views.

13. Kermit Pattison, "Selling Wine the Web 2.0 Way," *Fast Company,* September 16, 2008, http://www.fastcompany.com/articles/2008/09/interview-gary-vaynerchuk.html.

14. Channel views as measured on YouTube as of July 25, 2009: official YouTube channels youtube.com/totallytrucked, youtube.com/nutsaboutsouthwest, youtube.com/toysrusonline, and youtube.com/kodaktube.

15. Rita Chang, "Game Advertising Goes Mainstream," *Advertising Age,* July 13, 2009, http://adage.com/print?article_id=137829. Data from Frank N. Magid Associates and the Entertainment Software Association.

16. Chang, "Game Advertising Goes Mainstream," citing a study commissioned by MTV Networks.

17. This forecast is by IDC video game market analyst Billy Pidgeon, quoted in Matt Hartley, "In-Game Ad Market Comes of Age with Microsoft-EA Deal," *Globe and Mail,* March 18, 2008.

18. "Toys with a Second Life," *BusinessWeek,* December 20, 2007, http://www.businessweek.com/print/magazine/content/07_53/b4065091329372.htm. The sales estimate is by Sean McGowan, an analyst at Needham.

19. Business Insider, "Webkinz," *Silicon Alley Insider,* March 28, 2008, http://www.businessinsider.com/companies/webkinz. The figure for unique visitors is attributed to Compete (a Web analytics firm).

20. Sandy Carter, phone interview by David Rogers, December 18, 2009.

Chapter 5. CUSTOMIZE

1. Matt Richtel, "What Convergence? TV's Hesitant March to the Net," *New York Times,* February 15, 2009, http://www.nytimes.com/2009/02/16/technology/internet/16chip.html?_r=2. Quoting Greg Belloni, a spokesman for Sony.

2. "Top 1,000,000 Sites," Quantcast Corporation, http://www.quantcast .com/top-sites-4901. As of March 16, 2010, Quantcast's site registered 489,900 sites with average traffic of more than two thousand U.S. monthly visitors.

3. Raymond Williams, *Culture and Society, 1780–1950* (New York: Columbia University Press, 1983), 300.

4. Barry Schwartz, *The Paradox of Choice: Why More Is Less* (New York: Ecco, 2003).

5. Clive Thompson, "If You Liked This, You're Sure to Love That," *New York Times,* November 23, 2008, http://www.nytimes.com/2008/11/23/magazine/23Netflix-t.html. Thompson's article describes the Netflix Prize competition; the work of Bob Bell, Len Bertoni, and Martin Piotte; the Napoleon Dynamite Problem; and figures on the value of backlist catalog for Netflix and other DVD rental companies.

6. Sheena S. Iyengar and Mark R. Lepper, "When Choice Is Demotivating: Can One Desire Too Much of a Good Thing?" *Journal of Personality and Social Psychology* 79 (2000): 995–1006.

7. Schwartz, *Paradox of Choice*.

8. Clay Shirky, "How Social Media Can Make History" (lecture, TED@State, Washington, DC, June 14, 2009), http://www.ted.com/talks/clay_shirky_how_cellphones_twitter_facebook_can_make_history.html.

9. Thompson, "If You Liked This." Discussion of singular value decomposition in solutions to the Netflix Prize.

10. Fabrizio Salvador, Pablo Martin de Holan, and Frank Piller, "Cracking the Code of Mass Customization," *MIT Sloan Management Review*, April 1, 2009, http://sloanreview.mit.edu/the-magazine/articles/2009/spring/50315/cracking-the-code-of-mass-customization/.

11. Salvador, de Holan, and Piller, "Cracking the Code of Mass Customization."

12. The Pandora Music Genome Project is well described by Rob Walker, "The Song Decoders," *New York Times*, October 14, 2009, http://www.nytimes.com/2009/10/18/magazine/18Pandora-t.html?_r=1&ref=technology&pagewanted=all.

13. Number of custom radio stations (as of spring 2009), Salvador, de Holan and Piller, "Cracking the Code of Mass Customization," 72; number of users, Chris Nuttall, "Pandora Could Be a Hit in 2010 IPO parade," ft.com/tecblog, December 16, 2009, http://blogs.ft.com/techblog/2009/12/pandora-could-be-a-hit-in-2010-ipo-parade/.

14. Flannery's quotation is from Knowledge@Wharton, "When Small Loans Make a Big Difference," *Forbes*, June 3, 2008, http://www.forbes.com/2008/06/03/kiva-microfinance-uganda-ent-fin-cx_0603whartonkiva.html.

15. Paul Slovic, "'If I Look at the Mass I Will Never Act': Psychic Numbing and Genocide," *Judgment and Decision Making* 2 (April 2007): 79–95, http://journal.sjdm.org/7303a/jdm7303a.htm.

16. Bruce Kasanoff, "On Demand Books Grow Rapidly, While Traditional Titles Shrink," *Now Possible blog*, October 2009, http://www.nowpossible.com/2009/10/on-demand-books-grow-rapidly-while-traditional-titles-shrink/.

17. Stephen Baker, in-person interview by David Rogers, July 28, 2009.

Chapter 6. CONNECT

1. David Greene, "With Jobs Scarce, Soldiers Re-Enlist," *NPR*, April 10, 2009, http://www.npr.org/templates/story/story.php?storyId=102974015. Tells the story of Jeff and Sarah Taylor.

2. Dan Baum, "Battle Lessons: What the Generals Don't Know," *New Yorker*, January 17, 2005, http://www.newyorker.com/archive/2005/01/17/050117fa_fact. Tells the story of Nate Allen and Tony Burgess starting CompanyCommand.com.

3. Facebook, "Statistics," Facebook Press Room, 2010, http://www.face
book.com/press/info.php?statistics (accessed March 17, 2010).

4. Robin Wauters, "World Map of Social Networks Shows Rise of Facebook," TechCrunch, December 21, 2009, http://www.techcrunch.com/2009/12/21/
world-map-social-networks.

5. Justin Smith, "Fastest Growing Demographic on Facebook: Women
over 55," Inside Facebook, February 2, 2009, http://www.insidefacebook.
com/2009/02/02/fastest-growing-demographic-on-facebook-women-over-55/.

6. Phyllis Korkki, "An Online Outlet for Creating and Socializing," *New
York Times*, August 30, 2009, http://www.nytimes.com/2009/08/30/business/30count
.html. Korkki cites Forrester Research.

7. Ryan Junee, "Zoinks! 20 Hours of Video Uploaded Every Minute!"
YouTube Blog, May 20, 2009, http://www.youtube.com/blog?entry=on4EmafA5MA.

8. Clay Shirky, estimate of Twitter volume per minute, Twitter.com/
cshirky, July 13, 2009 approx. 10 pm EST, http://twitter.com/cshirky/status/26252
20015.

9. Erik Qualman, "Statistics Show Social Media Is Bigger Than You
Think," Socialnomics, Social Media Blog, August 11, 2009, http://socialnomics.
net/2009/08/11/statistics-show-social-media-is-bigger-than-you-think/.

10. "Wikipedia," Wikipedia, http://en.wikipedia.org/wiki/Wikipedia (accessed March 17, 2010). This is a semi-protected page.

11. Heather Champ, "4,000,000,000," Flickr blog, October 12, 2009,
http://blog.flickr.net/en/2009/10/12/4000000000/.

12. Facebook, "Statistics," Facebook Press Room, 2010, http://www.face
book.com/press/info.php?statistics (accessed March 17, 2010).

13. Jennifer Van Grove, "STUDY: 57 Percent of TV Viewers Use the Web
Simultaneously," *Mashable*, September 14, 2009, http://mashable.com/2009/09/14/
web-tv-study.

14. Clare Baldwin, "Twitter Helps Dell Rake in Sales," *Reuters*, June 12,
2009, http://www.reuters.com/article/idUSTRE55B0NU20090612?sp=true.

15. Simon Dumenco, "The Coming End of YouTube, Twitter and Face-
book Socialism," *Ad Age*, May 4, 2009, http://adage.com/mediaworks/article?article_
id=136388

16. Quoted by Ben Schott, "Twitturgy: Religious Tweeting. (Twitter +
liturgy.)," Schott's Vocab, March 26, 2009, http://schott.blogs.nytimes.com/2009/03/
26/twitturgy/.

17. Malia Wollen, "Lights, Camera, Contraction," *New York Times*, June
11, 2009, http://www.nytimes.com/2009/06/11/fashion/11BIRTHS.html. Tells the
stories of Rebecca Sloan and Sarah Griffith.

18. Seth Godin, *Tribes* (New York: Portfolio, 2008).

19. "Global Advertising: Consumers Trust Real Friends and Virtual
Strangers the Most," July 7, 2009, http://blog.nielsen.com/nielsenwire/consumer/

global-advertising-consumers-trust-real-friends-and-virtual-strangers-the-most/. Results are from the Nielsen Global Online Consumer Survey of more than twenty-five thousand Internet consumers from fifty countries.

20. Ibid.

21. Gita V. Johar, Matthias Birk, and Sabine Einwiller, *Brand Recovery: Communication in the Face of Crisis* (New York: Columbia Business School Case Study, 2008). Jarvis tells the story himself in Jeff Jarvis, *What Would Google Do?* (New York: HarperBusiness, 2009), 12–20.

22. Michael Sragow, "Hollywood's All A-twitter over Instant Fan Reviews," *Baltimore Sun*, August 19, 2009, http://articles.baltimoresun.com/2009–08–19/features/0908180074_1_twitter-tweets-bruno.

23. Andrew Hampp, "Forget Ebert: How Twitter Makes or Breaks Movie Marketing Today," October 5, 2009, http://adage.com/madisonandvine/article?article_id=139444.

24. Fred Wilson, "Is Momblogging the New Radio?" A VC, June 2, 2009, http://www.avc.com/a_vc/2009/06/is-momblogging-the-new-radio.html.

25. "The World's Most Popular Brands," ENGAGEMENTdb, July 2009, http://www.engagementdb.com/downloads/ENGAGEMENTdb_Report_2009.pdf.

26. Anthony DeBarros, Carol Memmott, and Bob Minzesheimer, "Book Buzz: What's New on the List and in Publishing," *USAToday.com*, April 8, 2009, http://www.usatoday.com/life/books/news/2009–04–08-book-buzz_N.htm.

27. Shashank Nigam, interview by David Rogers, November 5, 2009.

28. Lionel Menchaca, "Expanding Connections with Customers through Social Media," June 29, 2009, *Direct2Dell*, http://en.community.dell.com/blogs/direct2dell/archive/2009/12/08/expanding-connections-with-customers-through-social-media.aspx.

29. Lisa Hsia, "Bravo TV's Digital Media and Marketing Strategies" (BRITE '09 Conference, New York, March 4, 2009), http://www.briteconference.com/Videos/Hsia.aspx.

30. Brent Snavely, "100 Web-Savvy Drivers Review Ford Fiesta," *Free Press*, August 16, 2009, http://www.freep.com/article/20090816/BUSINESS01/908160432/1322/100-Web-savvy-drivers-review-Ford-Fiesta percent26template=fullarticle (accessed September 9, 2009).

31. Nielsen survey reported in Brian Stelter, "Water-Cooler Effect: Internet Can Be TV's Friend," *New York Times*, February 24, 2010, http:// www.nytimes.com/2010/02/24/business/media/24cooler.html.

32. Brian Quinton, "Doing Well by Doing Good," *Promo*, November 1, 2008, http://promomagazine.com/interactivemarketing/1101-amex-digitas-campaign/.

33. Idea markets are frequently confused with "prediction markets" such as the Iowa Electronic Markets, where users place bets up to five hundred dollars of real money on the outcome of future events, such as "Will John McCain Win the 2008 Presidential Election?" The Iowa Electronic Markets are famous for beating

many polls in predicting elections and were once considered by the Pentagon for an exchange that would bet on likely targets for terrorist attacks (the plan was canceled once it became public). In his book *The Wisdom of Crowds: Why the Many Are Smarter Than the Few and How Collective Wisdom Shapes Business, Economies, Societies and Nations* (New York: Doubleday, 2004), James Surowiecki argues that the accuracy of such prediction markets stems from the diversity of opinion, independence, decentralization, and aggregation of members' opinions.

However, while an idea market such as Cisco's or Motorola's or GE's also harnesses collective intelligence, it is fundamentally different from a prediction market. There is no binary prediction of a future event that either will or will not occur (McCain either wins or he doesn't), so there can be no final judgment call of whether the collective wisdom of an idea market was "correct." Investors in idea markets cannot be motivated by a reward for picking correctly. Fortunately, employee and customer networks usually have a great deal of intrinsic motivation to "invest" in the ideas they judge best based on their own unique knowledge.

34. David Hsieh, "Open Source Models of Innovation: Crowd-Sourcing, Open Platforms, and Customer Co-Creation" (BRITE '08 Conference, New York, February 8, 2008).

35. Stuart Elliott, "And the Recaps of the Super Bowl Spots Just Keep on Coming," *Media Decoder*, http://mediadecoder.blogs.nytimes.com/2010/02/09/and-the-recaps-of-the-super-bowl-spots-just-keep-on-coming/. Source on viewership is the Nielsen Company.

36. Reena Jana, "How Intuit Makes a Social Network Pay," *BusinessWeek*, July 2, 2009, http://www.businessweek.com/magazine/content/09_28/b4139066 365300.htm.

37. Shawndra Hill, Foster Provost, and Chris Volinsky, "Network-Based Marketing: Identifying Likely Adopters via Consumer Networks," *Statistical Science* 21 (2006): 256–276.

38. Brian Morrissey, "Connect the Thoughts," *Adweek*, June 28, 2009, http://www.adweek.com/aw/content_display/news/e3i344418db676344f04f7c79ca44 7c6e96.

Chapter 7. COLLABORATE

1. David Talbot, "How Obama Really Did It," *Technology Review*, September–October 2008. http:// www.technologyreview .com/web/21222. Subscription may be needed to access the full article.

2. Peter Overby and Renee Montagne, "Obama Campaign Shatters Fundraising Records," *NPR*, December 5, 2008, http://www.npr.org/templates/story/story .php?storyId=97843649.

3. Max Chafkin, "The Customer Is the Company," *Inc. Magazine*, June 2008, http://www.inc.com/magazine/20080601/the-customer-is-the-company.html.

4. Vivian Schiller, "Engaging Audiences in a Changing Media Landscape: The Future of Public Radio" (BRITE '10 Conference, New York, March 31, 2010).

5. Timeline Strategy Consulting, "How Much Profit Is Apple Making from the App Store?" *Seeking Alpha*, April 20, 2009, http://seekingalpha.com/article/131730-how-much-profit-is-apple-making-from-the-app-store. Apple does not disclose its revenue on paid iPhone apps, but this post offers a detailed analysis from public information, arguing that Apple's share of the revenue was approximately $150 million by the time it reached its one billionth (paid and unpaid) app download in April 2009.

6. Philip Elmer-DeWitt, "iPhone Sales Grew 245 Percent in 2008 — Gartner," *Fortune.com*, March 12, 2009, http://brainstormtech.blogs.fortune.cnn .com/2009/03/12/iphone-sales-grew-245-in-2008-gartner/.

7. Don Tapscott and Anthony D. Williams, *Wikinomics* (New York: Penguin, 2006).

8. Jeff Howe, *Crowdsourcing: Why the Power of the Crowd Is Driving the Future of Business* (New York: Random House, 2008).

9. Yochai Benkler, *The Wealth of Networks: How Social Production Transforms Markets and Freedom* (New Haven: Yale University Press, 2006), 59–90.

10. Thomas W. Malone, Robert Laubacher, and Chrysanthos Dellarocas, *Harnessing Crowds: Mapping the Genome of Collective Intelligence*, MIT Sloan Research Paper no. 4732-09, February 3, 2009.

11. Clay Shirky, "Supernova Talk: The Internet Runs on Love," *Shirky.com*, February 1, 2008, http://www.shirky.com/herecomeseverybody/2008/02/super nova-talk-the-internet-runs-on-love.html.

12. Dave Webb, "Why the Cisco I-Prize Is So Powerful," *ITbusiness.ca*, October 22, 2008, http://www.itbusiness.ca/it/client/en/home/News.asp?id=50430.

13. Cliff Kuang, "Crispin Porter + Bogusky's Crowdsourcing Experiment Backfires," *Fast Company*, August 28, 2009, http://www.fastcompany.com/blog/cliff-kuang/design-innovation/cripins-latest-experiment-backfires.

14. Howe, *Crowdsourcing*, 2008.

15. Eric Bonabeau, "Decisions 2.0: The Power of Collective Intelligence," *MIT Sloan Management Review*, January 9, 2009, http://sloanreview.mit .edu/the-magazine/articles/2009/winter/50211/decisions-20-the-power-of-collective-intelligence.

16. Darren Sharp and Mandy Salomon, "User-led Innovation: A New Framework for Co-creating Business and Social Value," Swinburne University of Technology (January 2008), 21.

17. Kevin Kelly, "The Bottom Is Not Enough," *The Technium*, February 12, 2008, http://www.kk.org/thetechnium/archives/2008/02/the_bottom_is_n.php.

18. John Geraci, "The Future of Our Cities: Open, Crowdsourced, and

Participatory," *O'Reilly Radar,* April 6, 2009, http://radar.oreilly.com/2009/04/the-future-of-our-cities-open.html.

19. Willy de Zutter, "SETI@home—Credit Overview," BOINCstats. http://www.boincstats.com/stats/project_graph.php?pr=sah (Retrieved June 28, 2009).

20. In some discussions of "collective intelligence," involuntary systems for harnessing user input are included, such as Amazon's collaborative filtering (which observes what books you look at on the site, so as to make better recommendations to others visiting the same pages). However, the involuntary and often unconscious nature of the user's contribution makes these cases less than a "collaboration" from the customer's point of view. Therefore, these cases are not included in this definition of passive contribution systems.

21. Scott Cook, "The Contribution Revolution: Letting Volunteers Build Your Business," *Harvard Business Review,* October 2008.

22. Michael Andersen, "Four Crowdsourcing Lessons from the Guardian's (Spectacular) Expenses-Scandal Experiment," *Nieman Journalism Lab,* June 23, 2009, http://www.niemanlab.org/2009/06/four-crowdsourcing-lessons-from-the-guardians-spectacular-expenses-scandal-experiment.

23. Dava Sobel, *Longitude: The True Story of a Lone Genius Who Solved the Greatest Scientific Problem of His Time* (New York: Penguin, 1995).

24. "The Rise of InnoCentive," *Economist,* September 17, 2009, http://www.economist.com/business-finance/displaystory.cfm?story_id=14460185.

25. Gary Wolf, "Why Craigslist Is Such a Mess," *Wired,* August 24, 2009, http://www.wired.com/entertainment/theweb/magazine/17–09/ff_craigslist.

26. Tony van Veen, "CD Baby 2008 Stats for CD and Download Sales," cdbaby, January 15, 2009, http://www.cdbaby.org/stories/09/01/15/8158752.html.

27. Tham Yuen-C, "Boy, 9, Writes Program Which Scores 480,000 Hits," *Straits Times,* April 1, 2009.

28. Claudine Beaumont, "Apple's iPhone Is a Developer's Goldmine," *Daily Telegraph,* April 16, 2009, http://www.telegraph.co.uk/technology/apple/5163678/Apples-iPhone-is-a-developers-goldmine.html. The figure given for Nicholas's earnings is £20,000.

29. Beaumont, "Apple's iPhone." The figure given for EuroSmartz's earnings is £160,000.

30. Howard Rheingold cited in Darren Sharp and Mandy Salomon, "User-led Innovation: A New Framework for Co-creating Business and Social Value," Swinburne University of Technology (January 2008), 20.

31. Yochai Benkler, "Openness in a Networked Society" (speech, NY Open Video Conference 2009, New York, June 19, 2009).

32. Thomas Gensemer, "From BarackObama.com to AT&T: Using Online Communities to Engage, Energize, and Mobilize Constituents" (BRITE Workshop on Online Communities, New York, October 16, 2008).

Chapter 8. Planning and Executing a Complete Customer Network Strategy

1. Julia Werdigier, "Burberry Looks Online for Ways to Gain Customers," *New York Times,* November 9, 2009, http://www.nytimes.com/2009/11/10/business/global/10burberry.html.

2. Erik Chang, "Costs around The World: Internet Access," billshrink .com, October 1, 2009, http://www.billshrink.com/blog/5787/internet-penetration-costs/.

3. Mark McClusky, "The Nike Experiment: How the Shoe Giant Unleashed the Power of Personal Metrics," *Wired,* June 22, 2009.

Chapter 9. Creating the Customer Network–Focused Organization

1. Ajay K. Kohli and Bernard J. Jaworski, "Market Orientation: The Construct, Research Propositions, and Managerial Implications," *Journal of Marketing* 54 (April 1990): 1–18.

2. Richard Binhammer, "Integrating Online Communities: From service and product forums to a holistic approach to customer communities" (BRITE Workshop on Online Communities, New York, October 16, 2008).

3. Richard Binhammer, phone interview by David Rogers, December 17, 2009.

4. Lionel Menchaca, "Expanding Connections with Customers through Social Media," June 29, 2009, *Direct2Dell,* http://en.community.dell.com/blogs/direct2dell/archive/2009/12/08/expanding-connections-with-customers-through-social-media.aspx.

5. Binhammer interview.

6. Mark Yolton, phone interview by David Rogers, December 21, 2009.

7. Yolton interview.

8. Thomas Gensemer, phone interview by David Rogers, December 22, 2009.

9. Gensemer interview.

10. Ben Elowitz and Charlene Li, "ENGAGEMENTdb: Ranking the Top 100 Global Brands," ENGAGEMENTdb, http://www.engagementdb.com/downloads/ENGAGEMENTdb_Report_2009.pdf.

11. Christopher Palmeri, "Hasbro Learns to Spell B-O-T-C-H," *Business-Week,* August 7, 2008, http://www.businessweek.com/magazine/content/08_33/b4096034648201.htm?campaign_id=rss_topStories.

12. Chip Heath and Dan Heath, *Made to Stick: Why Some Ideas Survive and Others Die* (New York: Random House, 2007), 25–28.

13. Tim Craig, "The 'What If' of Allen Haunts the GOP Race," *Washington Post,* February 6, 2008, http://www.washingtonpost.com/wp-dyn/content/article/2008/02/05/AR2008020503237_pf.html.

14. Michael Wesch, "The Machine Is (Changing) Us" (speech, Personal

Democracy Forum, New York, June 30, 2009), http://www.youtube.com/watch?v=X6eMdMZezAQ.

15. Binhammer interview, 2009.

16. Hillary Rodham Clinton, "Remarks on Internet Freedom" (speech, The Newseum, Washington, DC, January 21, 2010), http://www.state.gov/secretary/rm/2010/01/135519.htm. The complete text of the speech, well worth a read, is available in English, Arabic, Chinese, French, Persian, Russian, Spanish, and Urdu.

Index

Index

attention, scarcity of, 85
augmented reality, 77, 83, 90
authority, challenging, 6–7, 43, 214
automotive industry, with focus on
   customer networks, 258–59
awareness: building, through forums,
   158–59; as part of the purchase
   funnel, 46, 47

Baker, Stephen, 130
banking, on demand, 60
Bank of America, 60
Barakzai, Shukria, 54–55
bee colony, as networked intelligence,
   3–4
Bell, Bob, 111
bell curve, 36
benchmarking, 235
Benioff, Marc, 63
Benkler, Yochai, 214
Bennett, Claire, 94
Bertoni, Len, 111
Bessonnitsyn, Sergey, 187
Best, Charles, 126
Big Plays, 237
Big Seed strategy, 35
Big Switch, The (Carr), 64
billboards, as social media, 139
Binhammer, Richard, 246, 247, 273
Birch, Diane, 146–47
BlackBerry, 53–54, 74, 233
Blendtec, 91
Blink-182, 90
Blodget, Henry, 92
blog posts, 136
Blue State Digital, 176, 251
BMW, 123–24
books: on demand, 128; shortening of,
   104; as social media, 139
borderless, feature of customer net-
   work–focused organization, 253–54
Boston, city of, iPhone app, 155

bottom-up thinking, 190
Boxee, 107, 118–19
Boyd, Danah, 76
Brady, Sean, 141
brand assessment, 229
branding, as part of ENGAGE strategy,
   89, 90–92
brands: bashing of, 7–8; integrated into
   gaming, 101; loving, 8–9; shaped by
   conversations, 144–47
Branson, Richard, 92
Bravo Media, 157–58
BRITE conference, ix–x, xiii–xv, 23
Buck, James Earl, 140
Bug Battles, 203
Burberry, 228, 229
Burger King, 172
Burgess, Tony, 134–35
Burton, Jeremy, 70
businesses: needing to reorient to
   customer network model, 44–45;
   needing to view customers as network
   participants, 5; nurturing relationships, 45; viewing customers as
   isolated and passive, 5
business models: creating through customer networks, 9–10; fear of letting
   go of, 265
business objectives, lack of, 11
business process management, 102–3
business-to-business (B2B) content, 98

capabilities: leveraging across domains,
   237–38; new, developing within the
   organization, 238–39
Carr, Nicholas, 64
Carroll, Dave, 7–8, 42, 145, 272
car-share market, 61
Carter, Sandy, 103, 236
cause-related marketing, 274
CD Baby, 206–7
cell phone novel, 80–81

Index

Index

educational institutions, with focus on customer networks, 261–62

80–20 rule, 37

Eisenstein, Elizabeth, 44

Eliason, Frank, 155

embedded Internet access, as part of ACCESS strategy, 58, 71–73

employees: investing in an idea market for, 164–66; representing companies through social media, 154

ENGAGE strategy, 16, 17–18, 82–84; approaches to, 89–103; creating with customers in mind, 232–33; future of, 103–4; keys to, 104–5; self-assessment of, 278–79

Enterprise 2.0, 184, 255

Epicurious, 170

Erdős, Paul, 29

Espresso (ATM for books), 128

"Eternal Dream" (Mone), 80–81

Euler, Leonhard, 29, 30

events: organizing, 184; temporary forums tied to, 159–60

Evernote, 62

execution, of customer network strategy, 25, 223, 224, 237–39

Facebook, 136–37; and CNN during Obama inauguration, 159; Coca-Cola page on, 8–9; customer word of mouth on, 144; Facebook Connect, 116, 172; fan pages for brands, 146, 152–53; and HSBC customer protest, 38–39; impact of more connections, 34; linking with company's streaming content, 160; Scrabulous application, 264; and social graph, 171–73; use by U.S. military, 133–34; What happens in Vegas goes on, 271; Whopper Sacrifice, 172

faith, and spirituality online, 141

fashion industry, with focus on customer networks, 256–57

feasibility, as element of concept testing, 236

feature creep, 73

Fidelity Investments, 94

filter failure, 112

filters, for helping customers choose, 112–15

Fire Fighter Nation, 142–43

Firefox, 151–52

Flannery, Jessica, 125

Flannery, Matt, 125

Flickr, 137

Flip pocket video camera, 74–75

Ford Motor Company, FordFiesta Movement, 22, 158–59, 224–25, 230–31

forums, 148, 156–62; expectations from, 161–62; private, for loyal customers, 160–61; temporary, 159–60

FourSquare, 171, 257

freedom, of digital access as human right, 275–76

games, as part of ENGAGE strategy, 90, 100–103

games with a purpose (GWAP), 196

gaming: brand integration into, 101; increased appeal of, 100–103; interactive content in, 83; interactivity with other media, 102; as a lead generator for business, 103

Ganz, 21, 101–2, 224

Genentech, 66–67

General Electric, 98, 234

General Mills, 149

Gensemer, Thomas, 176–77, 215, 252

George Polk Awards, 139

geo-tagging, 68

Geraci, John, 193

glory, as motivation for collaboration, 186–87

Godin, Seth, 142

Goma publishing house, 81

Index

Index

Index

Index